The Speaker's Compact Handbook

Fourth Edition

Jo Sprague
San Jose State University,

Douglas Stuart
VMARE, Inc.

David Bodary
Sinclair Community College

WADSWORTH
CENGAGE Learning·

Australia • Brazil • Japan • Korea • Mexico • Singapor
Spain • United Kingdom • United Sta

WADSWORTH
CENGAGE Learning

The Speaker's Compact Handbook, Fourth Edition

Jo Sprague, Douglas Stuart, David Bodary

Publisher: Monica Eckman

Executive Editor: Lyn Uhl

Development Editor: Julie Martinez

Editorial Assistant: Colin Solan

Media Editor: Jessica Badiner

Brand Manager: Ben Rivera

Marketing Development Manager: Kara Parsons (Kindstrom)

Manufacturing Planner: Doug Bertke

Rights Acquisitions Specialist: Alexandra Ricciardi

Art and Design Direction, Production Management, and Composition: PreMediaGlobal

Cover Image Credit: ©koey/iStockphoto

For product information and technology assistance, contact us at
Cengage Learning Customer & Sales Support, 1-800-354-9706

For permission to use material from this text or product, submit all requests online at
www.cengage.com/permissions
Further permissions questions can be e-mailed to
permissionrequest@cengage.com

Library of Congress Control Number: 2012948756

ISBN-13: 978-0-8400-2815-0
ISBN-10: 0-8400-2815-6

Wadsworth
20 Channel Center Street
Boston, MA 02210
USA

Cengage Learning is a leading provider of customized learning solutions with office locations around the globe, including Singapore, the United Kingdom, Australia, Mexico, Brazil, and Japan. Locate your local office at
www.cengage.com/global

Cengage Learning products are represented in Canada by Nelson Education, Ltd.

To learn more about Wadsworth, visit
www.cengage.com/wadsworth

Purchase any of our products at your local college store or at our preferred online store
www.cengagebrain.com

Instructors: Please visit **login.cengage.com** and log in to access instructor-specific resources.

Printed in the United States of America
1 2 3 4 5 6 7 16 15 14 13 12

Using This Book

The Speaker's Compact Handbook provides a concise and portable resource for speakers. It is not coincidental that it shares these characteristics with its sister text, *The Speaker's Handbook,* the first handbook of its kind and now in its tenth edition. Even more concise and portable than that full handbook, *The Speaker's Compact Handbook* is appropriate for certain kinds of academic public speaking classes; for the student who has to give an individual or group presentation in a class from any department; for the beginning speaker who needs individual guidance in preparing for a particular kind of speaking situation; and for the professional who wants a quick refresher on the basics or quick pointers on topics such as the effective use of presentation slides.

Why a *Handbook*

A handbook differs from a textbook in a few important ways.

- First, handbooks are brief. They present a distilled version of the most useful advice gleaned from centuries of academic research and decades of practical experience.

- Second, handbooks are reference books. They are not intended to be read from cover to cover but are designed to help locate what you need, when you need it.

- Third, handbooks are *handy.* Quite literally, this compact edition fits in your hand. It is easy to keep on your desk or in your backpack, coat pocket, or purse without adding weight or bulk.

Starting Out in This Book

To make the most efficient use of the *Speaker's Compact Handbook,* we recommend that you first take a few minutes to look it over. You will see that the inside front cover and first page give an overview of part and chapter titles. The Table of Contents, which follows this introduction, gives a more in-depth picture of each chapter's content. Explore these chapters in any order that works for you. (See the section on page vi, "How to Put Together a Speech," for the quickest approach to getting started on a speech.) Here are two basic suggestions to help begin using this book as effectively as possible.

1. *Take time to establish a foundation.* In the first four chapters (Part 1—Approaching Public Speaking), we grouped together those topics that give you ways of thinking about and beginning the

task of preparing a speech. We suggest that you read these
chapters before delving deeper into the book.

2. *Consider the context in which you will be speaking.* Before you
   go about selecting sections of the book to guide you, it is
   essential that you understand the expectations of your
   particular situation, whether it is in the classroom, in the
   workplace, or in the public arena. We suggest that you look at
   Chapters 5 through 9 (Part 2—Speech Contexts), where you
   will find sections that discuss which elements of speaking are
   most relevant in each of four general contexts.

How to Put Together a Speech

Three important charts in this book provide an easy reference covering the basics of speech planning, creation, and
organization.

- **The Five Steps of Public Speaking,** Figure 1-1, page 7.
  This figure lays out the elements that go into almost every
  speech and cross-references the chapters that deal with each
  element.

- **Speech Planning and Practice,** Figure 10-1, page 62.
  This timetable graphically demonstrates the relationships
  between the elements described in Figure 1-1, and shows
  where tasks overlap and ways for progressing through
  them.

- **Speech Structure Chart,** Figure 32-1, page 192. This chart
  shows the relationships between a speech's main points, subpoints, supporting materials, transitions, introduction, and
  conclusion, as well as how they flow together in a standard
  speech.

Other Features to Help You

Emphasis and Review Tools

- **Key Points.** Throughout the text you will find Key Point
  boxes. These brief paragraphs summarize important aspects of
  the subject under discussion.

- **Quick Tips.** These boxes throughout the text present helpful
  hints about the subject under discussion.

- **Checklists.** The Checklists, also in boxes throughout the text,
  provide a summary of steps that must be taken in a process or
  list questions that must be asked to help define a situation or
  to find a solution to a problem.

Appendices

At the end of the book you'll find three supplemental sections for further reference:

- Appendix A: **Sample Speeches and Outlines.** This appendix contains an informative, an invitational, a persuasive, and a commemorative speech. It also includes a sample outline for an informative speech—the "comic book outline" referred to in various chapters of this handbook.

- Appendix B: **Citation Guidelines.** This appendix contains a sampling of citations for fifteen types of print, Internet, and other nonprint sources. The samples model how to cite sources, using either APA or MLA style.

- Appendix C: **Common Pronunciation and Usage Errors.** This is available for reference located online at your companion Web site. Using the wrong word, mispronouncing it, or using bad grammar can distract your audience from your message. This appendix lists some common errors to watch out for.

Remember, a handbook is a reference text—a resource that tells you how to do what you need to do when you're getting ready to do it, or are in the middle of doing it. This handbook, like all other handbooks, is therefore intended to be a lifelong tool. We hope that you will use it whenever you need, or want, to speak in public and that it contributes to the success of your presentations.

Acknowledgments

For their helpful suggestions that influenced several important decisions during this book's development, we owe thanks to past reviewers and the following dedicated public-speaking teachers:

Harlene Adams, *California State University—Sacramento*
Jacob Arndt, *Kalamazoo Valley Community College*
Heidi Arnold, *Sinclair Community College*
Julie Berman, *Savannah College of Art and Design*
Mardia Bishop, *University of Illinois*
Tina Bakehouse, *Creighton University*
Carl Christman, *San Bernardino Valley College*
Christopher Darr, *Indiana University—Kokomo*
Stacy Freed, *University of Tennessee—Martin*
Andrew Gooding, *Marshall University*
Anthony Hatcher, *Elon University*
Marilyn Johnson, *Cabrini College*
Eugene C. Jones, *Metropolitan Community College of Kansas City*
Sheree Keith, *Macon State College*

Patty Lamberti, *Loyola University Chicago*

Robert Leonard, *Sinclair Community College*

Felicia Stewart, *Clayton State University*

Cynthia Stohl, *University of California—Santa Barbara*

Jerry Thomas, *Lindsey Wilson College*

Kathleen Zaworski-Burke, *San Diego City College*

Online Technology Resources

While using this text, you have the option of using a rich array of resources to enhance and extend your learning. If your instructor did not request that these digital resources be packaged with this text, they are available to you for individual sale. Available resources include the Speech Builder Express program for customized coaching throughout the speechmaking and outlining processes; Speech Studio for uploading and sharing your speeches with instructors and peers; and the InfoTrac College Edition periodicals database. For more information and to access this book's online resources, visit **http://www.cengage.com.**

Contents

Contents

1 Approaching Public Speaking

CHAPTER 1. Understanding Public Speaking

Public speaking is the act of creating meaning with your listeners. As a speaker, you consciously combine communicative resources you already have at hand.

CHAPTER 2. Listening

Listening skills enhance your own speaking and help you meet your obligations as an audience member.

CHAPTER 3. Speaking Ethically

Ethical principles can guide you as a public speaker.

CHAPTER 4. Overcoming Fear of Speaking

Combining thorough preparation with relaxation and visualization techniques will increase your confidence.

CHAPTER 1
Understanding Public Speaking

Giving a speech is never a simple act. There are dozens—or perhaps hundreds—of decisions to make. However, this daunting task becomes more manageable if you have a few basic principles and theoretical frameworks to guide you.

As with any other skill (such as dancing, programming, or fly fishing), with public speaking there are principles to be mastered, there is a need for concentration and practice, and there are benefits to working with a skilled teacher and supportive co-learners. That is why so many colleges and universities require, or strongly recommend, courses in public speaking, why thousands of people join groups like Toastmasters International, and why corporations and public agencies spend millions of dollars on presentation training.

1a. What it means to be a speaker

You are a public speaker when you stand behind the podium at an awards banquet, or when you approach the floor microphone at a planning commission meeting, or when you sit at a table with three other members of your work group and present your proposal for tackling some problem. You are a speaker in class, at work, and among friends and family. In each of these settings, you apply communication skills differently. Though listeners contribute to the creation of meaning, as a speaker you are an originator and inventor. You bring something uniquely "you" to shape a transaction.

However, not all oral communication in a group setting is public speaking. Perhaps the distinguishing characteristic of **public speaking** is that it is an event where a group of people agree that one person—the speaker—will direct the event.

1b. Public speaking as meaning-centered communication

Viewing communication as simply the transmission of information from a sender to a receiver makes "giving a speech" a matter of selecting ideas, packaging them, shipping them efficiently, and verifying their receipt. For most purposes, speakers are better served by embracing a more collaborative and complex model of communication.

Think about a group of friends or a software design team. At any given time, one individual is putting forth ideas while the others listen and react. The result is a composite that did not exist in any one person's mind at the outset. The difference between *messages* (which are speaker controlled) and *meanings* (which are jointly created) has important implications.

1 Meaning is social

No individual, either sender or receiver, can control the "true meaning" of a statement. For example, a speaker who has violated a social norm cannot get off the hook simply by saying, "I did not intend that remark to be offensive, so it wasn't."

2 Meaning is contextual

Words take their meanings from the context that surrounds them as they are uttered. A statement can be repeated verbatim, but its meaning will not be identical if any part of the context has changed: when and where the statement is made; who is present; what happened previously; and what tone of voice, intonation, pauses, and expression accompany the utterance.

3 Meaning is contingent

The "true meaning" of a sentence or an act has to be interpreted within a chain of events. A speech may begin with an anecdote that initially seems to reflect the speaker's view but later is revealed as exemplifying what the speaker opposes. Meaning becomes clear as it unfolds in the interplay between speaker and listeners. Often, we do not know what something meant until we reflect on the entire encounter.

4 Meaning is negotiated by discourse communities

Sometimes the "true meaning" of a message has to be worked out over time by larger groups in society, whose members already agree on some things. An example is the definition of sexual harassment in the workplace, which was developed through court cases, legislative hearings, op-ed columns, and countless personal conversations.

1c. Familiar communicative resources

When you enter into an agreement that designates you as a speaker, your challenge is to adapt three communication skills that you already have in your repertoire. They are conversation, writing, and performance.

1 Conversation skills

In everyday conversations, you are probably relaxed, spontaneous, and responsive to the situation. You are able to express your changing feelings naturally. You do not worry about your exact words because meaning is clarified in the give-and-take of conversation.

One of the highest compliments a speaker can receive is to be called "conversational." The conversation skills that are useful to a public speaker include speaking in a comfortable and confident manner, listening to and considering the perspective of others, and adapting constantly to feedback. A lot of apprehension about public speaking can be dissipated if you use this conversational model.

2 Writing skills

The written word enables you to freeze your ideas on paper, allowing you to craft and tinker with them. Writing can create the distance you need to view your ideas objectively, test them for logical coherence, and see how well they fit together. In writing, you can also weave in multiple voices of authorities along with your own.

In writing, you pay close attention to word choices and organization in order to produce a carefully crafted message. You have the time to enjoy wordplay, to explore nuance, and to find elegant phrasing that makes the message memorable.

From writing, then, a speaker draws on the attention to language, the order of ideas, and the internal unity of the speech. Good writing requires time to rework and polish your words in order to achieve the most economical and forceful way to convey your message.

3 Performance skills

You are a performer whenever you *do* something rather than merely think about it. In this handbook, when we talk about performance skills, we mean your use of physical qualities—tone of voice, gestures, movement—to create a focal point for a group.

The performative aspects of public speaking make a speech more than a conversation, a PowerPoint presentation, or a transcript. *Performance* refers not to display or phoniness but to the enactment of an event between speaker and listeners that transcends the message or the exchange of information. The performance is what makes people say about a speech, "You had to be there."

Performance skills useful to the speaker include the ability to pay attention to the entire effect, the knowledge of how to use setting and timing, and the capacity to turn a collection of individuals into a cohesive group. Performers also know how to make use of the senses. They tie together visual effects, lighting, sound, music, humor, and drama. They develop a superb sense of timing and understand how to direct emotional buildup toward the right moment for climax. A speaker uses these skills by learning to visualize the desired impact and by carefully planning details that contribute to that overall effect.

CHECKLIST

Balancing Your Skills

Conversation skills

❏ Underreliance leads to stiffness, excessive formality, distance, and lack of spontaneity and immediacy.

❏ Overreliance leads to blunders, disorganization, vocal pauses, and the tendency to go off on tangents and lose focus.

Writing skills

❏ Underreliance leads to imprecise word choice, repetition, and lack of organization.

❏ Overreliance leads to a "canned" sound, inability to adapt to the audience, and an almost irresistible temptation to read or memorize the text.

Performance skills

❏ Underreliance leads to monotony and low emotional impact and energy level.

❏ Overreliance distracts from the message and leads to an unnatural or melodramatic persona, audience passivity, and questions of sincerity.

1d. The skill-learning process

We learn complex skills differently from the way we learn simple facts. Public speaking is a complex skill that combines a number of intellectual and physical operations. Most of these operations— such as how to raise and lower your voice, how to move your hands, and how to group ideas into categories—are already in

KEY POINT   The Four Stages of Skill Learning There are four stages in learning any skill, including public speaking:

1. unconscious incompetence (ui)
2. conscious incompetence (ci)
3. conscious competence (cc)
4. unconscious competence (uc)

As you move through the stages of learning public speaking skills, you will progress from not being aware that you are making errors or that you need to learn a particular skill (ui), to realizing that there's room for improvement (ci), to working toward improvement and being vigilant when you use the skill (cc), and finally to integrating the learned skills to the extent that competence comes naturally, and you no longer need to devote conscious attention to them (uc).

your repertoire. What you may not know is how to combine these skills to make an effective public speech.

A great deal of your communication behavior is unconscious. You do not think about how you move your lips to make sounds or why you speak one way with your friends and another with your boss. These are examples of skills of unconscious competence (uc), the first skill-learning stage listed in the Key Point box. At the same time, you may not be aware that you mispronounce *escape* or twirl your hair when you are nervous. These are examples of unconscious incompetence (ui).

When do your communication behaviors receive your conscious attention? Usually when you are learning a new skill or when you run into difficulties in communicating. As soon as you master a skill or solve a communication problem, your behavior becomes unconscious again.

1e. Common misconceptions about public speaking

There are many approaches to teaching public speaking and there is much folk wisdom about why some people are effective speakers. Four misconceptions can get in the way of becoming an effective public speaker.

- *Misconception 1: Good speakers are born, not made.* No one is born an effective speaker any more than one is born a good skateboarder or an accomplished violinist. Inborn predispositions and early learning help some people learn faster and go further. However, virtually anyone can learn to give a clear, effective public speech.

- *Misconception 2: Good speaking should be easy right away.* Many speakers think, "I know how to talk, so I must know how to give a speech." Skillful communicators can make public speaking look easy, but it takes work.

- *Misconception 3: Speaking will always be difficult.* Although learning a skill requires effort, performing the skill becomes much simpler once you reach a certain level of mastery (see the *Key Point: The Four Stages of Skill Learning*). When you get discouraged with a speech outline that just won't come together or with phrasing that just won't flow, remember: It *will* get easier.

- *Misconception 4: There are simple formulas.* Communicating with an audience is a complex act. Every public speaking event is unique. There is no all-purpose recipe for preparing or delivering a speech. The advice in this handbook comes from basic principles of public speaking that date back over two thousand years to Aristotle's *Rhetoric*. It continues to be refined through social science research. With these sound public-speaking techniques, you can be a flexible and an effective public speaker.

1f. Five steps for speech preparation

Preparing a speech is complex and can be daunting. Figure 1-1 is a list of the bare essentials that go into preparing any speech, even the most basic one. These basic steps will guide you as you get started. Later chapters explain these steps and describe different speech formats or types of speeches.

For simplicity, the basic steps are numbered in Figure 1-1, but a speaker is always revisiting steps in the *Plan–Investigate–Compose–Practice–Present* cycle to ensure thorough analysis and development and to polish the message. For a major speech, you might refine your analysis after some research. When practicing the speech, you may discover the need for one more piece of research.

The first four steps are developed in more elaborate form in Figure 10-1, which shows how they overlap in time and how important *oral* activity is at every step of the process.

THINK Initial decisions and analysis	Prepare plan 10 Select and narrow topic 11 Consider occasion 11 Clarify purpose 11 Determine mode of delivery 28 Frame thesis statement 11 Analyze topic 11 Analyze audience 12 Counter anxiety 4
INVESTIGATE Research for resources and materials	Locate resources 13 Investigate articles, books, and websites 14 Conduct interviews 15 Keep research notes 16
COMPOSE Development of speech materials	Develop rough working outline 17 Develop full-sentence outline 20 Add supporting materials 16 Add attention factors 30 Prepare introduction, conclusion, and transitions 31 Prepare presentation aids 27 Prepare speech notes 33
PRACTICE Preparation for oral performance	Give the speech aloud 33 Practice with presentation aids 36 Work on vocal delivery 34 Work on physical delivery 35 Get feedback 33
PRESENT The culmination of all your work	Relax, enjoy, connect with your audience, and debrief to learn something for next time.

© Cengage Learning

FIGURE 1-1 **The Five Steps of Public Speaking (with chapter references)**

QUICK TIP **More Than Dos and Don'ts** At the college level, the answer to all questions is "it depends." Although the chapters of this handbook are written as prescriptions, no simple dos and don'ts apply to every situation. The fundamentals of speaking are stated simply, but the application and combination of these principles depend on your good judgment in each speaking situation.

Critical Thinking Questions:

○ How does a meaning-centered perspective differ from a message-centered perspective?

○ What are your communicative resources and how can you maximize their impact?

○ Which of the five steps of the public speaking process do you find most challenging and why?

CHAPTER 2
Listening

Listening is a crucial communication skill. It is an essential component for most careers and an important factor in why relationships fail or succeed. Listening is not something experienced passively; it is a complex set of actions that requires conscious attention and practice. Listening is the active process of receiving, processing, and evaluating an oral message.

Effective speaking and listening go hand in hand. Listening closely and thoughtfully to public speakers gives you rich information about what works and what doesn't. You will be more appreciative of good speaking when you hear it. You will also be more critical of speaking that fails to measure up to the standards you set for yourself. Improving your habits and attitudes as a listener will directly enhance your effectiveness throughout the steps of preparing and delivering a speech.

2a. Prepare to listen

We need to prepare for situations that require skilled listening.

■ *Remove distractions and get physically set.* In our multitasking society, we are used to doing many things at once. However, when listening is a priority, we need to give the speaker our full attention by clearing away all materials except those needed for note taking, sitting up straight, and looking at him or her.

- Speaking in public takes courage and effort. Give the speaker the gift of your full attention whether you are an audience member or the next speaker. Avoid any verbal or nonverbal behavior that would distract the speaker or listeners.

- *Stop talking.* This principle applies not only to chatting with your neighbor but also to anything else that takes your attention away from the speaker, like planning your responses or texting. (See **2b.**) Similarly, when you interview someone, you should listen more than speak.

- *Decide on your purpose as a listener.* There are many possible objectives for listening. Those include learning, understanding a new point of view, evaluating a controversial argument, or enjoying a narrative. Think about the resources you will need—empathy, curiosity, critical analysis, concentration—to meet your goals as a listener.

2b. Be curious and think critically

Effective listeners balance a charitable and open receptiveness with a critical assessment based on their real-life experiences and common sense.

> QUICK TIP **Listening to Nonnative English Speakers** American businesses and classrooms have grown increasingly diverse. Developing a sensitivity to various accents will serve you well in our increasingly multicultural society. Practice listening to nonnative speakers and consider studying a second language yourself. Remember that to communicate with you, the speaker has learned American English vocabulary, grammar, and syntax, and then has risked speaking publicly in that new language. With a small amount of effort, most listeners can adjust to nonnative speakers' inflections, pronunciation, or pauses, and understand quite well.

- *Be open to the speaker's point of view.* Although people cannot help evaluating what they hear, you can make a conscious effort to substitute curiosity for condemnation. What exactly is this person saying? What led to that position? How did this person come to these conclusions and with what assumptions?

- *Follow the structure of the speech.* Try to identify the thesis, main points, supporting materials, and crucial links, whether these are explicitly stated or not. Looking for structure aids your retention of content and your evaluation of its validity.

■ *Assess the speaker's claims.* Whether or not the speaker is making a controversial claim, engage your critical thinking skills to test the validity of the argument. Use the *Checklist: Questions for Assessing a Speaker's Claims.*

■ *Ask questions at the designated time.* Your questions should deepen your understanding of what the speaker is trying to get across. Do not make a speech about your views or try to trap the speaker.

CHECKLIST

Questions for Assessing a Speaker's Claims

❑ Do the main points taken together justify the thesis? (See **18a.**)

❑ Is each claim stated clearly? (See **21a.**)

❑ Is this claim a proposition of fact, value, or policy? (See **11d.**)

❑ Is the support offered for each claim relevant to the point? (See **16.**)

❑ Does each piece of evidence meet the appropriate tests for examples, testimony, or statistics? (See **16.**)

❑ Are the links between the points logically drawn? (See **24d.**)

❑ What premises are taken for granted without being stated? Are these assumptions valid? (See **21c.**)

❑ Are any fallacies present? (See **21f.**)

❑ Does the speaker misuse emotional appeals or substitute them for intellectual argument? (See **25d.**)

2c. Listening to learn

Effective listening will enable you to reach a deeper understanding of the speaker's topic. It will also empower you to use your time efficiently when interviewing other people as you research your speeches. (See Chapter **15.**)

■ *Paraphrase.* Check your understanding of the points being made by paraphrasing and clarifying. Restate what you think you heard so that the speaker can confirm or correct your interpretations.

■ *Ask follow-up questions for clarification.* As the expert answers your open-ended question, careful listening will enable you to follow up with more-specific questions, such as: "You said a minute ago that the global impact of biofuels may be more harmful in the long run than the environmental impact of burning fossil fuels. Why do you say that?"

- *Take notes.* Be sure to take notes as you gather information from another person. It makes sense to employ this tool because the object is to optimize learning: You are required to think about what is being said so that you can write notes that make sense as well.

2d. Constructive feedback

In a class or a workplace, you may be asked to provide feedback on the decisions the speaker has made and the effectiveness of the presentation. The role of critic/consultant requires a special blend of honesty and tact. The supportive critic bears in mind the fragility of partially formed ideas and the close connection between the person's speaking personality and the person's self-image. The following guidelines are for listeners who have been asked to give feedback.

- *Start with the positive.* Acknowledge what the speaker has tried to do and how it has succeeded. By beginning with the positive, you reduce the speaker's defensiveness and increase openness for the constructive feedback to follow.

- *Make important comments first.* Before suggesting how to refine some sentence, think first about whether the message makes sense and whether the overall strategy is effective. When those issues are settled, move on to the refinements.

- *Be specific.* It is more helpful to say, "You were discussing causes of the problem in Point 1 and then again in Point 3" than to say "This speech was disorganized." With positive comments, it's better to describe what was effective.

- *Give suggestions, not orders.* Your comments should acknowledge that your response is the reaction of just one listener and that others may differ. For example: "I've never cared for a big, dramatic introduction, though I know it works for some people. Have you thought about . . .?"

- *Be realistic about the amount and kind of feedback a speaker can receive.* Always consider the speaker's feelings when deciding what to say and how to phrase it. Be aware of the time constraints a speaker faces. Early in the development of the speech, you can make some major suggestions for revision. However, if the speech is in final rehearsal, it's too late to suggest going back to the drawing board.

- *Use the 90/10 principle.* This principle, developed by one of the authors in teaching interpersonal communication, states that people's weaknesses are rarely the *opposite* of their strengths.

More often, they are the *excesses*. This awareness suggests a way of phrasing feedback: "The first 90 percent of quality A is a positive addition to your speech, but the last 10 percent of quality A begins to work in the opposite way." You are not suggesting that the speaker eliminate a characteristic behavior—just that he or she hold it in check. Here's an example: "Your informal conversational style works wonderfully for most of the speech, except at one or two points where it becomes so colloquial and casual that your credibility suffers a bit."

CHECKLIST

Constructive Feedback
❏ Start with the positive.
❏ Make important comments first.
❏ Be specific.
❏ Give suggestions, not orders.
❏ Be realistic about the amount and kind of feedback.
❏ Use the 90/10 principle.

2e. Common listening pitfalls

1 Daydreaming, doodling, and disengaging

It's easy for your mind to wander, in part because it takes a speaker longer to state an idea than for a listener to think the same thing. Listening experts recommend using that time differential constructively. Think of examples from your own life or of questions to ask later. Stay mentally active in ways that connect to the speech topic. (See **2a**.)

2 Being distracted by appearances

You may notice that a speaker sways back and forth, or has a vocal inflection that makes every statement sound like a question, or looks wonderful in that shade of blue. Letting yourself be distracted by these observations hinders your listening to the message of the speech.

3 Uncritically accepting a message

Don't automatically assume that if a speaker makes a statement, it must be true. If something sounds wrong, it may *be* wrong. Listeners share ethical responsibility for the meanings that come out of speeches. Show respect for speakers' ideas by giving them the scrutiny that they require. (See **2b**.)

4   Prematurely rejecting a message

Hear the speaker out. Listen attentively, and you may hear a new argument or find an intriguing point you hadn't considered. (See **2b**.)

5   Planning your rebuttal

You can certainly be critical and analytical, but unless you are in a debate that requires on-the-spot refutation, don't start composing your responses during the speech. (See **2a**.)

6   Looking inattentive

Even when you are confused, don't glaze over or look bored. When you disagree, don't grimace or roll your eyes. As a matter of courtesy and respect, assume a supportive and responsive listening demeanor.

The International Listening Association website **http://www. listen.org** provides resources about listening, including interesting listening facts.

Critical Thinking Questions:

- ○ Why is listening important to public speaking?
- ○ What can you do to improve your listening behavior?
- ○ What advice would you offer a friend required to give feedback to coworkers?
- ○ Which listening pitfall do you find most challenging and what could you do to change your behavior?

C H A P T E R 3
Speaking Ethically

Sometimes, a speaker succeeds in getting a point across or in persuading an audience but does so in a manner that is manipulative, exploitative, dishonest, or otherwise offensive. These cases raise questions about the ethical obligations of all speakers. Ethical questions do not ask, What works? Instead they ask, What is right?

In one sense, ethical beliefs are a matter of each person's own conscience. Yet our beliefs about right and wrong are highly influenced by other people. Codes of ethical conduct come to us through family, religion, and culture. The National Communication Association (NCA) has also established a code of ethics to guide communicators. It can be found on the NCA's website at **http://www. natcom.org/**.

3a. The ethical implications of your choices

No decision a speaker makes is morally neutral. We speak because we believe that what we say will make a difference. And it does. The results of a speech can be as serious as persuading others to follow a dangerous course of action or as apparently harmless as wasting the listeners' time with an unprepared and unfocused message. Every time you speak, you exercise power and assume responsibility for the consequences of what you do or do not say.

1 Ethical decisions are complex

Questions about what is the right or ethical course of action are complex. Our ethics grow from our values, and values sometimes conflict. Rarely are there black-and-white choices. The best we can do most of the time is to select the lightest shade of gray. As communicators, we are obligated to think in detail about each case and to make a judgment based on experience and reflection.

2 Ethical decisions vary with context

In a speech tournament, a debater might argue for medical marijuana at 9:00 and argue against it at 10:30. In this context, it is understood that the rules of the game are to defend the assigned side of a topic as vigorously and skillfully as possible. This is considered no more unethical than a football team's defense of the north goal in the first and third quarters and of the south goal in the second and fourth. However, we judge as very unethical a politician who takes one position when addressing voters in Oregon and the opposite position in Kansas. This politician fails the ethics test because we believe such public speeches should be sincere statements of the speaker's true beliefs.

What you can pass off as your own words varies as well. It is ethical for political leaders to employ speechwriters because the demands on public servants make it impossible for them to personally prepare each speech they give. However, in an academic environment, it is well understood that students should create and deliver their own speeches. Buying a speech online or having a friend write it is unethical for a student. (See **3b.**)

KEY POINT **Be True to Yourself and Your Listeners** As a public speaker, you are not simply a transmitter of messages; you also put yourself (your individual self) in contact with an audience. Though you may adapt, adjust, and accommodate to meet your goals, you have an ethical obligation to be true to yourself. When you have finished a speech, regardless of how anyone else responds, you should always feel good about what you said and how you said it.

Public speakers have a special kind of power. When audience members entrust you with their time and attention, you take on an obligation to treat them with fairness and concern. You have every right to pursue your own reasons for speaking, but not at the expense of your listeners' welfare.

3b. The integrity of ideas

A commitment to integrity requires us to take a larger view of how each individual speech either reinforces or weakens the fabric of society. To live and work together, we have to trust that, on the whole, other people are communicating honestly and reliably with us.

1   Don't plagiarize

Besides yourself and your audience, there are others who are not present to whom you have some ethical obligations. These are the people whose ideas and words you draw into the speech situation. The ethics of public speaking generally forbid using another's major ideas or exact words—or even paraphrasing them— without giving credit to the source. Anything short of that is equal to stealing. Plagiarism is a serious offense in academic institutions and in the world of publishing. Careers have been ruined when journalists and public figures have been exposed as plagiarists.

To avoid even the appearance of unethical appropriation of speech content, you should develop the habit of taking careful notes of the sources of all your ideas, statistics, and evidence. When you hear a wonderful anecdote, story, or phrase you might like to quote someday, make a note right then so you will remember to give credit to the source. (See **16d and 16f.**)

Do not copy passages from the Internet and paste them into your speech and then use them as if they were your own words. You also may run across websites that sell speeches or even write ones for money. But your instructor is familiar with these sites and will recognize speeches from them. In addition, many instructors use an originality checking service, such as the one at **http://turnitin.com** or similar online tools.

There are several online resources to help you avoid even the appearance of plagiarism. Refer to **http://www.northwestern. edu/provost/students/integrity/plagiarism.html** or **http:// owl.english.purdue.edu/owl/resource/589/01/**. For an online tool to help you collect, manage, and cite research sources, see **http://www.zotero.org/**.

2   Don't lie

Rarely do we live up to the standard of "the truth, the whole truth, and nothing but the truth" in everyday interactions. The phrase *it depends* always crops up in conversations about what counts as a lie, a white lie, a fib, or tactful phrasing. In public speaking, however, the following behaviors cross the line between honest and dishonest speech.

- *Making statements that are counterfactual.* This is pretty obvious. Saying, "I have no financial interest in this fitness center. I just care about your health" when you receive a commission for every new member you enroll is dishonest.

- *Playing word games to create a false impression.* Sometimes a speaker can use words with precise definition, being technically correct but totally misleading—for example, "In response to allegations of illegal drug use, let me say that I have never broken the laws of this country" (when the drug use was in another country).

- *Leaving out some part of "the whole truth" that, if known, would reverse the impact of the statement.* Saying, "We have totally dominated the Smurge Company in our market" is misleading if you neglect to mention that the domination happened in only one quarter out of four.

3   Don't oversimplify

Another dimension of the integrity of ideas has to do with faithfulness to the facts and realities of your subject matter. Although

---

CHECKLIST

Finding a Balance in Ethical Decisions

❑ Balance the value of using language in a lively and forceful manner against the risk of causing pain and offense.

❑ Balance the importance of appealing to your audience at an emotional level against the risk of abusing emotional appeals.

❑ Balance the need to support claims with evidence against the risk of introducing opinions as fact.

❑ Balance the right to use compelling persuasive appeals against the obligation to avoid simplistic persuasive techniques.

we can hardly say that there is one "real truth" on any complex issue, we can say that some accounts are so shallow or oversimplified as to provide a false picture. Before you speak in public—thus contributing to and shaping the public discourse on a topic—you have an ethical obligation to look beneath the surface.

Another form of oversimplification is exemplified by the classic list of propaganda devices identified by a group of journalists some decades ago. Unethical speakers use these techniques to short-circuit an audience's rational processes.[1]

- *Name-calling.* By attaching a negative label to an idea or a person, a speaker can provoke fear or hatred in an audience. The speaker hopes this tide of emotion will gloss over the lack of substance in his or her presentation.

- *Glittering generalities.* At the other extreme is the use of words or phrases that represent some abstract virtue like patriotism or motherhood in order to generate a positive response rather than dealing with the merits of a position.

- *Testimonials.* Another way to generate positive emotions is to link a popular figure with some cause or product. Here, the speaker replaces sound argument with a possibly inappropriate extension of the person's credibility from another area.

- *"Just plain folks."* It is fine to build identification with an audience so that members are receptive to the ideas presented. This process goes too far, though, when the speaker implies, "You should believe me, not because of the inherent validity of what I say, but because I'm just like you."

- *Card stacking.* In this method, a speaker carefully uses only facts or examples that bolster a particular position, and the highly biased selection is passed off as representative.

- *The bandwagon.* This technique is useful to a speaker who wishes to discourage independent thinking. The "everyone is doing it" approach appeals to the need for security and plays on fears of being different or left out. A proposition should be sold on its merits, not on its popularity.

This list is far from comprehensive. Effective persuaders also use such techniques as snob appeal (the opposite of "just plain folks") and stand-out-from-the-crowd (the opposite of the bandwagon). Such persuasive appeals are questionable whenever they serve to distract listeners from important issues, cloud important distinctions, introduce irrelevant factors, or use emotional appeals inappropriately or excessively. (For more about fallacies in logic, see **21f.** For fallacies in statistics, see **16b.**)

---

[1]Adapted from Alfred McClung Lee and Elizabeth Briant Lee, *The Art of Propaganda* (New York: Harcourt and Institute for Propaganda Analysis, 1939), 23–24.

Critical Thinking Questions:

○ Make a list of the ethical issues speakers face. Explain what balance has to do with managing any ethical speaking situation.

○ What makes plagiarism so serious, and how should a person who commits plagiarism be treated?

○ Which of the propaganda devices listed in this chapter have you used? Was it ethical to do so? Explain your answer.

CHAPTER 4

Overcoming Fear of Speaking

The ability to float doesn't make a person a proficient swimmer. Likewise, knowing how to talk doesn't make a person an effective public speaker. Both swimming and speaking require at least some ability to relax and focus on the situation at hand. Stage fright, communication apprehension, speech anxiety, reticence, and shyness reduce our ability to focus on communicating our message. Yet we need not become victims of this fear; instead, experts offer techniques that can help us become more comfortable and confident when speaking in public.

4a. Put your fear into perspective

Many speakers try to be calm in every speech situation. This is unrealistic.

1 Some fear is normal

All speakers feel some fear. For most of us the feeling can be managed and sometimes even turned into a positive effect. Like many athletes, you can use the adrenaline generated from fear to energize your performance.

The more speeches you give, the more confident you will become. You will recognize that the anxiety is usually worst just before the speech or during the introduction. Once your speech is under way and the audience responds to you, negative emotions are often replaced by exhilaration.

2   Identify your specific fears

Although one survey found that people list fear of public speaking ahead of fear of death, few people really expect the experience to be fatal. This kind of amorphous, ill-defined fear cannot be dealt with. Dealing logically with your fear of public speaking requires examining its components so that you can identify specific problems to be solved.

It is helpful to list your fears on paper. Be as specific as possible. If you write general statements like "I'm afraid I'll make a fool of myself," ask yourself these follow-up questions: "How will I do that?" ("I'll forget my speech") and "What will happen next?" ("The audience will think I'm dumb"). Use this format for your list of fears:

> I am afraid that [specific event] will occur and then that [specific result] will follow.

When you have generated your list, you can classify your fears. Common categories include: seeming incompetent, having physical responses that show your fear, failing to measure up to your ideal, and being negatively evaluated.

For items like "I'm afraid my visual aids won't be clear," the solution is simple. Check out the clarity of your visual aids with a few people, and, if there is any problem, redesign them. As **4b** points out, many fears have roots in inadequate preparation. The act of writing down the fears often points immediately to a solution.

Other fears on your list may relate to physical responses: "I'm afraid my hands will shake and my voice will crack." If many of your concerns fall into this category, pay special attention to the tension release and relaxation suggestions in **4c**.

A number of items on your list may relate to failure to meet your own high standards. Recognize this concern as a positive motivation to do the best you can. But also realize that the power of suggestion is great and that dwelling on failure can cause it to happen. Use some of the visualization and verbalization techniques recommended in **4d** to create positive self-expectations.

CHECKLIST

Steps for Specifically Identifying Your Fears

❑ **Step 1.** Make a list of your fears using the following format to phrase each one: I am afraid [specific event] will occur and then [specific result] will follow.

❑ **Step 2.** Consider the origin of that fear. What events in your life influenced your beliefs?

❑ **Step 3.** Create a list of alternative interpretations of your experience. Talk to colleagues and classmates as a way to gain perspective.

❑ **Step 4.** Decide not to be controlled by past experience.

Some speakers find themselves frozen by the fear of negative evaluation from their audience. Remind yourself that an audience is merely a group of individuals, and a speech is merely an enlarged conversation. If you would not be frightened to speak to any three or four of them, then it should not be frightening to speak to all of them together. Audience members would much rather listen to you speak than speak to themselves. They want you to succeed. See **4e** for suggestions about reconceptualizing the role of your audience.

4b. Prepare and practice

Although good speakers can make delivery seem effortless, their skill is based on extensive preparation over a period of time. The confidence they exude is also a result of preparation, not genes, fate, or dumb luck.

If you feel uneasy about starting your speech, perhaps your introduction needs more work. If you fear losing the continuity of the speech, you may need to practice it aloud several times to internalize the flow of ideas. If you find yourself becoming generally anxious, use this as a stimulus to review your preparation. Whatever else you do, remember that time spent fretting about the outcome could better be used taking positive action to ensure a positive outcome.

As you prepare, follow the suggestions on practice sessions in Chapter **33**. Avoid making last-minute changes in the speech.

4c. Use relaxation techniques

When too much adrenaline makes you jumpy, physical activity usually helps you cope with the physical effects of fear and release tension. A brisk walk around the block or a little pacing in the hall—or a few arm swings and neck rolls—can be enough to bring your body back to normal. If you are in sight of your audience before the speech, you may be able at least to clench and unclench your hands or toes unobtrusively. Don't risk your credibility by going through any bizarre preparatory rituals. Once the speech begins, take advantage of the extra energy from adrenaline to make your delivery more vigorous with appropriate dynamic gestures.

You can also handle symptoms of nervousness by learning and practicing relaxation techniques. Explore such methods as tightening and then relaxing muscles where your body is tense, breathing deeply, visualizing serene settings, or imagining sensations such as warmth or heaviness in parts of your body. Articles, books, and podcasts about stress and relaxation techniques are widely available.

Chemical aids to relaxation—alcohol, drugs, tranquilizers—are highly inadvisable. Their side effects will impair your mental and physical performance during the speech, and most will give you a false sense of security.

4d. Use positive self-suggestion

When you experience fear, you are visualizing the most negative outcome for your speech. It is possible, however, to turn these fearful visions around. Tennis players, field goal kickers, and speed skaters, among others, have found it helpful to visualize what they are striving for.

1 Visualize success

When you prepare a speech, do not let yourself think about failure. When you detect thoughts of failure, replace them with a positive scenario such as: "I will approach the lectern calmly, smile at the audience, and begin. My voice will sound strong and confident."

Do not, however, set unrealistic standards of perfection. Build some contingencies into your fantasy: "If I forget a point, I'll look down at my note card and concentrate on the main idea I am conveying."

Run through these positive visualizations a few times a day before your speech. As you practice, picture the audience responding favorably. And just before you get up to speak, remind yourself of the general tone and image you wish to project: "When I get up there, I am going to communicate my sincerity and concern in a warm, natural, confident manner."

2 Replace negative internal statements

One approach to reducing fears is to use the therapeutic technique of **cognitive restructuring** to probe our mental commentaries, to identify the unrealistic or irrational statements that cause fear and to replace them with more positive, logical, and realistic beliefs. We all have constant narrations running through our minds; they are so familiar that we are barely conscious of them. With some introspection, you can become aware of them and examine their effect on your behavior.

It is helpful to remember that these are not statements of fact but statements that you yourself have created and that you can choose to replace. Once you become fully aware of the mental commentaries that govern your response to public speaking, you can work on replacing the unproductive beliefs with more positive ones. Table 4-1 gives some examples.

Our unproductive responses are habitual and do not change easily. At first, you will have to repeat the replacement sentences

TABLE 4-1	Replacement Statements
False Belief	**Positive Replacement**
A good speaker never says "uh" or "er."	A few nonfluencies aren't even noticed unless attention is called to them.
I'm going to go blank.	I've practiced several times, and I know the basic structure of this speech.
I will make a mistake and ruin everything!	My speech doesn't have to be perfect to be worthwhile.
No one will be able to understand me because of my accent.	My listeners will want to hear what I have to say, not how I say it.

mechanically, over and over. Because the replacement sentences are so reasonable and logical, your mind will want to accept them. The reassuring nature of the words is likely to help you to become physically calmer, and feeling more comfortable reinforces the new beliefs.

4e. Reconceptualize the role of the audience

If one technique in particular has helped people cope with their fears, it is reconceptualizing the role of the audience.

- *Change the audience from "critic" to "recipient."* Remind yourself you are there not to *perform* but to share. Center your thoughts on audience members who appear sincere and responsive. What do you have to give these people? How will the ideas and information you offer enrich their lives?

- *Realize the listeners are on your side.* Most listeners are charitable and supportive. They want to hear a good speech given by a confident speaker. Recall a time when you listened to a nervous speaker. Your discomfort and embarrassment were probably almost as great as the speaker's. This is testimony to the basic empathy of most audiences. Listeners will notice the speaker's emotional tone. For example, you can actually feel an audience relax when a speaker who got off to a shaky start hits his or her stride, and the speech begins to flow more smoothly.

4f. Further assistance

Some fear of speaking is too deeply rooted to be remedied by the methods suggested here. If your fear of speaking is almost paralyzing and if none of the preceding suggestions work, you may need help in coping with it. Research shows that even severe fear of speaking can usually be reduced to a manageable level when treated by a qualified professional.

Many colleges and universities offer special sections of speech classes for fearful students. Others offer ungraded workshops to supplement regular classes. These programs use systematic desensitization, cognitive restructuring, skills training, or a combination of these and other methods. Psychologists and speech consultants also offer programs to help reduce fear of speaking. Such programs publicize using words like *stage fright, communication apprehension, speech anxiety, reticence,* or *shyness.*

KEY POINT   **Techniques for Coping with Speech Anxiety**

- Remember that all speakers feel some fear.
- Identify your specific fears so that you can deal with them.
- Give yourself time to prepare and thoroughly practice your speech.
- Use tension-release and relaxation techniques.
- Visualize yourself giving a successful speech.
- Replace negative internal statements with positive ones.
- Remind yourself that your purpose is not to perform but to share your ideas with your audience members, who want you to do well.

Critical Thinking Questions:

○ What are your greatest fears about speaking in public?
○ How might you restructure your beliefs to break free of old fears?
○ Which of the relaxation and tension-reduction techniques do you find most useful?
○ How will you prepare your next speech to better manage your apprehension?

CHAPTER 5
Analyzing Speech Contexts

The skills and recommendations discussed throughout this handbook are necessarily general. They become useful when you are able to tailor them to the demands and expectations of a particular context. A person with excellent generic speaking skills may be at a loss if a situation requires knowledge of a particular format. For example, it does a concerned citizen no good to prepare a compelling persuasive argument if the person cannot penetrate the rules of parliamentary procedure to gain recognition in order to speak. Ultimately, what is important to a speaker is not so much the words he or she speaks so much as the meaning created through the interplay between these words, the audience and the context in which they are spoken. Any given message or **text** takes on meaning from the circumstances that surround it—from the **context**. (See **1b.**) Both speakers and listeners rely on the context to make sense of messages. So knowing the rules and customs of a given speaking occasion will reduce the uncertainty you feel and thus minimize your fear.

5a. The basics

You will save time and work more efficiently if, before you even begin to plan a speech, you think carefully about the overall context of the speech. You can do this by starting with some fundamental questions: Who? Where? What? When? Why? How?

- To **Whom** will you be speaking? And **where** will you be speaking? It is virtually impossible to begin to design a speech without having some picture of the situation that you will be entering. The people gathered in a particular place, or linked electronically, constitute the audience that will help define the meaning of your speech. As soon as you identify them, you can use Chapter **12** to guide your more detailed audience analysis.

- **What** will you speak about? Topic selection is rarely completely under your control or completely out of your control. In every case, an early determination must be made about the general content area of your speech. Then, and only then, can you begin to gather materials and organize, develop, and craft them into an effective speech.

- **When** will you be speaking? Both the calendar and the clock have much to do with your overall approach to the speech. Be realistic about how soon you need to have the speech ready and how long you will be talking. This information is necessary to manage your preparation time (Chapter **10**) and to practice your speech (Chapter **33**).

- **Why** are you giving the speech? You always have some *reason* for speaking. Maybe you were invited to speak at some event, were assigned to speak in a class, or sought an opportunity to address a particular audience. Additionally, you have some *purpose* for speaking. In this handbook we classify general speaking purposes as to persuade, to inform, and to evoke. However, most situations involve a blend of these goals. Chapter **11** goes into more depth about how to identify these purposes and how to refine them into specific objectives and thesis statements.

■ *How will you be presenting the speech?* From the outset, decide whether your speech will be extemporaneous—that is, carefully planned and outlined but not planned word for word—delivered from a written manuscript, memorized, or impromptu (off the cuff). The decision will influence how you prepare. Guidelines for each mode of delivery are presented in Chapter **28**.

5b. The format and models

Just as there are genres of literature—for example, fiction, non-fiction, and poetry—each with multiple subgenres such as the thriller, romance, and space opera, there are familiar categories or contexts of speaking. When one conducts a training workshop, delivers a sermon, or participates in a debate, there are some well-known, albeit general, expectations about the shape that speech will take. In other situations, there are more specific formats that speakers typically follow. Examples of some educational, work-place, civic, and ceremonial formats are found in Chapters **6, 7, 8,** and **9.** Whenever such standard formats exist, it is your responsibility to learn about them and to adhere to them.

If you are not given a particular format to follow, your first research task should be to seek out models to study. How do social workers present case reports at staff meetings? What is included in a progress report on an engineering project? What kinds of speeches have been presented as keynote addresses to this particular organization? There may be a set of written guidelines to follow. If not, ask for manuscripts, outlines, and videos of previous presentations. Interview members of the organization about what is expected. Whenever possible, observe presentations of the type you will be making. Make note of the speech's organization, the kinds of arguments and evidence used, and the style and tone of the speaker. From these observations, generate a template for your presentation.

5c. The dimensions of the speaking situation

Besides finding out the essential information about a speech situation and researching existing formats, speakers benefit from thinking about factors that define every context for speaking. These dimensions might be arrayed along several scales. Locate where your speaking situation falls within each dimension.

◄──────────────────────────────────►
Public sphere   **Private sphere**

A context is established, in part, by where the speaking occurs. A particular set of expectations accompanies a meeting in a legislative hall, in a large city square, or in a cathedral. Quite different expectations will come into play if the speech takes place in a private office or in a living room.

◄──────────────────────────────────►
Formal demeanor   **Informal demeanor**

Some contexts are highly formal and require dressy attire; use of titles and respectful forms of address; dignified word choices; and ceremonial settings adorned by flags, corporate logos, and/or floral arrangements. The informality of other contexts is signaled by casual dress, use of first names, colloquial speech forms, and everyday physical arrangements.

◄──────────────────────────────────►
Monologic   **Dialogic**

Contexts are also defined by the role of the participants. In monologic situations, it is assumed that a featured primary speaker will dominate the event, taking primary responsibility for what is talked about. In dialogic situations, other participants can direct both the topic and the form of the interaction. As with all the other scales, there are many contexts that fall between the extremes or that blend the norms. At a public lecture, for example, the expectation is that the main speaker will be listened to without interruption or heckling until the question-and-answer period begins. Then the norms of dialogic speech take precedence, and it is considered inappropriate for the speaker to give another speech. Invitational speeches work this way.

◄──────────────────────────────────►
Highly prescribed rules of speaking   **More open rules of speaking**

All public speaking is rule-bound to some extent, but there is tremendous variation in how explicit those rules are. Some contexts have very rigid rules about who may speak, for how long, and on what topic. In a formal parliamentary meeting, a speaker must receive recognition and then link the discourse to a particular motion. In a legal proceeding, advocates can present arguments only during opening and closing statements. Contrast this to a meeting of a small task force in which participants might take the floor at any time and change subjects at will. The rules in this kind of small group either are implicit—group members may subtly penalize those who talk too much or too long—or they evolve on the spot, as when someone suggests that each person take a few minutes to state a position on the topic.

◄───►
Power resides with speakers   **Power resides with listeners**

Power differences between speakers and listeners inevitably influence context. Sometimes, the power resides with the listeners—bosses control paychecks, teachers assign grades, and judges make rulings. Whether motivated by common sense, self-preservation, or genuine respect, speakers usually show restraint in addressing those in higher-power positions. At other times, power resides with the speaker. Here, the expectations differ. The speaker doesn't deny having power but often chooses to downplay it in order to avoid being intimidating or threatening to listeners.

◄───►
Existing community   **One-time assembly**

The context of a speech differs based on the relationship among the participants. When an established group comes together, speeches typically include in-group jokes, use of abbreviations and shorthand expressions, and references to shared history. There is no need to spend time building a sense of community because the participants are already interested in a common topic or in the speaker. Extra time is needed when individuals gather for the first time.

◄───►
Immediate audience   **Extended audience**

Most often, a speech is intended for those who are present. However, there are occasions when everyone understands that the real context of the speech involves a much wider audience that will later read it or see its broadcast.

These dimensions illustrate the complexity of speech contexts. A speaker could be right on target in analyzing most of the factors in a situation but misreading just one of them—for example, the expected level of formality—could jeopardize effectiveness. Do not be afraid to ask questions about any new situation that you enter. If you are in charge of an event, be sure that invitations and announcements communicate shared expectations.

Another important determinant in each speaking context is culture. Mastering the marketing presentation in a U.S. business context will not prepare you to give a similar presentation in Japan. Knowing about different cultural norms and expectations will help you to be respectful of international guests and colleagues.

Each of the four chapters that follow offers preliminary suggestions for a particular kind of context—the educational, the business and professional, the civic and political, and the social and ceremonial. However, these generalizations need to be adapted for each specific event. For example, a training workshop within a company would combine the expectations of workplace and educational contexts.

Critical Thinking Questions:

○ How might skill requirements differ across each dimension?

○ What additional dimensions might you add?

○ What dimensions best describe the speaking situation you most often face?

CHAPTER 6
Educational Context

Although it is common to contrast academic life with the "real world," the classroom speaking context is a real one in all important respects. Classroom presentations include real people who are involved in the mutual creation of meaning with significant consequences. Speakers need to analyze the expectations and requirements of each educational situation. The first step is to determine the purpose of the oral assignment or the team presentation.

6a. Oral assignments to develop speaking skills

Academic speech classes, presentation skills training programs, speech contests, and Toastmasters' groups are contexts in which the presentation of a public speech is the primary activity. They are not a means to some other end. In these situations, the assignment is typically designed around the skills students need to practice and demonstrate. You may be required to give a speech to inform or to persuade, to include a variety of supporting material, or to use different kinds of reasoning. Admittedly, such speech experiences are artificial in some ways. For example, you may be asked to cover a great deal within a very short time or to provide a detailed outline with speech components labeled. But there is no need to resent the requirements of classroom speaking. Try to select topics that excite you and that could engage your listeners. Take advantage of this special opportunity to receive detailed feedback on both the impact of your message and the technical aspects of your presentation. To succeed in these assignments, it is important to learn exactly what each one entails and to touch every base.

6b. Oral assignments to provide practice for professional contexts

In advanced academic classes and in organizational training programs, you will have opportunities to learn how the generic speaking skills of analysis, research, organization, and delivery are modified in various contexts. To present a literary critique, a social science research report, an engineering design review, a health care plan for a patient, or a training program for employees (see **7e.**), you must master different sets of conventions. Oral assignments are designed to simulate situations you will face in career settings. Audience members may be asked to role-play colleagues, customers, or clients. Outside experts are sometimes invited to give feedback on presentations. It is particularly important in these projects to get detailed information on the purpose of your presentation and on the expectations of your listeners. See Chapter **7** for guidelines about various professional presentations and reports.

Though we always encourage you to "be yourself," assignments of this sort invite you to project yourself into a new persona. If you aspire to be, for example, a chemist or a journalist or a physical therapist, the classroom setting provides a safe environment to explore how you will communicate in the role. Step up to class assignments and try on the conventions, the speaking style, and even the clothing that will be expected in the new role.

6c. Oral assignments to help you master subject matter

The most common use of oral assignments in educational contexts is as a means to a broader end. Oral reports, debates, and group presentations are powerful ways to explore and master subject matter. When student presenters know they have to talk about ideas in public, they are forced to engage material deeply to synthesize points and make them clear to others. Members of classroom audiences often find that peer presentations help reinforce course content. This is possibly because classmates explain things in more accessible ways than professors sometimes do or because we listen differently to classmates than we do to our instructors. Instructors find oral presentations to be one important way to assess student learning, sometimes superior to papers or exams. These presentations show how fully students understand course material and how creatively they can apply it.

For these assignments, success depends on taking the extra time, after studying the topic and doing research, to follow the principles of effective speaking. An oral presentation doesn't consist of simply reading an academic paper. Clarify the expectations and time limits and then plan and rehearse a lively, well-organized presentation that will engage the audience and boost your credibility.

> ### CHECKLIST
>
> ### *Key Tasks for Classroom Presentations*
>
> ❏ Understand the instructor's purpose for the oral presentation, such as improving speaking skills, simulating a professional context, or enhancing comprehension of subject matter.
>
> ❏ Understand the criteria that will be used in evaluating the assignment. The ones used in history or business classes may be very different from those used in your public speaking class.
>
> ❏ Understand the format and time limits of the presentation.
>
> ❏ Practice thoroughly. Try to use an extemporaneous mode rather than memorization or reading. Practice with your presentation aids. For a group presentation, insist on a formal run-through with your group.
>
> ❏ Afterward, take time to consider what you learned about the subject matter, about speaking in an educational context, and about working cooperatively if it was a team presentation.

6d. Team presentations in the classroom

Team presentations may be assigned in a class to present the results of a collaborative project. Their purpose also may be to provide practice for presenting with a group in professional contexts. In either case, success depends not only on good speaking skills but also on planning, coordinating, and working in teams. General guidelines appear here, and more detailed discussions of team and group presentations can be found in **7b** and **8a**.

The first step of a team presentation is to establish a preparation plan as a group. A team presentation should be thought of as one "macro-speech" rather than a series of individual presentations. The group needs to create an outline of the entire presentation to ensure that all key points are covered in an organized way and that everyone gets to make a contribution. To provide coherent content, each team member must have a picture of the whole presentation and who will be responsible for each piece—specifically the introduction, main points, transitions, conclusion, and questions.

For the presentation to project the impression of unity, it should be clearly organized. Additionally, the main points should have parallel structures. If possible, everyone should use the same specialized terms and acronyms; each presenter should try to forecast or refer back to points by other presenters; and presentation slides, charts, and other visual aids should have a common look. Preparation meetings and at least two practice sessions will help ensure a smooth, unified presentation.

Critical Thinking Questions:

- ○ What makes classroom speaking different from speaking in other contexts?
- ○ How should you prepare for a classroom speech given by a team?
- ○ What audience behaviors might you expect when listening to a classroom speech?

CHAPTER 7
Workplace Context

Generally, in business and professional settings, the emphasis is on efficiency and clarity. Speech in workplace settings is expected to be streamlined and unadorned. A routine report to a work group typically does not begin with an attention getter. Rather it features a detailed, logical orientation to locate the topic within the organization's multiple tasks. Visual aids (including handouts) are central to professional presentations, in part so that technical details can be available for examination and reference. (See Chapter **27.**) Within organizations, listeners may ask each other tough questions and play devil's advocate. In a team environment, internal communication is a way to test ideas so that they can be improved before costly mistakes are made.

Typical presentations in a business and professional context include employment interviews, team presentations, project proposals, status reports, and training sessions. We also discuss chairing a meeting.

QUICK TIP **Professional Benefits** A quick glance at job descriptions on the Web reveals frequent use of phrases like "excellent oral and written skills," "strong ability to motivate others," and "excellent interpersonal and communication skills." The skills you develop as a public speaker will help you get a job. The candidate who gives answers that are concise, who can express ideas and desires in memorable ways, and who remains calm in a stressful situation will make the better impression. Once you get the job, you can use these communication skills to shape your career environment so that you gain personal satisfaction while being an effective and valued professional resource.

7a. Job interviews

Traditionally, the job interview consists of an applicant and a personnel director, with a desk as a prop. However, more interviews are now being done in a group, with a number of people from different departments and levels speaking with the applicant. In addition, preliminary interviews are often conducted by telephone. Other events that resemble interviews are the performance review and the sales presentation to a committee. In any of these situations, you may not be successful if you come prepared only to answer questions. Whenever you speak to a group, even a small one, you should apply several public speaking concepts. The following are the most important.

1   Audience analysis

Learn all you can about the people who will be interviewing you. If the organization has a website, check it for information. If possible, get a list with the attendees' names, so that you can learn to pronounce them, and with their positions, so that you can think about their various perspectives and interests. When you are introduced, you can quickly associate faces with the names and the roles you have studied. Throughout the interview, you can adapt your answers to their perspectives; for example, "That brings up the whole question of the cost effectiveness of surveys. I'm sure you have confronted that issue, Ms. Keenan, being director of marketing research."

2   Opening statement

The first question of a job interview most likely will be, "Tell us a little bit about your background—how you got to where you are now, and how you describe your orientation to our field." Seize this opportunity to set the tone. Make a brief statement that, like a speech introduction, gets the audience's attention, creates rapport, and establishes a framework for the main content to follow. Do not assume that, on the day of the interview, your résumé or sales brochure is fresh in the interviewers' minds. Besides reiterating what you sent earlier, you can add further information that would be of interest to the group.

You can use your opening statement to describe a general philosophy or position. You may highlight aspects of your experience to show trends or directions that led you to the present interview. Whether you are selling yourself, a service, a product, or an idea, use this opportunity to establish credibility.

It seldom hurts to compliment the organization. Be as specific as possible to show your knowledge of its workings.

3 Answers to questions

Review the guidelines for answering questions in Chapter **37.** Attempt to tie questions together in a group interview; for example, "This question spotlights another side of the training issue that Ms. Herman raised a few minutes ago." You can also demonstrate your powers of synthesis by relating certain common threads to your opening statement.

4 Problem–solution–result (PSR) statements

A **PSR statement** is a brief, memorable personal success story. In it, you succinctly state a *problem,* describe your *solution* to that problem, and then list the beneficial *results* of your solution—all in 90 seconds or less. If you prepare several PSRs, you will be ready to respond positively to a variety of questions about your skills and achievements. Ninety seconds is not much time, but brevity is important for PSRs.

Describing the problem should take no more than 45 seconds. You set the stage by laying out what was at stake, describing what the consequences would have been if the problem had not been solved, and noting any constraints you may have operated under. The solution should take no more than 20–25 seconds and describe what actions you took and what skills and abilities you brought into play. Summarize the key steps and avoid the temptation to go into details that would comprehensively demonstrate your understanding of your field. Save such details for follow-up questions. The outcome should show quantifiable results, and it should be a concise (20–25 seconds) and powerful description of the immediate and long-term benefits of your actions, including any awards or recognition that you received.

Here is a sample of a PSR:

Problem

> While I was the publications manager for a small software company, there was one time when my leadership, management, and organizational skills were really put to the test. We had a telecommunications management package under development and in trial for a large potential customer. At a status meeting, it became known that Sales had promised to have a complete documentation set for a week from Friday (eight days away), instead of the eight weeks agreed upon in the original development plan. Well, this was a major problem, because the documentation consisted of 10 manuals, many of which were not started yet. If we failed to produce the manuals, no matter how ridiculous the deadline, the image of the company would suffer, as would the chances for landing the customer.

Solution

> I immediately pulled my staff off all other projects and divided the workload according to their various talents. I made the rounds of the other departments in the company, negotiating new delivery dates for their existing projects while gaining assurance of easy access to subject matter experts for my staff. As the days passed, I adjusted workloads to respond to evolving needs, did subprojects where necessary, and continued to work on interdepartmental cooperation.

Result

> On the appointed Friday, three sets of a 10-manual, 800-page documentation suite went into the hands of DHL for delivery. As a result, my team was stronger, with the confidence that comes from meeting an impossible goal. The other departments knew they could count on us in a pinch. The potential customer was very pleased with the documentation and became a customer not long after—which landed the company a $12 million receivable.

By keeping your PSRs brief, you make them memorable, and you also allow your interviewers to set the level of detail. If the interviewers want to know more, they can ask additional questions, and, of course, you will have prepared more PSRs to cover the more in-depth questions. In the preceding example, an interviewer could ask more about how the speaker negotiated the new internal delivery dates or what the most difficult project assignment was.

PSRs are not only for job interviews. They are also useful in performance reviews and salary adjustment meetings, where you want a great many examples to demonstrate the benefits that accrue to the organization because of your presence. Although by no means exhaustive, Table 7-1 lists a representative set of topics for PSRs.

Prepare PSRs when events are still fresh in your mind. Don't wait until the annual performance review, until you start job hunting, or until you've finished school.

5   Effective delivery

You are "on stage" the entire time during the interview, even if you are sitting and in an informal setting or talking on the telephone. (See **7a.6.**) (Delivery skills are discussed in Chapters **34** and **35**.) When you answer a question from one member in a group interview, be sure to include the entire group with eye contact.

6   Telephone and video interviews

Increasingly, companies are turning to in-depth phone and video interviews, especially for out-of-town applicants. These

TABLE 7-1	Topics for Problem–Solution–Result Statements	
Specific personal attribute	**Decisiveness**	**Versatility**
	Creativity	Leadership
	Spoken/written communication	Confidence
	Fast learning curve	Analytical problem solving
	Adaptability	Organization
Specific work skill	Report writing	Accounts receivable
	Supervision	Medical knowledge
	Manual dexterity	Government relations
	Crisis management	Facility with computers
	Negotiating experience	Budget preparation
Accomplishment	Designed and implemented X	Improved productivity
	Lowered costs	Organized and directed
	Staffed X	Enhanced customer relations
	Set record for X	Met goals and objectives
	Recruited and trained X	Devised new strategies

interviews can last an hour or more and require the same kind of preparation as face-to-face interviews do. You should prepare a brief outline of answers to common interview questions and include statistics about your relevant accomplishments.

For phone or video interviews, there are additional considerations:

- Do not try to multitask. Make arrangements for pets and children. The interviewer can tell if you are not paying attention, especially if you need to ask him or her to repeat a question.

- Because the interviewer cannot see your body language or gestures, the tone of your voice should convey your interest and enthusiasm.

- Even though you may be talking from home, do not be overly casual. This is still an interview, not a chat with a friend.

- Try to answer the interviewer's questions directly and concisely—ideally, in less than two minutes. This shows that you can organize your thoughts and convey information effectively.

- Because you cannot see the interviewer's body language, it is okay to ask for feedback; for example, "Is there any area in which you want additional information?"

- Before hanging up, just as you would at the end of a face-to-face interview, ask the interviewer for his or her e-mail address so that you can send a thank-you note reiterating your interest in the job.

If you have a job interview via webcam, see the videoconferencing tips in **7g.**

QUICK TIP   **Your Online Image** If you are going onto the job market, you want to project an image of being competent and credible.

For a professional image in your online presence, is your Facebook page something you would want a potential employer to see? Are your electronic messages professional? Before you submit any message, make sure all words are spelled correctly, the grammar is correct, and the tone is appropriate. Also make sure you have double-checked the recipient list. Include your contact information so that the potential employer can easily contact you.

Do not use your current job's e-mail address. If your personal e-mail address is less than professional, such as fluzy465 or studman321, sign up for a second e-mail account just for your job searches. (Free accounts are available from Google, Yahoo, and other Internet companies.)

If you use social networking applications, such as Facebook, LinkedIn, and Twitter, check what the public—including potential employers—can see about you on those sites. Change that sexy photo of you to a more sedate one. Customize your privacy settings so that only the basic information is available to the general public. Additionally, as most potential employers will do, Google your own name to see what's out there.

7b. Team presentations

Often, teams form within an organization to make a **team presentation** about products, processes, or decisions to internal and external audiences. A team may be composed of people from the same department, or it may be interdepartmental. In either case, in addition to good speaking skills, success depends upon planning, coordinating, and working as a team.

1   Preparation plan

In the workplace, everyone is already over tasked. Therefore, it is crucial at the beginning of a project to make a plan that ensures people's time will be used efficiently. This responsibility usually falls to the project manager, who should initiate the first planning session well before the date of the presentation.

CHECKLIST

Key Tasks for Group Planning

❑ Clarify the purpose, including identifying who the stakeholders are, what their expectations are, and what constitutes success. (See **11c** and **22a**.)

❑ Agree on the core message—the equivalent of the thesis statement—that will serve as a touchstone against which all content will be evaluated. (See **11d**.)

❑ Divide the labor among team members.

❑ Establish the timeline, making sure to cover intermediate milestones and practice sessions.

❑ Preview the message, transition smoothly between speakers, and summarize.

---

2   Content outline with speakers' responsibilities

For the steps in organizing a presentation, see Chapters **10, 17, 18,** and **19.** We recommend that a team presentation be thought of as one "macro-speech" rather than as a series of individual presentations. We have all heard group presentations in which the speakers contradicted each other, overlapped in content, left out key points, jumped ahead, and stole the thunder of upcoming presenters. They even squabbled publicly about the order and coverage of points. To provide coherent content and project a professional image, each team member must have a picture of the whole presentation and how each piece relates to that whole.

Before deciding on an outline, the group should engage in initial brainstorming and preliminary decision making. After the topic is narrowed and focused, one person in the group needs to create a detailed outline of the presentation. The outline should be complete with an introduction and a conclusion, transitions, time limits for each segment, and a list of visual support and equipment needed.

In order to craft the outline of the presentation, the group should come to agreement on several issues:

- *The introduction.* This may be done by the team leader or the first speaker. In any case, the introduction should cover the basics— make the audience want to listen, tell them what will be discussed, and introduce the team members. (See Chapter **31**.)

- *The main points.* Each segment needs to serve a clear purpose in developing the core idea. If the group merely decides that, for example, Andrea will talk about her part of the project, and then Clint will talk about his, and so on, there is no guarantee that the components will be relevant and will fit together. As with a speech, it is best to cover only a few key ideas—which means only a few speakers. However, in an extended presentation, group leaders could present main ideas. Then additional speakers could present segments that function as subpoints under the various main ideas. No matter how simple or complex the organization, there needs to be prior agreement on the goal of each part of the presentation and on the time allotted for it.

- *The transitions.* Listeners need to be reminded of the overall road map for the presentation. The transition from segment to segment can be handled by a group leader, or each speaker can be responsible for building a bridge to the next. For the principles of transitions, see Chapter **31.** It is important to say more than "Here's Johnny"; instead, you should offer a statement like "Once the basic design has been completed, it needs to be tested. Here is where John Carlton and his able group come in. John is now going to tell you about the steps they go through to make sure our clever designs actually work."

- *The conclusion.* A group leader, or the final presenter, can review and integrate the material presented. The important point is to plan a wrap-up that ties things together and ends on a positive note. (See Chapter **31.**)

- *The question-and-answer period.* A long or technical presentation might have a question-and-answer period after each segment. Otherwise, time should be provided for questions at the end of the complete presentation. Decide who will field questions and direct them to the appropriate person. Sometimes, people who did not participate in the main presentation are available as resources during the question-and-answer period. (See Chapter **37.**)

3   Unifying elements

Potential customers or clients are greatly reassured if the organization seems to be a coordinated team. Projecting the impression of unity, mutual respect, and teamwork should be one of the goals of each presentation. Having a clearly organized presentation is the most important way to make this point. However, there are a few additional ways a team can show they are "on the same page."

- *Make the segments parallel.* Presenters might use common phrasing for the main idea: "With our technological innovations, we will own this marketspace next year. . . . With our dedicated and knowledgeable sales force, we will own this marketspace next year. . . . With our uncompromising support, we will own this marketspace next year." Or presenters might use parallel organization in their segments. In a cross-departmental status report, each department might follow this pattern: (1) review the goal, (2) report on progress to date, (3) report on problems encountered, (4) identify solutions, and (5) provide a current timetable.

- *Use common themes and phrases.* Develop a glossary of technical terms, abbreviations, and acronyms. Get agreement within the group to adhere to the "approved list." Once the substance of the presentation is in place, look for ways to emphasize your organization's unique approach or the special features you are offering. Just as the main ideas can have common phrasing, other central concepts and themes can be consciously woven throughout the presentation.

- *Find opportunities to connect to other presenters.* Speak of your co-presenters with respect and admiration. Use terms like *colleague.* Briefly forecast or refer back to their points and direct questions to them, acknowledging their expertise.

- *Present a consistent visual message.* Everyone's presentation slides, charts, and diagrams should have a common look. Agree on a template at the beginning of your preparation and designate a specialist to polish and unify the visual materials. Recognize that even team members who aren't speaking are communicating nonverbally throughout the presentation. Control your team's nonverbal cues.

4   Practice

Busy professionals who know their topic well often are reluctant to have formal practice sessions. But practice is essential for pulling together a team of speakers.

- *Schedule at least one early run-through even if some pieces are still under construction.* The goal is to get a sense of how the presentation fits together and to find opportunities to improve it.

- *Schedule at least one final run-through.* This will serve to polish the transitions and to familiarize the speakers with the equipment and visual aids.

- *Arrange for feedback on the presentations during the practice stage.* Participants may comment on one another's content and clarity. It is also common for managers or other organizational members to sit in on practice sessions and make suggestions. For very important presentations, simulations may be staged with people role-playing audience members. Also, communication consultants may be brought in to videotape the rehearsal and even to coach individuals on presentation skills.

- *Pay attention to the timing of the overall presentation, whatever the level of rehearsal.* You might also designate someone to give time signals during the actual presentation in order to keep the team on track.

5   Debriefing

Shortly after a presentation, the team should meet to talk candidly about what worked and what needs to be improved in the future.

7c.   Project proposals

To pursue a plan, you often have to convince others that your ideas are worth their time, money, and energy, by means of a **project proposal.** The project might be a research idea, services for a possible client, a course of action to reach an institutional goal, or an innovation you would like your organization to adopt. In each case, you are addressing the decision makers who will endorse or reject your plan.

1   The evaluation criteria

If you are proposing a research idea for your senior thesis, look at the standards set by the faculty. If you are applying for funds from an agency or bidding on a contract, carefully review the Request for Proposals (RFP) and be sure you address every point. If you are making a pitch to a client or customer, find out what is important for their decision among competing proposals. As with any form of audience analysis, listening is key. Talk to the decision maker directly or get information from documents and experts. If possible, study models of successful proposals.

2   The introduction

After greeting and introducing yourself and any colleagues, concisely state the problem that the proposal addresses. You should probably include a brief description of the background, showing your awareness of its significance. You might mention alternative approaches that have been tried or are available. In any case, within the first couple of minutes, state your proposal. (The proposal statement is similar to a thesis statement, described in **11d.**) Include the positive results of the proposed action, as in these examples:

- "My partner and I would like to contract to handle all your public relations and advertising placement needs, *freeing you to concentrate on your business operations.*"

- "Our agency is requesting funding from your foundation to provide a pilot program that will *empower senior citizens* by teaching them how to access health information online."

- "I would like to have 10 percent of my time released from my other assignments for the next six months to conduct research on a data security application that would *enhance several of our existing products.*"

3   The body of the presentation

Explain the overall strategy and the rationale for it. Move to an explanation of the steps you propose. Probably you will also discuss timelines, costs, personnel, and so on. If there are deliverables, such as product designs, prototypes, or documents, be specific in your commitments. It can sometimes be helpful to define what certain deliverables are *not*. For example, "We will deliver 6,000 widgets in bulk, but it will be up to you to provide the packaging." If there are limitations or risks, mention them briefly but don't dwell on them. Be ready, however, to discuss them if there are follow-up questions.

Presentation aids are especially helpful in making your vision clear. (See Chapter **27**.) Handouts can show that you have thought about specifics, while allowing your oral presentation to focus on the major concepts of the proposal.

4   The conclusion

After a short recap of your key points, make a direct appeal for the acceptance of your proposal. (See **31b.2**.) Once again, emphasize the benefits of your plan by linking to the needs and values of the decision makers.

> ***Not:***   Our consulting firm has an excellent reputation, and we take pride in doing exceptional work.
>
> ***But:***   Adopting our plan will help you refashion your website to better serve your current customers and attract new ones.

7d.   Project status reports

A **project status report** can be delivered to an advertising campaign's project team, a church's search committee for a new minister, or the funding agency for a multimillion-dollar government contract.

1   The introduction

Start your report with a very brief summary of what is being undertaken and where you are in the process. Assume that listeners are familiar with the overall project.

2   The body of the report

Depending on the project, this detailed account of the progress can be organized into categories such as task, objective, or department. For large projects, several speakers might report on different areas, such as the development, testing, documentation, and marketing of a software application. (See **7b** for suggestions on group presentations.)

When addressing problems such as delays in the schedule, be open and direct, but maintain a tone of confidence and optimism. Choose words carefully. Don't whine, apologize, or point fingers. Tell what you have done to rectify the situation and what adjustments you have made to minimize impact on the total project, as in these examples:

- "While we are waiting for delivery of replacement parts, we have shifted three production engineers to work on packaging."

- "Recent server problems at the university library have curtailed access for students, so I have not been able to see the appropriate research. However, I have applied for an account with the county library system so that I can log on to the necessary databases there."

3   The conclusion

End with a realistic assessment of the status of the project. If changes in budget or timelines are inevitable, state them directly. If you have proposals to overcome problems or to make improvements, declare them here. If things are going well, don't be shy about saying so!

Allow plenty of time to answer questions. Welcome them and respond directly and nondefensively. (See Chapter **37**.)

CHECKLIST

Sample Agenda for a Project Status Meeting

1. Welcome, introductions, overview
2. Goal review
3. Progress to date
4. Problems encountered
5. Identified solutions
6. Impact on timetable and budget
7. Summary, Q&A

7e.   Training sessions

Examples of **training presentations** include workshops for new employees about the corporate style guide for documents, training sessions for an organizational customer about a new software package, and health education classes for people who have recently been diagnosed with a disease or condition.

Making information clear and usable is the centerpiece of training. (For more on informative strategies, see Chapter **22**.) However, one key difference between training and informative speaking is that training is typically expected to produce some verifiable skills in the participants. To get people to change their behavior, you need not only a strong informative message but also persuasive skills of motivation. (The skill-learning process in **1d** can serve as a guide for planning a skill-related training program.)

1   The objectives

It is essential for trainers to discover what trainees already know and what they need to learn. A *needs analysis* is similar to an audience analysis. (See Chapter **12**.) However, the challenge for trainers is often to satisfy both the organizational decision makers who request the training and the participants who attend the training. For example, management might envision a training presentation on conflict resolution as a workshop in order to teach skills for responding to customer complaints. However, the employees might expect to learn how to deal with difficult coworkers or supervisors. Trainers should use a variety of sources of information, such as *interviews, observations,* and *questionnaires,* to identify the various perceived needs of organization members and to clarify expectations about what the training will cover.

In planning the training, you should use the needs analysis to identify the training objective or the behavioral outcomes you are aiming for. (See **11c.3**.) What, exactly, will participants be able to do after the training that they can't do now?

2   A mix of activities

A good workshop or training program always includes discussions and opportunities for practice. It is usually a mix of activities such as group exercises, analysis of case studies, role-playing, brainstorming, and sharing. Although selecting and facilitating such activities will build on your speaking skills, such activities usually require additional preparation in training techniques. Besides enrolling in train-the-trainer programs, you will find it useful to observe effective trainers in action and to work with an experienced co-trainer at first.

Another expectation of a training program is the extensive use of clear, useful, and professional visual and presentation aids. (Pay particular attention to the suggestions in Chapters **27** and **36**.)

3   The agenda

The training should follow principles of organizing any presentation. (See Chapter **19**.) The presentation should include a logical progression of content, coherent groupings, and effective transitions between points. (See **32b**.)

However, because you are involving the participants, you will not have complete control of the timing. You may have planned for 10 minutes of questions after your first "mini-lecture" but find that there is only one question, requiring a brief response. Later, an activity you thought would need about a half hour ignites the group, and they spend twice that long discussing it. Experienced trainers work from a careful plan, but they keep contingency plans available. Sometimes you may need to redesign on the spot, dropping some planned components and making smooth transitions between rearranged pieces. (Experience in impromptu speaking is valuable preparation for such occurrences! See **28b.**) At other times you will need to wrap up a discussion quickly and skillfully in order to move on.

To maintain your credibility as a trainer, avoid appearing rushed or disconcerted by the inevitable adjustments to your goals.

Not: "I had two more really great activities planned, but now I guess we don't have time for them."

But: "You've brought up most of the key points I wanted us to consider in this discussion. For a little more depth on [subject *x*] and [subject *y*], look over these pages in the printed materials you received."

Not: "Well, this framework has seven components, but I only have time to cover three of them."

But: "You see from this slide that this is a robust theory with several components. For our purposes in this workshop, we will be discussing three of them."

4   The introduction

Begin by explaining the importance of the material to be covered and then be quite specific about the objectives: "When this workshop is over, the participants will be able to [do these particular things]." Typically, the participants are invited to introduce themselves and to state their goals for the training. In dealing with busy adults, it is always a good idea to present a detailed agenda of what is to come and to be specific about timelines and breaks. You will also need to establish your credibility on the topic and to establish rapport with the participants. People learn better when they like and trust the instructor.

5   The two-part conclusion

The wrap-up of a training program differs from a simple conclusion in a speech. During the training, you provided opportunities for questions and comments throughout the session. You should also allow additional time for discussion during the wrap-up. In addition to a summary of what has been covered, it provides closure. It is valuable to have participants state what has been most meaningful and useful for them because training often includes explicit plans for the application of the concepts covered.

Participants might be asked to draw up an action plan for using the material on the job, or they might be invited to a follow-up session to discuss how the training has influenced their work. Finally, always save time at the end of training for feedback and a written evaluation of some sort.

7f. Chairing a meeting

Although individual speakers need to fit into an existing format, people who find themselves in leadership roles can often shape the context for speaking. Participants usually look to the leader to define the ground rules and facilitate the interactions. Here are general suggestions for leaders of meetings or programs.

1 Planning and preparing

You need to clarify the format, coordinate the participants, and anticipate contingencies.

- *Planning agenda.* Determine what will occur and in what order. Typically, the items of an **agenda** follow a hierarchical order. Routine reports, announcements, and introductions come first. They lead up to the major speaker, the presentation, or the discussion. For many organizations and governmental bodies, bylaws and custom set the general format. (See the *Checklist: Sample Meeting Agenda Based on Parliamentary Procedure* in this section.)

- Try to have all potential agenda items submitted to you well in advance. Many meetings have been thrown off schedule by the surprise request for a "brief announcement" that turned into a 15-minute speech. It is your responsibility to manage communication schedules so that the group's goals are efficiently met. Be firm in sticking to the agenda and moving the proceedings along.

- *Coordinating participants.* Give a *written* copy of the agenda to all participants in a formal business meeting. Confirm how and when they will participate: "I'll call on you for the treasurer's report right away. Save your idea for fund-raising, though, and introduce it under new business." For a decision-making session, let every participant know what to expect so that each can come prepared with the correct information and some prior thoughts. For an informal program such as a banquet, you might not write out the agenda, but you should still inform each person of the plan: "Right after the ventriloquist performs, I'll introduce you for the presentation of the Scholarship Award."

- *Managing logistics.* As chair of any event or session, you are a coordinator, facilitator, and host. You are not the "star." You are there to serve the group by helping members meet *their* goals efficiently and pleasantly. To this end, prepare by visualizing the event. Anticipate issues that may arise.

Will the group need information for its discussion? Perhaps you should bring minutes, policies, reports, and data for reference. Prepare handouts, slides, or charts to put key information before the group.

Consider the comfort and convenience of the participants. At a business meeting, will there be writing materials, name tags, refreshments, and scheduled breaks? At a banquet or public program, oversee or delegate even such small details as seating arrangements, water at the speakers' table, and audiovisual equipment.

CHECKLIST

Sample Meeting Agenda Based on Parliamentary Procedure

1. Call to order includes: checking credentials; calling roll; introducing observers, parliamentarian; honoring any ceremonial functions
2. Approval of agenda
3. Reading (or distribution) and approval of minutes of previous meeting
4. Treasurer's report
5. Reports of other officers
6. Reports of standing committees
7. Reports of special committees, task forces
8. Old business
9. New business
10. Announcements
11. Adjournment

---

2   During the meeting

Beyond the logistical concerns of agenda setting and troubleshooting, an effective leader can shape a context that helps a group meet its goals for communicating.

- *Introduction, transitions, and conclusion.* Carefully plan your opening and closing statements. Try to develop coherent, even graceful, transitions to bridge the parts of the program so that you do not fall back on statements like "We're moving right along" or "Last, but not least, . . ."

■ *Communication ground rules.* As the person who speaks first and from a position of leadership, you can model appropriate communication by the way you present yourself, the tone you take, and the level of formality you assume. Sometimes, however, it is necessary to be more explicit about the way communication will proceed. In these cases, a leader should *metacommunicate,* or talk about talk. For example, you might say:

  ■ "At our meetings, we agree to seek the floor by raising a hand and letting the speaker call on individuals."

  ■ "Because of the sensitive nature of our topic, we request that you do not use names or identify information when sharing examples from your organization."

  ■ "So that more people have time to participate, we request that you keep questions and comments brief."

  ■ "This morning, we will only discuss the problems that have brought us together and the causes we can identify. After lunch, we will get into possible solutions. If we start to jump ahead of ourselves, I will remind you to hold the thought until later."

Deal promptly and diplomatically with violations of communication rules and norms. Remind the entire group of the ground rules: "Remember, we agreed not to make any personal attacks in this discussion."

If ground rules have not explicitly been set, ask the group if it wishes to set some: "I notice that we have covered only two points on our agenda. Because we have to finish by four o'clock, would the group like to set a policy of limiting discussions to 10 minutes per point? Once we've covered everything, we can return to discuss any point in more depth."

If you must single out an individual, try to do so with a compliment: "Mr. [last name], you have so many experiences to share that you have already given us a great deal to think about. Now we need to move on to the next area of discussion."

7g. Videoconferencing and distance meetings

For telecommuters, colleagues in different cities, clients or vendors on different continents, and even some job interviewers, videoconferencing is becoming popular. In addition to a computer and a broadband Internet connection, you need a webcam and video-chat software, such as Skype. Here are some tips for looking professional while videoconferencing:

■ **Do not dress too casually for the meeting.** Avoid white, bright colors, and busy patterns, which can be distracting on screen.

■ **When you are speaking, look at the camera.** That is how you make eye contact in a videoconference. When other people are talking, it is okay to look at their image on the screen. However, be aware that the camera can turn back to you at any time, so look interested even if you aren't speaking.

■ **Consider the background.** Bright light from a window behind you will put your face into shadows. A messy dorm room or office will harm your credibility.

■ **Pay attention to your posture.** If you face the camera straight on, you risk looking like a mug shot, especially if there's a white wall behind you. Instead, slightly angle your body and then turn your head to look at the camera. But don't lean in too close—your colleagues don't need a close-up of your nose. You should be far enough away so that your shoulders are visible. Otherwise you will end up looking like a talking head.

When you first try videoconferencing, do a dry run with a friend to check for color, sound, and your facial expressions.

If you are videoconferencing with people from different cultures, be aware that your expectations for behavior at meetings may differ. For example, in some cultures, it is common to begin with polite "small talk" before getting down to business. Gestures can also have different meanings in different cultures. In Thailand and many Arab cultures, for example, showing the soles of your shoes can be a grave insult instead of a sign of extreme informality. Japanese people often nod their heads as they listen, but this means only that they are listening and is not a sign of agreement.

For more information about cultural differences, see

International Business Etiquette, Culture, and Manners at **http://www.cyborlink.com/** *Geert Hofstede Cultural Dimensions* at **http://geert-hofstede.com/countries.html**

Samovar, Larry A., Richard A. Porter, and Edwin R. McDaniel. *Communication Between Cultures,* 7th ed. Boston, MA: Wadsworth/Cengage Learning, 2010.

Samovar, Larry A., Richard A. Porter, and Edwin R. McDaniel. *Intercultural Communication: A Reader,* 12th ed. Boston, MA: Wadsworth/Cengage Learning, 2010.

Critical Thinking Questions:

○ Why is an agenda so vital to conducting effective meetings?

○ How do meetings with clear agendas still get off track?

○ How can the communication skills of a leader keep a meeting on track?

CHAPTER 8
Civic and Political Context

When you speak as a member of a community or a political body, you may be entering a context in which there are conflicts of interest. For a diverse group to come to a consensus, communicators need to work to build bonds. Civic and political contexts are often characterized by statements of respect and common ground. Notice, for example, how representatives from opposing political parties say things like "My distinguished colleague from South Carolina . . ." and "The esteemed senator and I have cosponsored legislature in the past, and it is with regret that I must reluctantly disagree with her remarks."

In a democratic society, we allow for the testing of ideas through vigorous debate and argument. We maintain social order by setting fairly strict rules constraining the form of speech. The ideal is that personal attacks be avoided, as are arguments made from pure self-interest. We do not argue for restricted parking in the neighborhood around a university campus by saying, "I am inconvenienced and my property value may be jeopardized." Instead, we state that the community needs to maintain its special character and to continue to attract residents who will be good neighbors to the university. Passion and eloquence are not out of place in this context. Sound argument and evidence are frequently combined with appeals to common values.

Typical speaking situations in this context include public debates, town hall forums, legal arguments, panel discussions, political conventions, appearances before community agencies, rallies, and talk shows.

8a. Group formats

Group formats include, but are not limited to, the symposium, panel, forum, and debate.

1   Confirm the format and clarify expectations

There are many versions of group presentations, and, too often, their standard labels are used interchangeably and inconsistently. You may be invited to be part of a "panel" and prepare accordingly, only to discover that the organizer has actually set up a debate. Here are the definitions most commonly used in speech communication texts:

Symposium: A series of short speeches, usually informative, on various aspects of the same general topic. Audience questions often follow.

Panel: A group of experts publicly discussing a topic among themselves. Individually prepared speeches, if any, are limited to very brief opening statements.

Forum: Essentially a question-and-answer format. One or more experts may be questioned by a panel of other experts, journalists, and/or the audience.

Debate: A structured argument in which participants speak for or against a preannounced proposition. The proposition is worded so that one side has the burden of proof, and that same side has the benefit of speaking first and last. Speakers assume an advocacy role and attempt to persuade the audience, not each other.

Do not assume that the person arranging the program uses the terms this way. Find out as much as possible about the program, such as its purpose, its audience, the amount of time allotted to each speaker, and rules or taboo topics. Ask about the format. Will there be a moderator, discussion among participants, a timer, or questions from the audience? Who are the other speakers, and what will they talk about?

2   Prepare carefully for a group presentation

Do not be lulled into thinking that a group presentation is merely a conversation. Even if you already know your topic very well, you should brush up on your research, plan a general outline, and bring along notes with key facts and statistics. Prepare visual aids if appropriate. Plan an introduction and a conclusion for your formal part of the session.

Be ready to adapt, however, in your best extemporaneous style. Because you are in a group, make frequent references to the other panelists: "Ms. Larsen has pointed out some of the reasons mental health care is so expensive." Also, unless the panelists coordinate beforehand, overlap on related topics is inevitable. If you hear your favorite example or best statistic being presented, quickly reorganize and substitute a personal story or equally compelling statistic. See Chapter **37** for suggestions to use in the question-and-answer exchange.

3   Be aware of your nonverbal communication

When you speak in a group, you should still follow the guidelines for effective delivery. In fact, if you are seated, you may need to project a little more energy to compensate for the lack of visibility and movement. Nevertheless, you should avoid rocking or spinning your chair.

Far too many speakers seem to forget that they are "on stage" during the whole presentation. While other speakers are talking, look attentive and be courteous. Nod and respond facially in ways sufficiently subtle so that you do not upstage the speaker. Above all, do not distract the audience by whispering, fidgeting, texting, or grimacing in disbelief. Do not hurt your own credibility by looking bored, slouching, or frantically going over your notes. Consider taking brief notes on what others say that you might wish to address.

CHECKLIST

Moderating a Symposium, Forum, Panel, or Debate

If you are called on to moderate a group presentation, here are some guidelines:

❏ Be sure the format and ground rules are clear to all participants well in advance. Let them know who the other speakers are and what they will cover.

❏ Plan an introduction. Engage and motivate the audience toward the topic to be discussed. (See **31a**.)

❏ Make a *brief,* one- or two-sentence transition between each segment of the presentation.

❏ Strictly enforce time limits. Emphasize the importance of these limits to speakers before the program, and arrange an unobtrusive signal for when time is almost up. If a speaker goes well past the time limit, you should interrupt politely but not apologetically.

❏ Moderate discussion aspects of the session by keeping the participation balanced. If one topic, speaker, or audience member is consuming too much time, interrupt politely and move the discussion along. Do not, however, take over the discussion to develop your own ideas.

❏ Wrap up the parts of the presentation with a conclusion. (See **31b**.) The logical closure should be an extemporaneous summary of the points that have emerged during the presentation.

The previous suggestions, combined with general speaking skills, should get you through most group situations. The public debate presents some additional challenges.

8b. Public debates

Formal academic debating and competitive tournament debating require skills beyond the scope of this handbook. Any good public speaker, though, can handle informal debates—such as those held during election campaigns or at public meetings or club functions—by remembering and applying the following prescriptions.

■ *Consider the opposing point of view.* Research both sides of the topic to see what evidence you will encounter. Look at the strongest points of your opponent's case and the weakest points of your own. This helps you anticipate the arguments and prepare for them.

- *Organize your ideas, arguments, and evidence.* First, develop your own best case for your position, which will be your opening statement or constructive speech. Next, plan attacks on, or challenges to, the opposing position, which you will use to respond to or to refute their case. Finally, compile defense material, which you will probably need to answer challenges to your position.

- *Prepare your opening speech carefully.* Pay particular attention to organizational clarity and to sound support of assertions. Follow the general suggestions for speaking to an unfavorable audience. (See **23b.3**.)

- *Address major issues during the refutation phase.* When you refute a point, explain the argumentative impact and show what damage you have done to the underlying logical structure of your opponent's argument. If you weaken an opponent's case, drive home the point by issuing a specific challenge so that the opponent can repair the damage.

- *Save time for a summary of the argument.* Debates can be confusing, with points flying back and forth. So, even if you have to skip some additional specifics, use the final few minutes to focus on the controversy, interpreting how it has emerged during the discussion. End with a persuasive closing statement and a clincher that capitalizes on your strongest point.

- *Maintain a calm and professional demeanor.* As with sports, poker games, or any other competitive activity, emotions can sometimes get out of hand. Do not lose perspective—getting the last word on every single point is less important than maintaining your long-term credibility. Even if another debater distorts or misleads, you should remain courteous and unflappable. Your tone may be vigorous, but it should never be hostile. Address your arguments to the audience and refer to the other speaker by name—not as "my opponent." Treat the person's arguments respectfully, and grant good points that are made. Always assume the honesty and good intentions of the other speaker. Never say, "That's a lie." Rather, say, "I think those figures are inaccurate. Here's what I found." Keep in mind the wisdom of the maxim, "You can disagree without being disagreeable."

Critical Thinking Questions:

○ What makes civic and political speaking different from speaking in other contexts?

○ How should you prepare for a political discussion with a bipartisan audience?

○ How might lack of civility affect your credibility in a democratic society?

CHAPTER 9

Social and Ceremonial Context

Arguably, the most ancient forms of speech are those that people developed simply to affirm their connectedness. We make small talk to share our everyday experiences, and we draw together to share joy, grief, outrage, and reverence. The expectation in social and ceremonial contexts is that the participants are united. This is not a time to mention difference or to actively build consensus. Just assume consensus and celebrate it. Typical speaking situations in this context include presenting an award, proposing a toast, or nominating a candidate.

Some speeches, classified in this book as **evocative,** are designed more to fill a ritualistic function than to transmit information or change behavior. These follow standard forms, and, as with all rituals, the familiarity of the form is one reason people like them. Happy moments, like winning an Olympic medal, and sad ones, like mourning a death, take on added meaning when accompanied by traditional, familiar ceremony. Certain words, gestures, and acts are expected. For example, the Olympic athlete would undoubtedly be disappointed if the medal award ceremony and playing of the national anthem were replaced by a gift certificate presented at a pizza house get-together. When you give a ceremonial speech, you are necessarily forced to tread the line separating tradition and triteness.

9a. The language of ritual

Cover the expected bases no matter how predictable they are. Do not be *too* creative but instead strive to find ways to make these ceremonial moments special and fresh. Above all, this means avoiding overused phrases and constructions. Unless you prepare carefully, you will hear yourself ad-libbing clichés that you would never use otherwise:

On this auspicious occasion . . .

This small token of our esteem . . .

Without further ado . . .

Information exchange is of secondary importance in these speeches. Style becomes crucial. Because the two or three ideas you transmit will be fairly basic, you should expend your energy crafting ways to express them—polishing your language and working on timing. This process is made easier by the fact that ceremonial speeches are usually short. Frequently, a memorized or partially memorized mode of delivery is best. (See **28d.**) Your language should be more elevated than in everyday speech but not so formal as to seem stiff or unnatural.

9b. Audience analysis

In preparing all ceremonial speeches, consider two questions.

1. *What are the needs of the person to whom or about whom I speak?*

   Suppose that, as company president, you give a safety award each year and so, for you, it is old hat. However, it is a special moment for the recipient. What can you say that he or she will remember with pride? Address the *uniqueness* of that person. Although the form of the speech may be stylized, the content should be personalized.

2. *What are the needs of the people for whom I speak?*

   In most ceremonial or ritualistic addresses, you can think of yourself as speaking on behalf of some group or community and not just for yourself. People have come together to share emotions as well as—or instead of—information. Yet these emotions may be unfocused. When you deliver a thoughtful and moving speech, you symbolize the feelings of audience members and are thus bonding them. You also help them gain perspective and find deeper meanings in their experiences. As you prepare for this sort of speech, envision yourself as expressing the feelings of the audience.

9c. Guidelines for various events

1 Presenting an award or honor

- Unless suspense or surprise is part of the tradition, announce the person's name early in the speech.
- Explain how the person was selected for the honor and by whom.
- Besides listing achievements or qualities, use a brief anecdote or description to capture some unique qualities of the person.
- If a tangible object such as a plaque, certificate, or key to the city is presented, explain what it symbolizes.

2 Delivering a eulogy or memorial address

- Do not accept this assignment unless you feel able to keep your composure.
- Acknowledge shared feelings of sadness and loss but do not dwell on them.

- Highlight and celebrate the value of the one being eulogized. Some people present may have known the person only professionally, or only socially, or only long ago, or only recently. Touch on several aspects of the person's life. Do not be reluctant to share light, and even humorous, moments.

- Use phrases that bond the group together: "All of us who cared for Eleanor . . ." or "I see many people here who . . ." or "We all know how persistent she could be when she believed in an idea."

- Try to place the loss in some larger, more optimistic perspective. Themes of the continuity of life, appreciation of each moment, and growth through pain are timeless and universal. These philosophical concepts remain a source of comfort.

- Do not play on the grief of a captive audience to promote a specific religious belief or social or political cause.

3 Giving a toast

- If the toast is a formal part of the event, make arrangements ahead so that everyone will have a beverage in hand at the proper time. Be sure that nonalcoholic beverages are available so that everyone can participate.

- Refine your basic idea into a short message of goodwill, and memorize it.

- Choose the words carefully. Humor, wordplay, rhymes, metaphors, and proverbs all find their way into toasts. If no witty inspiration comes to you and if the toasts in books all seem corny and contrived, there is absolutely nothing wrong with taking a sincere thought and stating it gracefully.

- If the toast is more than a few sentences—really a short speech—do not make listeners hold up their glasses the full time. Start out as a speech. Then at the end say something like, "Let's raise our glasses to our new laboratory director. Sheila, we wish you luck, and success, and may all your troubles be microscopic!"

4 Accepting an award or a tribute

- Unless asked in advance to prepare a major acceptance speech, limit your remarks to a few sentences.

- Accept the honor with pride. Do not let humility and embarrassment make you seem to reject the gesture.

- Share the honor with those who deserve it. However, do not get into an endless thank-you litany of the sort that tends to make the Academy Awards presentation run overtime.

- Give a gift back to the audience. Can you offer them a genuine tribute, an insight, or a funny story related to your relationship with them?
- End with a future-oriented statement about what the honor means to you.

5   Emceeing a ceremony or banquet

- Plan opening remarks that establish an appropriate mood. Whether the occasion is a solemn one, a celebration, or a regular monthly luncheon, make guests feel welcome and set the tone for the rest of the program.
- Make gracious and concise introductions. When you introduce people, direct the audience's response by asking them to hold their applause or by signaling for applause through your phrasing and inflection.
- Invite or control applause at other times during the event, if appropriate.

CHECKLIST

Sample Agenda for a Banquet or Ceremony

1. Greeting: brief statement of purpose by emcee
   - ❑ Invocation, song, patriotic ritual, group ritual
   - ❑ More extended theme-setting remarks by emcee
   - ❑ Formal welcome (from mayor, governor, etc.)
2. Introduction of honored guests at platform or head table
   - ❑ Introduction of special guests in audience
   - ❑ Reading of telegrams or messages from those not present
3. Ceremonial event (when an award is the central purpose of the program, items 3 and 4 are usually reversed)
   - ❑ Thanks to committees or planners
   - ❑ Announcements of elections, election results, and similar issues
   - ❑ Awards or presentations
4. Introduction and presentation of featured speaker or event
5. Closing by emcee
   - ❑ Quick announcements
   - ❑ Benediction, song, ritual

Light entertainment such as comedy, skits, or musical interludes may be inserted before item 2, 3, or 4.

Critical Thinking Questions:

- ○ What makes ceremonial speaking different from speaking in other contexts?
- ○ How should you prepare for a ceremonial speech such as a wedding toast?
- ○ What behaviors might you expect from the audience when they are listening to a ceremonial speech?

3 Planning Your Speech

CHAPTER 10. **Your Preparation Schedule**

Have a schedule to structure the preparation of your speech.

CHAPTER 11. **Topic Selection**

Select an interesting and manageable topic and determine what response you hope to evoke with the topic.

CHAPTER 12. **Audience Analysis**

Base your speech preparation on thorough audience analysis.

CHAPTER 10
Your Preparation Schedule

Experienced speakers save time and avoid wasted effort by organizing their preparation. An effective preparation plan will give you some time for creativity within the constraints of the deadline.

10a. The four phases of creativity

The creative process has four phases: preparation, incubation, illumination, and refinement. Here is how they apply to creating a speech.

1. The *preparation* phase includes gathering the materials, analyzing the topic and audience, and making the first attempts at putting the parts together.

2. *Incubation* is a phase marked by frustration, and the speech is often set aside. During this phase, your unconscious mind and your peripheral awareness work on the problems.

3. *Illumination* occurs when, suddenly, the pieces fit together. Illumination may occur while you are working on the project. However, it is just as likely to occur when you are driving down the freeway, taking a shower, or even sleeping. Exhilaration and relief accompany this phase. You work eagerly and fluidly, accomplishing more in a few hours than you have in several days.

4. *Refinement* comes next. After the creative burst, there follows a comparatively long period of checking details, fine tuning, and polishing. Like the preparation phase, this phase is largely cognitive and requires concentration and discipline.

It is essential to allocate time for *each* of the four phases. Many creative products have never been shared because the creator gave up during the refinement phase. Other fine ideas have failed because the speaker presented them directly after the illumination phase, without spending time on refinement. The rest of this chapter supplies guidance for optimizing your planning so that none of the creative phase is slighted.

10b. A realistic timetable

At one university, a group of public-speaking instructors informally survey their students at the end of each term, asking what advice they would pass on to the next group of students. Consistently, the surveyed students' response is "Start early." To know what is "early" enough for you, you need to create a detailed timetable.

1   List the tasks and the time needed

Be sure to include intellectual tasks such as analyzing your topic and not just physical tasks such as going to the library or making visual aids. For each task, jot down the most and the least optimistic estimate of the time needed. Always build in some extra time to allow for emergencies. Speech research and rehearsal can go on when you have a headache, but the creative aspects of speech organization require physical and psychological alertness.

2   Determine the order of the tasks

Professional project managers call this step *determining the critical path*. It consists of listing all the tasks in chronological order with the time estimates for each one. Speech practice must occur after the speech outline is completed. The outline cannot be completed until you have articulated your speech purpose, goals, and so on. When you lay out the entire project in this linear fashion and add up the time estimates for all the tasks, you will see if it is possible to reach your goals. Often, you may discover that in order to succeed, some preliminary steps must be taken *now*. Suppose your speech is due in three weeks, and the critical path adds up to five weeks. If you discover now that your plans are too ambitious, you have time to scale them down. Perhaps you don't really need eight interviews or professionally designed visual aids.

3   Set intermediate deadlines

In Figure 10-1, speech planning and practice is divided into four stages: initial decisions and analysis, research, development of speech materials, and practice. For each stage, the central tasks are contained in a box with a solid border. The related but less time-bound tasks are surrounded by a broken border. Generally, time flows downward and to the right in this chart.

The figure also shows the transitions between stages where deadlines fall naturally. That is, the central tasks of one stage cannot really be started until the central tasks of the previous stage have been completed. For example, you must make preliminary decisions regarding a narrowed and focused topic, purpose, and thesis before you can get into the serious research. At some point, you must stop gathering material and put the speech together. In addition, without a speech outline, you cannot begin the first stage of practice. There is no point in feedback practice sessions that come too late for you to make adjustments based on the feedback.

Sometimes, however, you must briefly retrace a few steps. For instance, important new evidence may present itself, or a feedback session may show that a different visual aid is needed. Such backward steps should be minimal, and under almost no circumstances should you be changing basic decisions, such as your

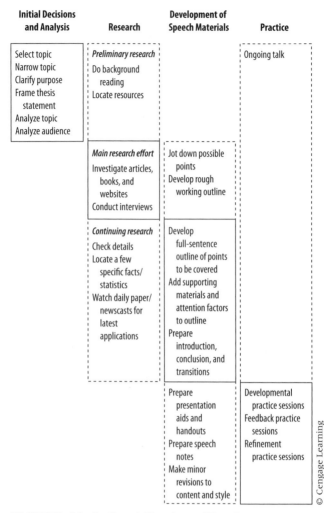

Initial Decisions and Analysis	Research	Development of Speech Materials	Practice
Select topic Narrow topic Clarify purpose Frame thesis statement Analyze topic Analyze audience	*Preliminary research* Do background reading Locate resources		Ongoing talk
	Main research effort Investigate articles, books, and websites Conduct interviews	Jot down possible points Develop rough working outline	
	Continuing research Check details Locate a few specific facts/statistics Watch daily paper/newscasts for latest applications	Develop full-sentence outline of points to be covered Add supporting materials and attention factors to outline Prepare introduction, conclusion, and transitions	
		Prepare presentation aids and handouts Prepare speech notes Make minor revisions to content and style	Developmental practice sessions Feedback practice sessions Refinement practice sessions

© Cengage Learning

FIGURE 10-1 Speech Planning and Practice

topic. Especially, do not make any major changes to the speech at the last minute. During the final practice sessions, you should have complete mastery of the organization and basic content. In that way, you can focus on refining your phrasing, delivery, and timing in order to obtain the desired audience response.

10c. Oral composition

Because a speech is delivered orally, it should be composed orally. Also, because the meaning of a speech is dependent on the interaction between speaker and listeners, it should be created collaboratively. Accomplish this goal by keeping the speech "conversational" even during those parts of preparation that require you to draw on your skills as a writer or performer.

Although you cannot practice the speech until your basic outline exists, one form of oral preparation begins with your first idea. This is the "ongoing talk" in the large, dotted section in the *Practice* column of Figure 10-1. Talk to yourself about your topic. Talk to other people. Try out your ideas and words; see if they make sense. Work your ideas into conversations over lunch and chats with friends. After talking ideas through with a number of people, you will find that you have begun to work out the speech wording.

If you are fortunate, you may be able to continue this oral and collaborative process by structuring your practice sessions as a more formal method for obtaining feedback and support. (See Chapter **33**.)

CHECKLIST

Avoid Common Planning Pitfalls

❏ *Give yourself time for incubation.* Try to live with your topic for a while before you start composing your speech. Plan an hour of preparation for each speech minute.

❏ *Build in some time for unexpected emergencies.* Don't overrate your efficiency and cut your preparation time too close. As insurance, put some breathing room in your schedule.

❏ *Work through writer's block.* Don't give in to the temptation to do "a little more" research or planning. For your speech to succeed, you must stop getting ready to create and start creating well before the final deadline.

❏ *Start early to practice orally.* You will need to practice a speech aloud several times to be successful. Plan to orally practice for three days before your actual speech date. The first time you give the speech aloud should not be in front of the audience.

Critical Thinking Questions:

○ Why is it necessary to plan for creativity when developing a speech?

○ Why is oral preparation preferable to practice "in your head"?

○ How will you overcome your personal planning pitfalls?

C H A P T E R   1 1

Topic Selection

Do not settle on the first topic that occurs to you. Consider a number of different topics and assess whether they are interesting, manageable, and likely to evoke the response you want. When you have chosen a promising topic, crystallize your reasons for speaking about that subject.

11a. Looking for a topic

Speakers have varying degrees of freedom in topic choice, depending on their situation. At one end of the spectrum is the assistant manager who is told to give an oral report on the effectiveness of the current employee scheduling system. At the other end is the student who is told, "Friday morning you will be the third speaker and persuade us to do something, anything." Most speaking situations fall between these extremes. Even when the general topic is set, you need to develop an approach that will fit you, the audience, and the situation.

1   Your experience, expertise, and interests

You bring a body of knowledge to the speech situation. Perhaps this is why you have been asked to speak. Your background may be the springboard for discovering a twist on a topic that can develop into an interesting and compelling speech. You should ask yourself a number of questions to help progress with this.

Brainstorm answers to the following questions. Do not stop to evaluate every answer as you write it down. Respond to these questions in as many different ways as you can think of, even if some seem silly. Later, you will select your best topic in terms of audience and occasion.

- *What unusual experiences have you had?* Consider places you have traveled, jobs you have held, and events in which you have participated. Do not overlook experiences that you take for granted but that might be unfamiliar and interesting to others.

- *What special knowledge or expertise do you have?* Each of us has developed mastery in certain areas. This may be in relation to how you make your living or to people you meet in the context of work. Your course of study in school has increased your knowledge in areas that might be of interest to your potential audience. Think, too, about the talents, hobbies, and skills you have developed.

- *How are you uniquely prepared to assist your audience?* Perhaps your role at work or in an organization affords you knowledge or insights that others need.

- *What strong opinions and beliefs do you hold?* What topics stir your passions? Issues that touch on your core values frequently make good speech topics. (See Chapter **25.**) These are the kinds of topics that can provoke you into heated debate or that fascinate you intellectually. Explaining the basis of a pet theory or favorite area of inquiry can grow into an excellent speech.

- *What would you like to know more about?* Use the occasion of giving a speech as an opportunity to research a topic that has piqued your curiosity.

2   The audience and occasion

By brainstorming answers to the questions in **11a.1,** you will create a great list. To choose the one topic on which you will speak, you next need to think about who the audience members are and what they expect. This step can help you rule out a number of the possible ideas on your list. Remember that the occasion for a speech is closely related to its context. (See Part **2.**)

To find the most appropriate topic from those remaining, empathy is your best tool. Imagine you are one of the audience members sitting on those hard chairs in the boardroom or classroom. What topic would make you want to listen?

3   A timely and timeless topic

You may still have more than one possible topic on your list even after going through the processes in **11a.1** and **11a.2.** Other things being equal, the best topics are those that are both timely and timeless. For example, people were discussing the rights of the individual versus the rights of the group and the need for security versus the need for adventure both 1,000 years ago and this past year. Our descendants most likely will continue to discuss these issues. When you tie a contemporary event to one of these enduring concerns, you link the timely and the timeless.

Neither of these conditions by itself is an indication that the topic will be a good one. If an event has been front-page news for two weeks, a speech on that topic may be timely. However, unless you can tell your audience what it means in more universal terms, you probably will give them little information that they do not already know. The reverse is true as well. Your audience can miss or fail to be interested in the relevance of your topic if you do not tie it into the fabric of their current existence. A profound, timeless topic should have a timely application, and a timely speech should show the timeless implication of the subject.

Table 11-1 shows how topics that are too narrowly contemporary or too broadly universal may be altered to meet these criteria. Notice the variety of speeches to which the timely/timeless standard can apply.

TABLE 11-1	Timely and Timeless Topics	
Timely (but Potentially Trivial)	**Timeless (but Potentially Diffuse)**	**Timely and Timeless**
There was a major confrontation last week when the Ku Klux Klan held a rally downtown.	Freedom of assembly must be protected for everyone.	Last week's confrontation over the Ku Klux Klan rally raised important questions about what restrictions, if any, should be placed on freedom of assembly.
I took a trip to Quebec.	Travel helps people understand diversity of human cultures.	My trip to Quebec helped me to understand my own culture by contrasting it with another.
Our company has adopted a new profit-sharing plan.	The best management philosophy is one that treats the employees like partners.	Our new profit-sharing plan will benefit the employees directly, and it reflects an enlightened philosophy of management.

11b. Narrowing your topic

The selection of a topic is not complete until that topic has been narrowed to accommodate the constraints of time. You have to limit yourself to the number of points that can be adequately developed in the time available. You can simplify your research and preparation by narrowing your topic at the beginning. For example, instead of looking up every book and article about the impact of the Internet on society, you can focus on those related to the influence of social network sites in higher education.

1 Determine the number of ideas

The average speaker utters 100 to 150 words per minute. If you speak very rapidly or very slowly, you may fall outside of this range. Chances are, though, that your rate of speaking is somewhere near 125 words per minute. Conveniently, a typical paragraph of simple sentences runs about 125 words. Thus, on average, a speaker delivers roughly one short paragraph per minute. If your material is highly technical or has a lot of statistics, dialogue, or dramatic pauses, or if you speak slowly, you had better allot two minutes per paragraph.

This formula, though simple, allows you to make a fairly realistic estimate of the length of your speech. For instance, if you plan on speaking informatively for eight to ten minutes, you need to set aside at least one to two minutes for the introduction and one minute for the conclusion. This leaves six to seven minutes for the body of your speech—or six to seven short paragraphs.

The same formula can be applied to longer speeches, business presentations, and lectures. A 20-minute speech can be thought of as 20 short, simple paragraphs or 10 longer, more developed paragraphs.

2   Select a few main ideas

Knowing that a speech should be limited to two or three main points does not tell you *which* two or three to select. Consider the following questions, which can help you narrow your topic effectively.

- *Which aspects of your topic are best covered in the public, oral mode?* A speech should not be used to repeat common knowledge, to discuss specialized problems of a small portion of the audience, or, of course, to indulge the speaker's ego.

- *Which aspects of your topic are best suited to this audience and occasion?* Select those points that relate most directly to the needs, attitudes, knowledge, and expectations of your listeners. (See Chapter **12**.)

- *Which aspects of your topic can you present most effectively?* Select those points on which you have the most knowledge; in which you have the most interest; and which best fit your strengths and abilities, for example, explaining complex material or telling stories.

11c. Clarifying the reasons for your speech

Each speech has a general purpose, a specific purpose, and a set of desired outcomes. Like a speech's occasion, the purposes and desired outcomes of a speech are also closely related to its context. (See Part **2**.)

1   The general purpose

What is your intention? Are you trying to change people's minds? To teach them something? To move them?

The general purpose of a speech can be classified in one of four ways:

Inform: A speech designed to explain, instruct, define, clarify, demonstrate, or teach

Invite: A speech designed to explore a topic with an audience or invite the audience to respond

Persuade: A speech designed to influence, convince, motivate, sell, preach, or stimulate action

Evoke: A speech designed to entertain, inspire, celebrate, commemorate, or bond, or to help listeners relive a significant event

In reality, no speech has only one purpose. Most have a combination, but one purpose is usually dominant. For instance, a classroom lecture is used primarily to teach, but at the same time it can be used to shape attitudes. The purpose of a campaign speech is to drum up support for the candidate, but the speech can also entertain. An excellent sermon might do all four: inform, invite, persuade, and evoke.

Within these general categories of informative, invitational, persuasive, and evocative speeches, of course, there are many more specialized formats and genres. Strategic guidelines for informative speaking (Chapter **22**) and persuasive speaking (Chapter **23**) give insight into how these purposes are realized in common types of speeches. All of Part **2** addresses adapting speeches for different contexts.

2   The specific purpose

Knowing which of the three purposes—to inform, persuade, or evoke—will be predominant in your speech will help you in the next step: deciding what you really want to accomplish with your topic. In phrasing your specific purpose, identify your central reason for speaking. Do not go any further until you can complete this sentence:

If there is one goal I want to achieve in this speech, it is to . . .

At this point, your topic should have a clear focus:

Not: My specific purpose is to inform the audience about politics.

But: My specific purpose is to inform the audience about the role of the two-party system in American politics.

Not: My specific purpose is to invite the audience to discuss traffic safety.

But: My specific purpose is to invite audience members to understand red-light-camera laws and to share their perspectives about them.

Not: My specific purpose is to persuade the audience against illegal immigration.

But: My specific purpose is to persuade the audience of the need for stronger enforcement of existing immigration laws.

3   The desired outcomes

Once your goal is phrased in the terms of what you want to do, turn it around and phrase it in terms of what you want your *audience* to do:

> If there is one action I want my listeners to take away after my speech, it is to . . .

In other words, if your speech is a success, what will your audience do? This is called the **primary audience outcome.**

> ***Not:*** My desired outcome is to sell this product.
>
> ***But:*** My desired outcome is to *have you buy* this product.
>
> ***Not:*** My desired outcome is to explain photosynthesis.
>
> ***But:*** My desired outcome is to *have you understand* the workings of photosynthesis.

The desired outcome is the behavior you want the audience to adopt.

Next, break the primary audience outcome into a series of *contributing audience outcomes*. In phrasing these components, use verbs that describe *actions*. "I want my audience to *appreciate* art" is fine for a primary audience outcome, but you must go further and ask yourself how you will know if you have succeeded. What, exactly, are people doing when they are appreciating art? If you think about the specific behaviors that indicate appreciation of art, you will probably come up with a list like this:

- Go to galleries and museums
- Read books on art
- Create pieces of art

Here is how speech purposes and desired outcomes can be crystallized for a persuasive speech about eating habits:

> *General purpose:* To persuade
> *Specific purpose:* To convince audience members to change their eating habits
> *Primary audience outcome:* I want my audience to start eating locally grown, organic foods
> *Contributing audience outcomes:* I want my audience to

- *minimize* consumption of fast food
- *shop* at local farm markets when in season
- *buy* organic food when possible
- *eat* organically grown food when possible

11d. Developing a thesis statement

In contrast to your "purpose" and "outcomes," the thesis sentence states your topic as a proposition to be proved or a theme to be developed. A thesis statement gives you something concrete against which to test ideas.

1   A single declarative sentence

The thesis statement, sometimes referred to as the **central idea,** gives your speech a focus. This sentence helps you make the transition from thinking about where you want to end up (your goal) to thinking about how to get there.

A thesis statement should not merely name your topic. It should briefly summarize what you plan to say about the topic. The rationale for wording it as a complete sentence is the clarity of thought that comes when you must delineate both what you are talking about, or the subject of the sentence, and what you are saying about it, or the predicate of the sentence. The sentence "Today I will talk about cell phone plans" has *you* as the subject and the fact that you *are talking* as the predicate—but your speech is not about you talking. That sentence is not an example of a thesis statement.

However, in the sentence "Cell phone plans are confusing," the topic—cell phone plans—is the sentence's subject, and the point being made about the topic—they are confusing—is the predicate. (See **11d.3** for further discussion of the role of propositional phrasing in testing the relevance and completeness of ideas.) Be sure that the thesis statement includes enough information to differentiate your approach from other possibilities.

Invitational Speech

Not:	Exploring credit promises and pitfalls.
Or even:	There are many credit promises and pitfalls.
But:	Today, we will explore the promises and pitfalls associated with credit card use.

Persuasive Speech

Not:	Something must be done about human papillomavirus.
Or even:	HPV is on the increase and should be stopped.
But:	The threat of human papillomavirus requires a program of education and treatment.

2   Questions about the thesis statement

What questions will your listeners ask themselves during your speech before they accept your thesis? Try to identify these questions before proceeding with your research.

Consider this thesis for a persuasive speech:

"Today I will demonstrate the problem of homelessness in our community, share a solution being offered at St. Vincent Hotel, and help you to recognize the benefits of supporting this organization."

Audience members might ask these questions as they listen:

- Is homelessness a problem that needs to be addressed?
- Does the St. Vincent Hotel effectively address the problem?
- Do the benefits outweigh the costs necessary to move listeners to action?

A speech about comic books might have the following thesis sentence:

"With their scope, history, and influence, comic books are an interesting component of American popular culture."

The audience might ask themselves the following questions during this informative speech:

- What is the scope of comic book themes?
- What is the history of the comic book?
- What influence have comic books had?
- Are comic books an interesting component of American popular culture?

The answers to such questions will not necessarily be the main points of your speech, and you might not develop your ideas in this order. However, the analysis can direct your research and help ensure that you cover essential information.

3   The kinds of propositions

In a persuasive speech, the speaker *proposes* something to the audience. Thus, the thesis of a speech and the claim of an argument are described as propositions. There are three kinds of propositions: the **proposition of fact,** the **proposition of value,** and the **proposition of policy.** When you are developing a persuasive speech, discovering which kind of proposition lies at the heart of your speech is essential to planning your persuasive strategy. (See Chapter **23** for a full discussion of persuasive speaking.)

Proposition of fact   It may seem that if something is a fact, there is no need to use persuasion to establish it. However, there are issues in the factual domain that cannot be verified directly. For instance, there either is or is not life on other planets. The question is one of fact, but because we lack the means to find the answer, we must draw inferences from the data we have. Here are some other examples of propositions of fact:

Lack of physical activity increases the risk of developing type II diabetes.

Converting to solar energy can save the average homeowner money.

Proposition of value Persuasive speakers are often attempting to prove evaluative positions. Their goal is to judge the worth of something in order to establish that it is good or bad, wise or foolish, just or unjust, ethical or unethical, beautiful or ugly, competent or incompetent. Here are some examples of propositions of value:

> It is wrong to try to avoid jury duty.
>
> The free enterprise system is the best economic model for the working class.

Proposition of policy Most common and most complex of the persuasive theses is the proposition of policy, which advocates a specific course of action. Here are some examples of propositions of policy:

> The federal government should legalize marijuana for private use.
>
> You should send your children to a charter school.

KEY POINT   **Kinds of Propositions**

1. Propositions of fact: IS/IS NOT
2. Propositions of value: GOOD/BAD
3. Propositions of policy: SHOULD/SHOULD NOT

11e. Speech titles

Although every speech needs a thesis and a purpose, a title is necessary only when there is to be advance publicity, when there is a printed program, and usually, when the speaker is going to be formally introduced. Unless there is a definite deadline set for submitting the title, you can defer selecting one until the speech is composed.

An effective title should pique interest in your subject and make the audience eager to listen. Sometimes a metaphor, a quotation, or an allusion that is central to the speech can be part of the title. A title can take any grammatical form. It can be a declarative sentence, a question, a phrase, or a fragment, for example:

> "Freedom of Speech Is in Jeopardy"
> "Is Free Speech Really Free?"
> "Threats to Free Speech"
> "Free Speech: An Endangered Species"

QUICK TIP   **Thesis Statement versus Speech Title** Do not confuse the thesis statement with the speech title. The thesis statement is a declarative sentence essential for organizing and composing the speech. The title can be a word or a phrase. Its purpose is not only to indicate the topic but also to arouse interest.

Critical Thinking Questions:

○ Explain the process and benefit of selecting a topic appropriate to audience and occasion.

○ How might one's audience influence topic selection?

○ Brainstorm a list of possible speech topics and create a general purpose, specific purpose, primary audience outcome, and contributing audience outcome for this speech.

CHAPTER 12
Audience Analysis

Speakers do not give speeches to audiences; they jointly create meaning with audiences. The outcome of any speech situation is a product of what the speaker actually says and how the listeners process and interpret what is said. Audience analysis, therefore, is much more than a step in planning a speech. It involves the coming to understand and consider the "coauthors" of your speech—your listeners.

You speak to a particular group of people because you want a certain response from them. If you do not know the composition of that group, you cannot make intelligent decisions about what to include, what to emphasize, and how best to arrange and present your ideas. Therefore it is necessary to research your audience thoroughly. Their age, gender, attitudes, and expectations are all relevant to your planning. This chapter approaches each of these audience demographics separately. You have to mix and match these techniques as you discover the actual composition of your potential audience.

12a. Sources of information

When you ask an audience to listen to your ideas, you are asking them to come partway into your experience. It is your obligation, in turn, to go partway into theirs.

The following are valuable sources of information to understand your audience. It may be necessary to use more than one of these sources.

■ *Direct observation.* If possible, try to observe the audience, perhaps at a business meeting or while they listen to another speaker.

- *Systematic data collection.* One excellent way to understand your audience is to ask them about themselves. Even a simple form of data gathering can be useful, such as distributing a three- or four-item questionnaire at a meeting before the one where you will speak. Another option is to use an online survey tool such as SurveyMonkey.com to gather audience attitudes and background.

- *Interviews/focus groups.* When you cannot get information on the whole audience, talk to some members of the group. In these individual or group sessions, try to find out not just what people think but also how they think. Ask open-ended questions and encourage respondents to expand on their answers by framing follow-up questions in a nonargumentative tone. Ask them for examples and anecdotes.

- *Contact person.* The person who asked you to speak has certain expectations about the interaction between you and the audience. Ask this contact person specific questions about his or her perceptions of the audience. Ask about previous speakers—both best and worst—to better understand what to do and what to avoid.

- *Inference and empathy.* When you do not have much specific information about an audience, draw on your general knowledge of human behavior and groups. Let empathy round out the image. What, for example, would be reasonable assumptions about a college audience at 9:00 a.m. on your campus, or at a Rotary Club monthly luncheon? Get outside yourself and adopt your listeners' frames of reference.

12b. Audience demographics

Obtaining each audience's vital statistics enables you to make certain general predictions about their responses. The *Checklist: Pertinent Demographic Questions* lists useful kinds of statistics. However, there is no such thing as an average audience. A speaker would be more than a little surprised to stand before a group of listeners whose composition followed exactly the distribution of the most recent census with regard to age, gender, race, socioeconomic status, and religion.

CHECKLIST

Pertinent Demographic Questions
- ❑ What is the average age of the audience members?
- ❑ What is the age range of the audience members?
- ❑ With what generational group would audience members most closely associate?

❏ What is the proportion of males and females in the audience?

❏ What relational arrangements are represented (married, single, divorced, domestic partnership)?

❏ What cultural groups are represented, in what proportion?

❏ What is the socioeconomic composition of the group?

❏ What occupations are represented?

❏ What religious groups are represented?

❏ How homogeneous (similar) or heterogeneous (diverse) are the audience members for each of the preceding characteristics?

Obviously, all demographic characteristics are not equally important for any given speech. Knowledge of the religious orientation of your audience will be important in preparing a speech on euthanasia. However, religious orientation might have no bearing whatsoever on another topic. Despite differences in relative importance to a particular topic, try to find out the following demographic characteristics, if only to give you a general picture.

You can gather information about your audience from the person who asked you to speak. In addition, you can use the Internet to find demographic information about the people who live in a particular town or region. Look for official city websites, population profiles at **http://www.city-data.com,** and websites of local newspapers for local current events. If you are speaking to members of a specific organization or company, the organization or company may have its own website, which will give you information about its activities or products. Nevertheless, it is important to keep in mind the limits of demographic generalizations and to avoid stereotyping.

K E Y   P O I N T   **Limitations of Demographic Generalizations** Very few generalizations can be made on the basis of demographic factors. Social science research, even when carefully controlled and well designed, provides *probability statements* about how one group *on average* differs from another group *on average*. For example, with respect to almost any trait you might select, the differences among individual women and among individual men are far greater than the differences between the average man and the average woman. You can say that many people in an audience *are likely to* respond in a certain way; you cannot say that any individual in that audience definitely *will* respond in a given way.

1   Generational culture

It is likely that your classroom or workplace contains three different generational groups, which may include Traditionalists, Boomers, Gen Xers, and Millennials. These groups have been influenced by very different environmental, political, and sociological circumstances, leading to quite different perspectives. Of course not every person in a particular generation will espouse the values of that generation, but some tendencies are worth consideration.

- Traditionalists have been shaped directly or indirectly by the Great Depression and World War II. They tend to value privacy, hard work, trustworthiness, formal communication authority, and social order, and tend to be fiscally conservative.

- Boomers have been shaped by the post–World War II economic boom. They tend to value competition, change, hard work, and inclusion, and take more collaborative approaches to work.

- Generation X has been shaped by greater independence at a younger age than previous generations (i.e., latchkey kids). Members of this group tend to be highly independent, creative, entrepreneurial, and comfortable with change. They tend to value feedback, balance, fun, informality, and information, and to expect instant access to information.

- Millennials have been shaped by technology and instant access to information. They tend to value positive reinforcement, autonomy, flexibility, diversity, technology, multitasking, and constant access to information available through their extensive social network.

> QUICK TIP   **Generational Identity** You can infer certain specific experiences audience members may have had based on their generational identity. What world events, socio-political shifts, movies, TV shows, songs, and sports figures have been central to your audience members' lives? What terms, examples, or concepts will be unfamiliar to them?

2   Gender

The issue is not how many males and females are present, but what audience members think about masculinity and femininity. These gender expectations are highly culture bound and have changed during the last few generations.

Traditionally, women were socialized to be nurturing, sensitive, compassionate, and emotional. So, in the past, appeals to home, family, and the safety of loved ones usually were effective with women. Traditionally, men were socialized to be dominant, aggressive, ambitious, and unemotional (except when it came to sports). So, a speech to a predominantly male group used appeals to power, success, competitive values, and logic.

In recent decades, however, women and men have been experimenting with more equal roles and divisions of labor in both public and private life. Today, stereotypical assumptions about social roles and power relationships are likely to offend a sizable portion of your audience. Avoid such comments as "To Mr. Davis's left, the charming young lady in the pretty blue dress is our regional sales manager, Linda."

3 Race/ethnicity

As with the differences between women and men, the differences between ethnic groups are not innate. The differences that do exist result from variations in socialization and experience. In the United States, we daily encounter newcomers who migrated here voluntarily to be with their families or to improve their opportunities. Some came involuntarily as refugees. Conversations with such diverse members of our communities encourage those who have been in the United States longer to remember why their ancestors came. Some came seeking opportunity, some came to escape economic hardship or political and religious oppression, and others came involuntarily as slaves.

This expanding ethnic and cultural diversity can be seen as either a problem or an opportunity. In the past, when there were three or four predominant ethnic groups in an area, it might have been a reasonable goal to become somewhat expert on the cultural values and symbols of those groups. Today, when dozens of cultures are part of a single community or organization, this approach to audience analysis becomes more challenging. Moreover, some audience members are likely to have a multicultural heritage.

Because people's experiences, not their traits, shape them as listeners, there are no prescriptions for how to relate to predominantly white, African American, Native American, Latino/Latina, Hispanic, or Asian American audiences. Instead, you need to familiarize yourself as much as possible with the experiences of each group. The common experience of nonwhite racial groups and most other ethnic minorities in the United States has included discrimination and oppression. Members of these groups are justifiably sensitive to any communication that reduces their status or reflects old stereotypes especially when delivered from members of a historically dominant group.

KEY POINT **Multiple Identities of Audience Members** Age, race, and gender all contribute to a person's interpretation of the world. So too do religion, social class, educational level, economic status, sexual orientation, health, physical ability, and many other factors. As an example, consider President Barack Obama, whose mother was from Kansas and whose father was from Kenya, and who went to elementary school in Indonesia and to high school in Hawaii. After college in Los Angeles and New York, he worked as a community organizer in Chicago and then went to Harvard Law School.

The demographic profile of U.S. society is constantly changing, and no formula can tell a speaker how each of these variables relates to a particular topic—let alone how they all interact. As a speaker, your task is to consider how the various traits of your listeners might affect their core values (or worldviews, frames of reference, or master narratives). (See **25c.**) What do your listeners draw on to organize their experience and make sense of it?

Forms of address, both collective and individual, are very important. Never refer to people by first names, diminutives, or nicknames unless invited to do so. Never address white males by titles such as "Mr. Jones," "Dr. Smith," or "Colonel Taylor" while addressing anyone else by their first names. Find out what group designations your audience prefers and respect their wishes.

Beyond showing sensitivity to the variety of cultural groups, a speaker can also demonstrate an appreciation of cultural diversity. People of any ethnic group can tend to look at things from the standpoint of their group's own history and culture. Taking the time to investigate other cultural views can open up a number of different avenues for good communication. Making the effort to pronounce unfamiliar names and phrases correctly and avoiding stereotypical cultural generalizations will show your goodwill and openness.

12c. Audience attitudes toward your topic

Audience reactions to the thesis of your speech can range from strong disagreement to strong agreement. Much social science research is based on asking people to clarify their attitudes on scales like this one:

Strongly disagree	Moderately disagree	Slightly disagree	Neither agree nor disagree	Slightly agree	Moderately agree	Strongly agree

If your goal is to bring your audience to take some specific action, your listeners' responses will range across these categories:

Opposed to action	Uninclined to act	Ready to act	Taking action

If the majority of your audience falls to the left on either continuum, that audience should be considered *unfavorable,* and if it falls to the right, it is *favorable.* If it falls in the middle, it is *neutral.*

Most speakers agree that knowing the audience's predisposition toward the topic is the single most important piece of information in planning their speech strategy. If your speech deals with a controversial topic, it is crucial that you interview people who have different attitudes and experiences. Listen carefully and respectfully to their accounts of the world. At the information-gathering stage, your goal is not to plan a strategy for changing their beliefs, but rather to try to see how their views and yours might be connected. Once you determine whether your audience is favorable, neutral, or unfavorable, you can follow the specific suggestions offered in Chapter **23.** Although attitudes toward your topic are most obviously relevant to persuasive speaking, they can influence the speech to inform or evoke as well.

12d. Audience expectations

Anticipate what your audience expects from your speech. We have stressed the importance of knowing your purpose in speaking, but what is your audience's purpose in listening? Perhaps they are required to attend your speech as part of a class or job assignment. Maybe they are present voluntarily but for a reason unrelated to you or your topic. Perhaps, if you are fortunate, they are there because of an interest in what you have to say. In any audience, you will find combinations of these and other motivations. Knowing the predominant audience expectation is vital to the preparation of your speech. An excellent speech can fail miserably if the audience expected a different sort of talk.

This is not to say that you must be bound by the audience's expectations. You can lead them to a new mind-set, but to do that, you need to discover what they know and expect. Start with the questions in the *Checklist: Audience Analysis.*

CHECKLIST

Audience Analysis

❏ *What do they know about your topic?* Make no broad assumptions about the sophistication of your audience; rather, use the techniques of audience analysis to know it. People listen and learn best when exposed to information that is just beyond their current level of comprehension.

❏ *What do they think about you?* Learn what your audience has heard, read, or assumed about you. You want to build on their positive expectations and overcome their

negative ones. Knowing what your credibility is prior
to the speech helps you decide how much you need to
bolster it during the speech. (See **26a**.)

❑ *What is the history of your audience as a group?* Audiences
come in many different forms, with varied levels of
group cohesion. Most audiences have some common
history, which may range from a long association in a
business or club to a few weeks together in a classroom.
Learn all you can about what they have done together.
You may find some connections to your speech topic.

❑ *What is the program surrounding your speech?* To
understand an audience's expectations of you, it is
essential to learn your speech's place in the context of
their immediate situation. Familiarize yourself with the
agenda and where you fit into it.

Critical Thinking Questions:

○ What demographic information would you request in the
event that you couldn't gather the information directly?

○ How would you determine your audience's attitude and
expectations toward you and your topic?

○ How is audience analysis useful in the process of speech
development and delivery?

○ How might an online survey tool like SurveyMonkey.com
be useful in gathering information about your audience
members' knowledge and attitudes toward your topic?

PART 4

Finding and Using Resources

CHAPTER 13
Your Research Strategy

To make the best use of your time, plan a research strategy. You need to think about what you want to find before opening your Web browser or dashing off to the library. How much time do you have for research? What are your objectives? What questions require investigation? What information can best be found in the library? Which research can be done online? Whom can you interview about your topic?

13a. Fit your research to your time

Chapter **10** recommends having a realistic timetable for preparation. In one day, you cannot make an exhaustive study of the literature. However, you can draw from general references like encyclopedias, whether at the library or online. With more time, a broader effort is possible.

13b. Progress from the general to the specific

Start by investigating the "big picture" with encyclopedias and even Wikipedia. As you begin to understand what is and what is not essential to your topic, you can get more specific. An encyclopedia article should be the starting point, not the end point, of your research.

> QUICK TIP   **Wikipedia**   The online encyclopedia Wikipedia (**http://en.wikipedia.org/wiki/Main_Page**) can sometimes be a good source of information because it is constantly updated. But this self-described "free encyclopedia that anyone can edit" is also more likely to contain errors—both unintentional and malicious—than are traditionally edited encyclopedias. Although the administrators of the site are working to make it more reliable, the wisest approach is to read the Wikipedia articles but not to use them as your sole source of information. The same is true of the growing family of "wiki" references, including Wikiquote (**http://en.wikiquote.org/wiki/Main_Page**); Wikispecies, a taxonomic directory of life forms (**http://species.wikimedia.org/wiki/Main_Page**); and Wikinews (**http://en.wikinews.org/wiki/Main_Page**). The Wikimedia Foundation is also building libraries of copyright-free books (Wikibooks **http://en.wikibooks.org/wiki/Main_Page** and Wikisource **http://en.wikisource.org/wiki/Main_Page**), as well as a collection of public-domain images, sound, and video (Wikimedia Commons **http://commons.wikimedia.org/wiki/Main_Page**).

There are two basic sources to tap for research: recorded information and interviews with people. It is usually best to start with the recorded information, so that you will be able to ask knowledgeable questions when you interview experts. (See Chapter **15** for detailed information about interviewing.)

One of the most useful talents in the early stages of research is the ability to skim. Do not try to read every book and article on your topic. Instead, try to get a feel for the most important approaches and theories. Look at the table of contents, skim the first and last chapters of the book, or read the first and last paragraphs of the chapter or article. Jot down the names of key people who are frequently cited in addition to recurring concepts and studies.

Similarly, on the Web, it is easy to be seduced by links that look interesting but have little to do with what you are researching. (See **14c** for advice about efficient Web research.)

As you begin your research, look for summary or state-of-the-art articles, books, and websites that synthesize current thinking on your subject. Pieces that trace the history of your topic can also be useful. Often, these sources are readily identifiable by their titles:

"What Is a Working Woman?" [H. H. Stipp, *American Demographics*]

"The Lasting Changes Brought by Women Workers" [*Business Week*]

Women in the American Economy [Juanita M. Kreps, Prentice-Hall]

Skimming several sources and reading a few general ones will give you a good overview of your topic. You can then narrow your topic and focus on the remainder of the research.

13c. Develop a list of key terms for your topic

As you start exploring your topic, make a list of key terms that appear often. Familiarity with the language of your topic is essential as you continue your research. Key terms are particularly useful in online searches—one way to reduce an Internet search engine's hits to a manageable number is to use precise language.

13d. Use audience analysis questions to direct your research

When you've done some background research, go back and analyze your topic. Consider whether you should narrow it, adjust your speech objectives, or fine-tune the wording of your thesis statement. See **11d.2** for the kinds of questions your audience might have as they listen to your speech. These questions can become the basis of your research objectives.

Suppose that your thesis is this:

"Since the beginning of the Industrial Revolution, women in the United States have been exploited as a cheap and expendable source of labor."

Your audience will want to hear the answers to questions like these:

Are women a cheap source of labor?

Are women an expendable source of labor?

Can the labor practices appropriately be labeled as exploitation?

Has the treatment of women been consistent since the Industrial Revolution?

Therefore, your list of research objectives should include goals like these:

Find out how women's salaries compare with those of men who do the same job.

Find specific examples of women who have been treated as an expendable source of labor.

Find an expert definition of *exploitation.*

Find out how women's work changed at the time of the Industrial Revolution.

Armed with this list of research objectives, you are ready to make the best use of your research time and to ask for the help you need.

Critical Thinking Questions:

○ What are the advantages and disadvantages of using a source like Wikipedia in the early stages of research?

○ What are the advantages and disadvantages of local interviews as a source of information on a topic?

○ In what situation might a "Google search" be adequate research?

CHAPTER 14
Print, Internet, and Other Electronic Resources

The vast amount of information available, literally at your fingertips, can seem overwhelming. Stay focused on your research objectives as you explore various electronic and print resources. (See Chapter **13.**)

14a. The library

Even with the advent of the Internet, the library is still the place to find the widest variety of research tools—including access to the Internet—as well as professional researchers primed to give you direction and help.

> QUICK TIP **Talk to a Librarian** Librarians are information specialists and are there to help find the materials you need. Do not hesitate to ask them questions. They welcome the challenge of trying to understand your requirements and can help direct you to the answers you seek, whether your questions are about key terms, general resources for your topic, or Internet search strategies.

14b. Books and articles

In addition to the librarian, important library resources include the book catalogue, periodical indexes and databases, and special dictionaries and encyclopedias.

The book catalogue In most libraries, the book catalogue is a computer database. These database systems let you search for entries in a number of ways. You can choose to search by some combination of subject, author, and title. You can focus on subjects as they are grouped in the Dewey decimal system or the Library of Congress classification. You can search by keywords or *descriptors*—words or short phrases that the database uses to identify entries on related topics. Additionally, in some cases, you may make a *free text search,* in which the computer does not limit itself to defined descriptors. Rather, it looks for words and combinations of words that you have chosen within the titles and content summaries of the books in the database. The list of terms you developed in **13c** will be helpful in both keyword and free text searches. If you encounter difficulty, do not hesitate to ask for help from a librarian.

Periodical indexes and databases You can locate magazine, journal, and newspaper articles on your topic using the periodical indexes and databases available at the library. Some of these are general in their coverage, while others are about a specific field such as criminal justice, religion, engineering, business, music, or tax law. There also are separate indexes for many major newspapers, such as *The New York Times.* Once again, do not hesitate to ask a librarian for guidance in finding these sources.

Gale, InfoTrac®, LexisNexis, EBSCO, ProQuest, and Wilson OmniFile are some of the services that provide information retrieval. A service can have hundreds of databases to choose from—each can cover hundreds of thousands of articles and papers. Most public libraries subscribe to at least one of these services. College and university libraries are likely to have more than one, which usually are available only to students, staff, and faculty. Many companies have access to at least one of the major systems. Figure 14-1 shows a search conducted

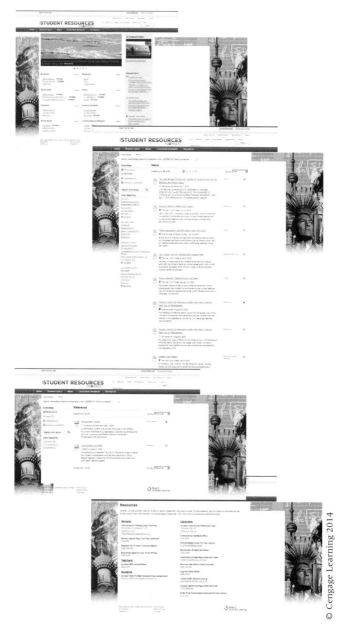

© Cengage Learning 2014

FIGURE 14-1 A Search Using Gale

on a Gale database using the keywords *comparable worth* and *equal pay.*

Specialized dictionaries, encyclopedias, and other resources Special dictionaries and encyclopedias are useful tools, especially for clarifying terms and concepts as they are used in fields where you may have little knowledge. The library may have other sources of information in a variety of media, including atlases, photographs, art collections, compact discs, and all manner of digital media.

14c. The Internet

Information accessible via personal computer ranges from Web pages and weblogs (blogs) to online editions of encyclopedias and news magazines, stock market reports, government statistics, and news on sports and entertainment.

Search engines and metasearch engines are like indexes for the World Wide Web. You type in a keyword or a URL and the engine looks for links. Metasearch engines combine results from several search engines. Here are examples of both:

- Google

  http://www.google.com

- Yahoo!

  http://search.yahoo.com

- Bing (MSN Search)

  http://bing.com

- Yippy (metasearch engine that clusters results by topic, source, or URL)

  http://yippy.com

- Dogpile (metasearch engine)

  http://www.dogpile.com

If a search engine is like the index of a book, a subject directory is like the library's book catalogue. You find the general subject and then browse through it to see what may be useful. Subject directories consist of links organized by topic. The topics on the first page of a directory are general, but each of them leads to lists of more specific subtopics. In addition, subject experts and librarians have created smaller, but more select, subject guides. Here is a sampling:

- About.com (summaries and links from experts in 750 subjects)

  http://www.about.com

- Internet Public Library (subject directory and general reference books)

  http://www.ipl.org

- INFOMINE (searchable virtual college-level library with 100,000 links)

  http://infomine.ucr.edu

- The Scout Report Archives (searchable virtual library of more than 28,000 resources)

  http://scout.wisc.edu/Archives/

- **WWW Virtual Library** (links to virtual libraries on 300 academic subjects)

  http://www.vlib.org

- Pinakes (a metasubject directory for 50 subjects)

  http://www.hw.ac.uk/libWWW/irn/pinakes/pinakes.html

In addition, a few search engines look for information on "invisible Web" databases (such as Census Bureau statistics and reports from government agencies) whose contents are not accessible via standard search engines.

- USA.gov (search or browse U.S., state, local, and tribal government websites)

  http://www.usa.gov

- GPOAccess (search or browse information databases produced by the U.S. government)

  http://www.gpo.gov/fdsys/

- Thomas (search engine for legislative information such as U.S. Congress bills, treaties, votes, and more)

  http://thomas.loc.gov/

Also invisible to standard search engines are the messages and articles on blogs. If you know your subject well and want a specialized piece of information, these may be worth checking out. Some search engines do special searches of blogs. Here are a few:

- Google Blogsearch

  http://www.google.com/blogsearch

- Technorati (blog search engine)

  http://technorati.com/

- Yippy Blogs (metasearch of four blog search engines)

  http://blogs.yippy.com/

Subject directories of selected blogs can be found at

- Internet Public Library: Blogs

  http://www.ipl.org/div/blogs

- DeepBlog.com
  http://www.deepblog.com/index.html

1 Search effectively and efficiently

Approach the available search engines and directories with a search technique that maximizes focus and minimizes ambiguity. Use Boolean operators ("this AND that," "this OR that," "this NOT that") if the search engine allows, in order to avoid being overwhelmed by tens of thousands of hits. Many engines permit users to specify that one word in the search should be near another and to use other tools (such as wildcards and required terms) to be as precise as possible. Check the "Help" feature of your favorite search engine to learn its shortcuts. Most search engines also have an "Advanced Search" option with additional tools. For example, you can limit your search to a specific domain (such as .edu or educational sites) or to pages that have been updated recently.

An excellent place to find information on the various search engines and strategies for using them is the Internet Public Library (**www.ipl.org**). Especially see its "Web Searching Tips." Also extremely valuable is the UC Berkeley Library's "Finding Information on the Internet: A Tutorial" (**www.lib.berkeley.edu/ TeachingLib/Guides/Internet/FindInfo.html**).

For the most efficient Internet search, you must have a research strategy. (See Chapter **13.**) After you have narrowed your topic, you can decide what are the most likely categories and keywords to identify information related to your topic.

Table 14-1 lists some useful reference sites to help fill the holes in your background knowledge and double-check facts. You will find many other sites through links on *The Speaker's Compact Handbook* website.

2 Carefully evaluate Internet sources

Scrutinize Web-based materials with special caution, although *any* information you gather in the course of research should be subjected to tests of credibility and reliability, as described in **16c.** Information on the World Wide Web requires a particularly critical eye. In contrast to the various review processes required before ideas can get into print or onto film, the only thing it takes to mount a website is the necessary software and a server. As you look at websites, ask the questions in the *Checklist: Evaluating a Website.*

Appendix B provides templates and examples for citing Internet as well as print sources in APA and MLA styles.

TABLE 14-1	Some Useful Reference Sites

Dictionaries and Pronunciation Guides

Dictionary.com Online Dictionary and Thesaurus (includes audio pronunciations)

http://www.dictionary.com/

VOA Pronunciation Guide—audio guide for names of people and places in the news

http://names.voa.gov

Specialty Dictionaries—links to dictionaries on topics from Accounting to Wine

http://www.yourdictionary.com/specialty.html

Encyclopedias and Other Reference Works

Encyclopedia Britannica (free condensed articles; full articles available to subscribers)

http://www.britannica.com/

Bartleby.com—reference collection with *Columbia Encyclopedia, Encyclopedia of World History, New Dictionary of Cultural Literacy, Columbia Gazetteer,* and *World Factbook*

http://www.bartleby.com/reference/

Quotations

Quotations at Bartleby.com—search *Bartlett's Familiar Quotations* (1919 edition) and *Respectfully Quoted* (1989)

http://www.bartleby.com/quotations/

The Quotations Page—26,000 quotations from 3,100 historical and contemporary authors

http://www.quotationspage.com/

Statistics

FedStats—links to statistics collected by U.S. government agencies

http://www.fedstats.gov

NationMaster.com—creates graphs for comparisons among countries

http://www.nationmaster.com/index.php

StateMaster.com—creates graphs from comparisons among U.S. states

http://www.statemaster.com/index.php

Population Reference Bureau—data by country and region about population trends, health, and the environment

http://www.prb.org/

Media Links

Online newspapers.com—links to newspapers around the world

http://www.onlinenewspapers.com/

ABYZ News Links—links to newspapers, magazines, and TV stations around the world

http://www.abyznewslinks.com/

U.S. History and Government

Library of Congress—U.S. history resources

http://www.loc.gov

Thomas—searchable database of federal legislation

http://thomas.loc.gov/

U.S. National Archives and Records Administration—historically important U.S. government documents and records

http://www.archives.gov

| **TABLE 14-1** | (Continued) |

Science	BrightSurf.com—science news stories
Eric Weisstein's World of Science—links about math, chemistry, physics, astronomy	http://www.brightsurf.com/
	How Stuff Works—brief articles and links about how all sorts of things work
http://scienceworld.wolfram.com	http://www.howstuffworks.com/index.htm

CHECKLIST

Evaluating a Website

Ask these questions as you look at a website:

❏ *Who created it?* Is it a personal page? If so, what are the person's credentials and how compelling are they? If it is an organization's page, does it provide enough background information (*for example,* an "About us" page) for you to make a judgment about its credibility?

❏ *What is its slant?* Why was this site created? Was it to provide information, advocate a position, or just rant? If it is providing information, how is that information influenced by the underlying assumptions embraced by the site's creator?

❏ *Is it up-to-date?* Does the site have regular maintenance that keeps it on top of changes in the topic?

❏ *What company does it keep?* That is, to whom does it link, and who links to it? How would you assess the credibility and competence of those linked sites?

For more on evaluating websites, see the UC Berkeley Library's tutorial (**http://www.lib.berkeley.edu/TeachingLib/Guides/Internet/Evaluate.html**) and the guidelines from Johns Hopkins University's Sheridan Library (**http://guides.library.jhu.edu/evaluatinginformation**).

Critical Thinking Questions:

○ How does searching for newspaper articles in newspaper databases different from a general Internet search?

○ What kinds of information can you get from a librarian?

○ Why does information on the Internet need to be scrutinized more carefully than information in published sources?

CHAPTER 15

Interviewing People About Your Topic

You are surrounded by potential sources of information in the form of other people, both as individuals and as members of informal or formal information networks. These sources can complement and supplement your library and electronic research.

15a. Finding people with relevant information

Look for experts to interview at home, at school and work, and in the community.

1 Acquaintances, family, and coworkers

As you start developing ideas on your topic, begin to talk about them with the people you see every day. You may find surprising sources of expertise. In addition, on many topics, these people can offer you a lay perspective that you will not find in any book. You could even do an informal survey or a brief questionnaire.

2 Experts

In every community, there are people with information about a variety of topics.

- *Educators.* Dissemination of information is an educator's business. Call the appropriate department or school. They will direct you to someone knowledgeable.

- *Public officials and agencies.* People elected to public office consider it one of their duties to make information available to their constituents. If you do not know where to start, call your local or regional government office and ask for assistance in gathering up-to-date information.

- *Independent organizations and special interest groups.* Groups such as the American Cancer Society or the local Rotary Club can be excellent sources of information. When possible, interview experts with differing opinions about your subject, especially if the subject is controversial. A useful resource for making contact with such groups is the *Encyclopedia of Associations,* available at the library.

- *Acquaintances.* Athletes, businesspeople, police officers, doctors, and accountants can all be experts. If you do not know a person in a particular field, see if you have a link to one through a colleague or friend.

You can also tap into an enormous pool of talent by computer. The newsgroups and social networks available online can introduce you to knowledgeable people at national, and even global, levels. In these groups and on message boards, people carry on extended dialogue on many issues. Before asking a specific question, check to see if it is one that has come up many times. Newsgroups usually have a "Frequently Asked Questions" (FAQ) file. Links to Usenet FAQs of all kinds can be found at the Internet FAQ Archives: **http://www.faqs.org/faqs/.**

15b. Conducting interviews

As with all aspects of public speaking, in interviewing, preparation is just as important as the process itself.

1 Preparing for the interview

Ask yourself in what ways your interviewee can best contribute to your research. Devise a list of questions that are specific. You do not want to waste this person's time by asking for information you could have found in the encyclopedia or in a book or an article that he or she has written. Prepare open-ended, but focused, questions.

> *Not:* How many women are there in the workforce in this county? [You could look up this figure.]
>
> *Not:* What are the problems working women encounter? [This is too vague.]
>
> *But:* I've read that in this county the average woman's salary is 32 percent less than the average man's. To what do you attribute this disparity?

2 During the interview

First, establish rapport and set a context. Briefly explain who you are, why you need the information, and how far you have gotten in your research. Also, confirm your understanding of the time available. If you wish to record the interview with a digital voice recorder, ask permission at this point. Be ready with a notepad in case you do not get the permission. Even if you record the interview, take notes. They will provide a written key to help you find statements on the recording that you might want to quote. Also use notes for potential questions and clarifications during the interview.

When you begin to ask questions, be sure to let the expert do most of the talking. (See the suggestions on listening in **2d.**) Do not interrupt, disagree, or offer your own opinions. Use questions to summarize and direct the interview: "So far you've talked about four problems working women face—unequal pay, lack of training, sexual harassment, and inadequate child care. Are there others?"

Allow for a closing phase for the interview. Consider a clearing-house question such as, "Is there anything else you can share that might be useful to me?" Respect the interviewee's time limit. If you are approaching it, stop—even if you have gone through only half of your questions. Summarize your perspective of the interview. Of course, convey your thanks.

> QUICK TIP **After the Interview** As soon as possible after the interview, read through your notes, making sure they are legible and make sense. Jot down any additional details that come to mind. If you recorded the interview, label it clearly. Clarify immediately anything that may be confusing, verify any quotes you'd like to use, and follow up the interview with a personal thank-you note.

Critical Thinking Questions:

○ How might your social network be useful in locating an expert to interview?

○ What are the advantages of information gathered locally through an interview over information located on the Internet?

○ Why would public officials be good sources of information? Why would they be willing to speak to you?

CHAPTER 16
Identifying and Recording Evidence

Carefully review your supporting materials: the print and electronic texts you have gathered and the interview notes you have taken. **Supporting materials** can clarify or expand on ideas, or they can provide evidence for the claims made in your speech. Select the support for your ideas first on the basis of relevance, then on soundness, and then on interest value. Use a variety of the following methods to develop your speech.

16a. Examples

Beyond the universal appeal of a good story, examples provide audience members with a chance to check their understanding of a speaker's message. As a speaker, you need to decide whether to use real examples or hypothetical ones and how brief or how long these examples should be.

1   Factual examples

A **factual example** relies on an assertion that is universally accepted. Sometimes it is directly verifiable, as in "Elena Kagan is a justice of the Supreme Court." Even if you were not at the swearing-in, there is enough corroborative evidence from many sources to satisfy you that this is a factual statement. "The earth is 93 million miles from the sun" is another assertion accepted as a fact, although it is not directly verifiable using any of the five senses. But we accept it because we have constructed theoretical frameworks based on consistent results of observation and can make scientific predictions of near-absolute certainty.

When you use examples to prove a point, though, specific logical tests must be met.

CHECKLIST

Tests of Factual Examples

❑ *Are sufficient examples given?* The more examples you give, the less likely your listeners are to dismiss the phenomenon as the product of chance.

❑ *Are the examples representative?* To be credible, examples should represent a cross section of cases.

❑ *Are negative instances accounted for?* When you reason by example, you must look into and account for dramatic negative examples. Your obligation, if you wish to carry your point, is to show how these negative examples are atypical.

---

2   Hypothetical examples

Sometimes, when no factual example quite suits your purpose or when you are speculating about the future, you might give a brief or extended **hypothetical example.** Here is an illustration of an extended hypothetical example:

> How should you get out of debt? Well, let's imagine that you have $1,000 worth of debt. If you pay only the minimum amount on a credit card with 18% interest, it would take you 12 years and $1,115 in interest fees to pay off the debt.

In this speech segment, three brief hypothetical examples bring members of the audience into the speech:

> What would happen if this tax law were to pass? Well, Miguel over there couldn't deduct his business lunches. Audrey wouldn't be able to depreciate her buildings. You, Tom, with kids about to start college . . .

Be aware that the examples you pick reflect a set of assumptions about the world. Be sensitive to racist or sexist implications in your illustrations and avoid unintentional stereotypes.

> QUICK TIP **The Appropriate Amount of Detail** When you use examples, you must decide how long or short to make each one. The factual and hypothetical examples in a speech can be kept brief when you can safely assume that the audience is already familiar with them. If a succession of quick references will not illuminate a point for your listeners, however, you need to develop the example into an illustration.
>
> Ideally, a speech blends several short examples with a few extended ones. Properly selected, these show the audience both the breadth of your subject and some of its in-depth aspects.

16b. Statistical evidence

Statistical evidence is based on examples that have been systematically collected and coded in numerical form. An excellent source of governmental statistical information—classified by topic, state, and agency—can be found at **http://factfinder2.census.gov.**

1   Check the accuracy

For any statistics you cite, investigate the methods and motivations of those who collected them.

CHECKLIST

Tests of Statistical Evidence

❏ *Who collected the data?* Investigate the qualifications and competence of the researchers. Was the work done by a professional pollster or the host of a call-in radio show?

❏ *Why were the data collected?* The motivation behind collecting certain information can make the resulting data suspect. Most people have more confidence in inquiries rooted in a desire to advance knowledge rather than to sell a product or promote a cause.

❏ *When were the data collected?* Be sure your evidence is up-to-date. Attitudes change as swiftly as prices, and some data are collected every week or every month.

❏ *How were the data collected?* Find out as much as you can about the design of the research and the details of its execution. Track it back to the original study. Check how the cases or participants were chosen and how many there were. Evaluate the method of data collection— observation, experiment, or survey conducted by phone, mail, or personal interview.

2   Avoid misleading statistics

We know that language is ambiguous, but we tend to believe that numbers make straightforward statements. There is no mystery in 2 + 2 = 4. However, numbers *can* be ambiguous, with statistical pitfalls to trap the unwary.

The fallacy of the average   Although the average can be a useful tool for analysis, it sometimes gives a picture absurdly at odds with reality. An example is a report that shows an average of six computer scanners per department when, in fact, the marketing department has 40 scanners and most other departments have one or none. As this demonstrates, the mathematical *mean* is not appropriate when one or two extreme cases skew the distribution. The *median*—the number or score that falls at the midpoint of the range of numbers or scores— or the *mode*—the most frequently occurring score or number—can be more meaningful averages. See Figure 16-1 for a graphic representation of the scanner distribution. Although the *mean* is 6, the *median* is 2, with scores of 0 and 1 below it, scores of 3 and 40 above it. The *mode* is 1—the largest number of departments (three) have this score.

The fallacy of the unknown base   A speaker using percentages and proportions can sometimes give the mistaken impression that a large population has been sampled. In fact, data are sometimes reported in this manner to give credibility to unscientific or skimpy evidence; for example, "Two out of three mechanics recommend this synthetic oil." Most listeners would see this as shorthand for "We polled 300 mechanics around the country, and 200 of them recommended this synthetic oil." How valid would this recommendation seem if, in reality, only *three* were polled?

The fallacy of the atypical or arbitrary time frame   An executive of a computer circuit board company once told us that sales in February were double those of the previous month. This information could be misleading unless you know that January is always the worst month in the yearly cycle of the computer industry.

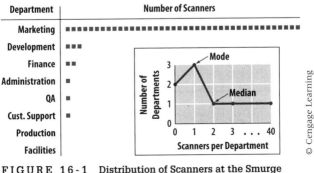

FIGURE   16-1   Distribution of Scanners at the Smurge Company

3 Make your numbers meaningful

The stereotypical dry, plodding speech is one that is overloaded with statistics. After a short while, the audience becomes overloaded too, and listeners start to build a mental dike against the numbers flowing over them.

When you do use statistics, round them off. Say "about fifteen hundred" instead of "one thousand four hundred eighty-nine point six." Use visual representations such as charts and graphs. (See **27a**.)

Use comparisons to make the numbers more understandable:

> For the amount of money they propose to spend on this weapons system, we could provide educational grants in aid to all the needy students in the 11 western states; or triple the government funding for cancer research; or upgrade the highway system in this state and its three neighbors.

16c. Testimony from authorities

Often, we call on statements from other people to get our point across. For instance, even if you have never been arrested or never been a public safety officer, you can give a credible speech on the penal system. You can do this by making judicious use of **testimony** from experts or eyewitnesses.

CHECKLIST

Tests of Testimony

❑ *Does the authority have access to the necessary information?* A person does not have to be famous to be an authority. However, when you use an authority, be sure that the person had firsthand experience, direct observation, or personal access to relevant facts and files.

❑ *Is the authority qualified to interpret data?* When an authority starts making interpretations, forming opinions and conclusions, and proposing recommendations, the standards of credibility become stricter. People earn the right to be considered experts either by holding relevant credentials or by establishing a record of success and experience.

❑ *Is the person acknowledged as an expert on this subject?* Just because a person is famous, it doesn't follow that he or she is an expert in all fields.

❑ *Is the authority figure free of bias and self-interest?* We give more credence to the opinion of an authority who appears to have no personal stake—ideological or financial—in an issue. If you can find testimony from a person speaking *against* his or her interests, then it certainly will be an effective addition to your presentation.

1 Evaluate the credibility of the authorities

It is easy to find **quotations** that say almost anything. It is much more difficult to select those that provide legitimate support for your points. This requires scrutinizing the people that you quote for support.

2 Do not distort quotations

Shortening quotations to highlight the basic thrust of the message is perfectly acceptable. What is unacceptable is editing a person's statements to such a degree that they appear to support different, or even opposite, positions. There is an old joke about the movie critic who wrote, "The wretchedness of the acting in this film is nothing short of amazing!" The critic later found out that an advertisement for the movie had quoted him as saying "This film . . . is amazing!"

Do not edit a quotation so radically that it loses all substance. Virtually content-free quotations are sometimes deliberately used to confuse listeners or to overwhelm them with an apparent preponderance of evidence.

16d. A complete record of your sources

Form the habit of recording complete bibliographic information for each source and of identifying the source for every piece of information you use in your speech. With electronic catalogues, you may be able to print out the bibliographic information for each of your potential sources or perhaps download it onto a portable storage medium. When you print pages from the Internet, make sure your "Print" command will include the headers and footers from your browser. Those contain the page title and the page's uniform resource locator (URL). Some people use an online tool called Zotero (**http://www.zotero.org/**) to collect, manage, and cite research sources. In other situations, you will need to record the information yourself. Writing down volume numbers of journals, or the cities of publication of books, or the telephone numbers of interviewees—details that you will never mention in your speech—may seem unnecessary. Routinely recording all such information, however, will help you retrieve sources if you need to check them again.

> **K E Y   P O I N T** **Citing Sources for a List of References**
> We recommend that you master one of the standard formats for citing references. In case you need to add a reference list to an outline or decide to produce a handout for your audience, the sources of your research will all contain complete information and will be in the same order. Three of the most popular formats are found in the *Publication Manual of the American Psychological Association*, 6th edition (2010), usually referred to simply as APA style; the *MLA Handbook for Writers of Research Papers*, 7th edition (2009), referred

to as MLA style; and *The Chicago Manual of Style (CMS),* 16th edition (2010), referred to as Chicago style. APA and MLA styles are the ones most likely to be used in speech classes. More information about these two styles is available online from Purdue's Online Writing Lab, Research and Citation section **(http://owl.english. purdue.edu/owl/).**

Individual variations notwithstanding, all three styles require an alphabetical listing of research sources that includes author, title, date, and publication details. In other words, include who, what, when, and where for every source. In addition to the conventions for citing books, articles, chapters, and websites, there are correct ways to cite nearly every type of source, including interviews, personal correspondence, photographs, TV shows, and e-mail. **Appendix B** shows the APA and MLA styles for 15 types of reference citation.

16e. Your research notes

In the process of doing your research, you want to gather and record your information and ideas in a way that makes it easy to find them later and to work with them creatively. Whole chapters of books that you have photocopied or pages and pages of text that you have downloaded from the Web are not easy to review. Smaller units of information will promote creative flexibility as you arrange and rearrange, structure and restructure your thoughts and data.

We talk about note cards in this section. However, the important thing is not the media but the activity. If you use an outlining tool or idea-development software on a computer, these suggestions are still pertinent.

1   Note cards from print and electronic sources

As you read the book or article, jot down each idea or bit of information on a separate card. Be sure to add an identifying code—such as author or title—and the page number. Use only one side of each card.

There are three kinds of data you might record: direct quotations or citations, paraphrased ideas, and references for later use. Be sure to do this for materials you find online. Even if you have a printout, it is valuable to go through the process of paraphrasing or quoting so that you internalize the key points that drew you to the source in the first place.

If you decide you must copy entire articles or chapters, be sure to make a bibliography card for each. If you photocopy the title page and copyright page of the book or the cover and table of contents of the periodical, you will have the necessary publication information for your reference list.

2 Note cards from interviews and surveys

The suggestions in **16e.1** relate to printed information but are easily adapted to information acquired through interviews and surveys. Make a bibliography card for each interview, citing the person interviewed, his or her qualifications, the date of the interview, and the person's telephone number or address. As you listen to the voice recording or review your notes, transcribe the information on cards.

3 Grouping your cards

When you have gathered many note cards, you may want to stack them under cover cards with titles such as "History," "Causes," and "Solutions." You may decide to put these keywords in the upper-right corner.

16f. Citing sources in your speech

In **32a** we talk about weaving supporting materials and their source information smoothly into the speech. The form this citation takes is, like many choices in speaking, dependent on the context. The college debate or speech contest may have a strict form, developed by tradition. Otherwise, you can choose how much information you need to include about the source as you speak—according to how much you think your audience has to hear to accept the source as legitimate.

One context is your listeners' attitude toward you and your topic, and **23b** describes adjustments you may need to make, depending on whether your audience is favorable, neutral, or unfavorable. Another determinant for the detail of your citations is your judgment on projecting credibility. (See **26c.**)

Critical Thinking Questions:

- ○ Why is it wise to use a variety of supporting materials such as definitions, quotes, examples, statistics, and stories from a variety of sources?
- ○ What are the tests of accuracy for statistical evidence? How is that process of testing similar to or different from establishing the credibility of an expert?
- ○ Why is it important to carefully track your sources in the preparation stage of speech development?
- ○ What level of citation within your speech is necessary for your audience?

PART 5

Organizing Your Ideas and Information

CHAPTER 17
Exploring Your Ideas

You may have lots of good ideas, but you need a procedure to assess which are the most important and where you want to go with them. This process cannot be ignored. Starting to develop the main points and subpoints of your speech entails four stages:

1. Generating many ideas
2. Grouping them into clusters
3. Labeling each cluster
4. Reworking and thinning out the ideas until you have two to five major groups that cover the most important ideas and that can be developed in your allotted time

17a. Assembling ideas and information

When you begin to prepare a speech, jot down every item you might possibly cover, drawn both from your research and from ideas that have been percolating. Follow the techniques of brainstorming and go for quantity rather than quality at this point. Do not judge or dismiss any idea. Write all ideas down as they occur to you and don't worry about duplication. You cannot start organizing until you have some raw material to organize.

17b. Identifying potential points

Read the brainstorming list you made and consider how you might cluster the entries. There is no one correct way to group these ideas. Almost certainly, some ideas will be omitted altogether and others may have to be adapted a bit to fit into a category. Sometimes, an idea from your brainstorming list will serve as a category in which to group smaller points. Other times, you will need to create a heading for several related ideas.

1 A working outline

Perhaps the most traditional technique of speech organization is to arrange ideas in the hierarchical, indented outline format. At this early stage of development, however, you do not want to be constrained by the requirements of the formal, full-sentence outline. The full-sentence outline will help you elaborate your points and subpoints, but a less rigid form, the **topic outline,** is more useful at this point. (See **20b** for examples of full-sentence and topic outlines.)

Because you might experiment with several different groupings of ideas, don't spend time at this stage on phrasing or formatting. Just try to fit ideas together, nesting them in various ways until you discover the pattern that seems to flow best.

If this is a comfortable method for you, you will have a head start on developing the full-sentence outline. But there are other, more spatially oriented ways to organize your thoughts, which we will describe next.

2 Concept mapping

Concept mapping is a visual method of showing how your ideas relate to each other. In its most basic form, you quickly draw a simple diagram made of labeled circles and squares, connecting them with lines.

Write your central idea—your topic—in a box or circle in the center of a sheet of paper. Jot down some major ideas from your brainstorming list around the topic, leaving enough room to add subpoints. As you write each idea, draw a line to connect it to its related point. This doesn't have to be done hierarchically, however. Subpoints might come to you before a broader point does. You can redraw connections as new relationships become clear.

There are a variety of styles of concept mapping, called *clustering, mind mapping, branching,* and *ballooning.* Figure 17-1 shows a simple concept map, one that could have been part of the organizational process that led to the sample informative speech outline about comic books in **Appendix A.**

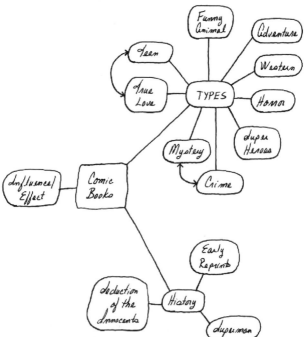

© Cengage Learning

FIGURE 17-1 **Simple Concept Map**

3   Idea notes

You can manipulate notes spatially or in linear form. For example, you can jot down your ideas on Post-It™ notes and stick them to a wall or a desktop. Cluster the notes according to themes, moving them from group to group until you are happy with the organization.

Another possibility is to start with your research notecards and additional cards capturing your own thoughts. In **16e,** we suggest grouping the research notecards under subject cover cards. You can write ideas, transitions, and syntheses on additional cards and plug them in where you think they fit. As with the Post-It™ notes, you can easily reorganize the cards to experiment with a variety of approaches. You can also group and regroup your ideas on a computer, using the simple outlining function of word-processing software or its diagram function. Mobile applications such as MindMeister.com also work well.

Once you have a set of potential points for your speech, the next step is to choose the points that are most suitable for your purpose and that work best together.

Critical Thinking Questions:

○ Why should you use brainstorming to start the speech organization process?

○ How might a mind mapping application or the sticky-note technique simplify the process of preparing your speech?

CHAPTER 18
Choosing Points That Work

A few basic principles for selecting main points and subpoints will help you craft a speech that is well structured, coherent, and effective.

18a. Main points that develop your thesis

Main points are primary ideas—the ones that are essential to the development of the thesis. To decide which main points to include in your speech, first look at your general purpose, your specific purpose, and your thesis statement. Then consider the likely questions your audience will have. (See **11d.2.**) Once you know what a complete development of your topic requires, use your thesis statement as a standard against which to test your main points. Ask yourself:

- Is there any part of my thesis that is not developed in the speech?

- Is there any main idea of the speech that is not reflected in the thesis?

If necessary, revise your thesis or add another main point.

18b. Main points that are mutually exclusive

Main points should be mutually exclusive for maximum clarity. That is, each category should cover different ideas. The challenge for the speaker lies in finding the best place for each idea.

Sometimes, when you are grouping ideas under potential main points, you will find that some fit into two or more categories. This is a sign that you have not yet found an effective system for classifying your ideas. Having a clear organizational pattern is essential. If you do not know where an idea fits, your audience certainly will not.

For example, let's examine a speech on the topic of great films. Our speaker has come up with an outline that looks at great dramas as the first main point, great comedies as the second, and great black-and-white films as the third. Apparently, the speaker was unable to decide whether to discuss film by dramatic category, by color, or by lack of color. Dramas and comedies can be shot on either color or black-and-white stock. The three main points—drama, comedy, and black and white—are not mutually exclusive categories.

With a system of mutually exclusive main points, a film cannot be listed under more than one point. If we put the sample organization to the test, however, we encounter uncertainty. For instance, *Raging Bull* is a drama and it was shot in black and white. Which main point would it go under? So, although each main point by itself seems a plausible way to classify movies, the three main points taken together do not constitute a sensible way to look at the topic.

What *would* be a sensible way to organize a speech about great films? One possibility is to divide the topic into main points along a single dimension—for example, color or lack of it. These main points could each have the same two subpoints—for example, drama and comedy. The topic of great films could also be organized chronologically (1920s, 1930s, etc.), with each decade having the subpoints of comedy and drama.

The important principle is to choose a classification scheme that makes it easy to fit each example under only one main point.

18c. Two to five main points

If your speech treats every thought as a main point, you will have no time to develop any of them. Your audience will probably be confused about what you are trying to say. If you have only one main point, your speech will be a string of examples of your topic. Your audience will probably be bored. Understand, too, that audiences are not able to remember more than a few main points. However, at the conclusion of your speech, you want them to remember your most important ideas. For all these reasons, you should have no less than two main points and no more than five.

18d. Relationships among points

Ideas of equal importance or of parallel logical function are called **coordinate points.** Points of lesser significance that support, explain, or contribute steps of logical development to other ideas are called **subordinate points.** The relationship of the main points and the other points in your speech must be clear in your mind. The next two chapters (**19** and **20**) will help you see and shape those relationships.

KEY POINT **Types of Points** Subordinate points, or subpoints, should fit inside, or support, a larger idea. Coordinate points—and subpoints—should be of equal importance. Be sure that each subpoint directly relates to the main point it is supposed to support.

Critical Thinking Questions:

○ What would you do if you found that your main points didn't fit your proposed thesis?
○ How does understanding the effort required to transform ideas into main points change the way you will prepare your next speech?
○ Why should you limit the number of main points in your speech?

CHAPTER 19

Arranging Points

Once you have selected the main ideas for your speech, you need to arrange them in the order that will maximize their effectiveness. In some cases, the decision is virtually made for you. Closing arguments to juries unfold according to stock patterns, and many ceremonial and special-occasion speeches—such as commencement speeches—follow a formula. (See Chapter **9.**) For the usual informative or persuasive speech, however, there is no given pattern. You, as the speaker, must select the best arrangement of ideas.

19a. Types of patterns

Patterns arise either from the subject matter or from the requirements of the thesis statement. There are five traditional patterns of speech arrangement: chronological, spatial, cause–effect, problem–solution, and topical.

1   The chronological pattern

Probably the oldest form of extended discourse is the narrative unfolding of a story. A time-ordered format that sequences information still undergirds many contemporary speeches. *Historical* development is the most common **chronological pattern.** If you were giving a speech on the early history of rock music, you might arrange it this way:

  I. Rhythm and blues (1940s–1950s)
 II. Rockabilly (mid 1950s)
III. The British Invasion (mid 1960s)

For another example, look at the outline on women workers in **20b.**
   A second way to look at a subject chronologically is to analyze a process *step by step.* The topic "How to repair a hole in drywall" could generate this outline:

  I. Gather materials, including a tin can lid, string, a small stick or pencil, patching compound, and tools.
 II. Punch holes in the lid and place string through the holes.
III. Holding the string, place the tin can lid inside the wall and position it behind the hole; tie the string to a pencil or a small stick, and twist until solidly in place.
 IV. Fill the hole with plaster and let dry; add a finish coat, let dry, and sand until smooth.

2   The spatial pattern

The **spatial pattern** is often based on geography or location. For example, the outline for a speech on the U.S. military deployment in Afghanistan might look like this:

    I. Northern zone
   II. Central zone
 III. South central zone
 IV. Southern zone

Or a geographically organized speech might look at health care systems in Europe (for example, England, France, and Germany) and Canada. Geography is not only areas on a map but also other spatial divisions of society such as rural, suburban, and urban.

The spatial pattern can also be applied to smaller areas such as the floor plan of a house. The following example of a spatial pattern describes a very small area indeed—an aircraft instrument panel:

  I. Instruments needed to maintain controlled flight are on the left side of the panel.
    A. Compass
    B. Altimeter
    C. Artificial horizon
    D. Turn and bank indicator
    E. Air speed indicator
 II. Instruments providing information on the aircraft's operating condition are on the right side.
    A. Tachometer
    B. Manifold pressure gauge
    C. Oil temperature gauge
    D. Oil pressure gauge
    E. Fuel gauge

3   The cause–effect pattern

This pattern is used to show that events occurring in sequence are, in fact, causally related. A **cause–effect pattern** is well suited to a speech in which the goal is to achieve understanding or agreement rather than action, as here:

  I. The recent economic recession has decreased housing values in many communities.
 II. [*This is the result*.] Real estate prices have dropped to record lows in many areas, making it a good time to buy some properties.

Occasionally, the pattern may be reversed to an effect–cause sequence:

  I. Mortgage rates and housing prices are at record lows.
 II. [*This is the cause*.] There has been a sharp drop in home values.

Of course, when using the cause–effect pattern, you must be sure that the causal relationship you propose is a valid one. (See the discussion of causal reasoning in **21d**.)

4 The problem–solution pattern

The **problem–solution pattern** is used to examine the symptoms of a problem and then propose a remedy. It is often used in persuasive speeches that advocate a new policy or a course of action, as in the following:

I. The current system of financing health care in the United States is inadequate.

II. [*This is the solution.*] A system of national health insurance would provide medical care to all citizens.

5 The topical pattern

The **topical pattern** is the most frequently used speech pattern. It is employed to divide a speech into elements that have no chronological or spatial pattern but are simply aspects of the topic. This is also the most difficult pattern. When subjects do not lend themselves to any of the arrangements discussed so far, you need to figure out the most effective order for your points.

Often, the best structure for a speech is a list of the components of a whole or a list of reasons that add up to the thesis. The following is an example of a topical pattern that lists reasons for a conclusion:

Thesis statement: Capital punishment should be abolished.

I. Capital punishment does not deter crime.

II. Capital punishment is ultimately more costly than life imprisonment.

III. The risk of executing an innocent person is morally unacceptable.

KEY POINT **Types of Speech Organization**

- *Chronological pattern* to describe the historical development of a topic or for step-by-step instructions.
- *Spatial pattern* to compare the occurrence of a topic in global, national, regional, or local areas or to describe the components of a small area or object.
- *Cause–effect pattern* to describe the origins of a condition or to show that a sequence of events is causally related.
- *Problem–solution pattern* to examine the symptoms of a problem and propose a remedy.
- *Topical pattern* to discuss aspects of a topic that do not lend themselves to any of the preceding patterns. For example, list the components of a whole or the reasons that add up to the thesis.

Chapters **21, 23,** and **24** discuss organizational patterns for speeches that are arguments for the thesis.

19b. Organizing subpoints

After your main ideas have been set, look at the subpoints under each. These, too, need to be arranged in some effective order—topical, chronological, whatever. You do not need to repeat the pattern used for the main points. You can choose the format that makes the most sense for each set of subpoints. Notice the different arrangements in the detailed outlines in **Appendix A.**

Critical Thinking Questions:

○ How would you arrange a speech addressing the equipment used in the game of lacrosse?

○ What type of speech is a problem–solution format best suited for? Why?

○ What makes topical pattern both easy and difficult to use effectively?

CHAPTER 20
Outlining

The speech outline is an indispensable tool of speech organization. A clear outline helps you keep track of the points you want to cover. Laying your ideas out on paper forces you to select points that support your thesis and fit together well. As the planning and practice chart in Chapter **10** illustrates, you need a logical outline of your points and supporting materials before you can finalize the oral version of your speech. Although you will probably refine some wording while developing the full-sentence outline, your focus should be the creative process. Oral composition and oral practice should surround this excursion into writing.

KEY POINT **The Benefits of Outlining** Frequently speakers prefer to write out entire speeches rather than to utilize the benefits of outlining. However, we believe that using the outlining process results in a clearer and more flexible and organized speech structure. If it helps to get your ideas on paper, consider using a concept or mind map.

20a. The conventional outline format

By following the standard rules of outlining, you will be able to visualize the relationships among the ideas of your speech.

1   The symbols

It is conventional to use Roman numerals to label the main ideas of the speech and to alternate between letters and numbers for each successive level of subordination, in the following manner:

   I. Main point
     A. First level of subordination
       1. Second level of subordination
         a. Third level of subordination
           (1) Fourth level of subordination
             (a) Fifth level of subordination

Do not skip levels. If your speech has only main points and subpoints, use I, II, III and A, B, C. If your outline includes sub-subpoints, use 1, 2, 3 for them.

Most word-processing programs have a formatting feature for creating an outline-numbered list.

2   Indentation

Each subordinate idea should be indented to align under the first word of the point it supports. Each subordinate idea should also align with the other subordinate ideas of the same level—in other words, all subpoints should be indented the same amount and all sub-subpoints should be indented a greater amount. This makes the relationship among ideas visually obvious. The points in your outline should not all begin at the left margin. The purpose of your outline is to clarify the structure of your ideas. Note how the indentation in the following outline shows the structure: a main point illustrated with two subpoints, one of which has two sub-subpoints.

   I. Bagpipes are not solely a Scottish instrument.
     A. Bagpipes originated in Asia Minor.
     B. There are various forms of bagpipes in Ireland and Spain, for example.
       1. Spanish bagpipes are similar in construction to Scottish pipes, with the sizes of the parts being different.
       2. Uilleann bagpipes in Ireland differ from Scottish pipes in that the piper uses bellows under the arm to keep the bag full rather than blowing into the bag.

3   Two or more subpoints for each point

English teachers are fond of saying, "Never have a 1 without a 2 or an A without a B." Generally, this is good advice. If a main point has only one subpoint, it probably does not have enough support. For example, the following main point needs more than subpoint A to be convincing:

I. Redwood City is the best California city in which to live.
  A. It has the best climate.

If this is your only example, you are guilty of hasty generalization. To avoid this fallacy, you should have *at least* two supporting points at each level of subordination.

20b. The full-sentence outline

The **full-sentence outline** is a tool to ensure coherent development of your speech. Your thesis statement (see **11d**), the main points, and at least the first level of subpoints should be stated as declarative sentences. A declarative sentence is, in effect, a proposition that can be proved or disproved, accepted or rejected.

Look at the following sentence:

I. Secondhand smoke harms nonsmokers.

If this sentence were presented to you on a true/false test, you could, with adequate knowledge, answer one way or the other. But what would you do if you encountered the following items on a true/false test?

I. Nonsmokers' rights
II. What is the effect of secondhand smoke on nonsmokers?

Obviously, an answer of true or false to either of these examples is impossible.

Far too many speeches are constructed around such vague phrases, questions, and uncompleted ideas. Listeners can identify the speaker's general topic but cannot always recognize the specific points the speaker is trying to make. Consider these examples:

Wrong: I. What are the causes of crime?

Right: I. Crime is caused by a combination of sociological and psychological factors.

Wrong: I. The history of the feminist movement in the United States.

Right: I. U.S. feminism can be divided into four historical periods.

Using declarative sentences in your outline helps you see whether you are actually making the exact points you want to make. Once the thesis and main points are stated in propositional form, they will provide a basis against which you can test all other speech content.

The following full-sentence and topic outlines deal with a subject—the history of working women in the United States—that could fill many volumes. In the following full-sentence outline, observe how the thesis statement and full-sentence main and secondary points provide a basis for the speaker to decide what to include.

Full-Sentence Outline

Thesis Statement: *Since the beginning of the Industrial Revolution, women in the United States have been exploited as a cheap and expendable source of labor.*

I. In preindustrial colonial settings, the boundaries between men's and women's spheres were indistinct.
   A. Colonial women ran self-sufficient factories in their homes.
      1. Women produced candles, the major source of artificial light.
      2. Clothing and bedding were made by women.
      3. The making of soap was a major contribution by women.
   B. The rigors of frontier life decreed a more equal division of labor between women and men than was found on the rapidly industrializing eastern seaboard.
      1. Men and women shared long hours of joint farmwork.
      2. Women were often left alone for long periods to run the farm.
II. Between the Revolution and the Civil War, increased industrialization led to increased exploitation of women workers.
   A. Factories undercut home production.
   B. When the westward migration caused shortages of male workers, women became a cheap source of labor for the factories.
      1. The percentage of women in the workforce increased.
      2. In 1829, women earned one quarter of what men did.
   C. Working women's efforts to improve their lot were not successful.
      1. The first women's strike was in 1824, but poor organization made it and others ineffective.
      2. Associations of working women failed because of the women's isolation and inexperience.

III. In spite of increasing unionization between the Civil War
and World War II, women's positions in the workforce
remained inferior.
  A. Women were an unwelcome minority in trade
  organizations.
    1. Male union leaders did not believe in equal pay for
    equal work.
    2. According to men, women were barred from union
    offices because "no conveniences were available."
  B. Before 1900, attempts by women to organize among
  themselves met with failure.
    1. Women's unions were not taken seriously.
    2. Female workers were usually too impoverished to
    strike successfully.
  C. Important gains by working women in the first decades
  of the 20th century yielded little net improvement.
    1. Women's situation had improved in some areas.
      a. Unionization of the garment industry was successful.
      b. New job classifications were opened to women
      during World War I.
    2. Female workers still had neither security nor equality.
      a. Men got their jobs back after the war.
      b. Women received one half of comparable men's pay.
IV. During World War II and after, women were used as a
dispensable and secondary source of labor.
  A. Traditional views of femininity were conveniently set
  aside according to economic needs.
    1. Three million women were recruited to replace our
    fighting men.
    2. "Rosie the Riveter" became a mythic ideal.
  B. After the war, labor, government, and industry
  cooperated to push women out of their new jobs.
    1. Although most women wanted to keep working, by
    1946 four million were gone from the workforce.
    2. When plants began to rehire men, women's
    seniority was often ignored.
    3. With the unions' tacit approval, many jobs held by
    women during the war were reclassified as men's jobs.
    4. Many of the laid-off women were denied
    unemployment insurance.
    5. Articles and pamphlets exhorted women to return
    to their "primary role."
      a. Women were needed to provide a haven for
      returning men.
      b. Women were needed to nurture the nuclear family.

In contrast, here is a topic outline of the first main point and
its subordinate points.

Topic Outline

Topic: *The history of working women in the United States*

   I. Preindustrial
      A. Colonial women
         1. Candles
         2. Clothing and bedding
         3. Soap
      B. Frontier women
         1. Joint farmwork
         2. Left alone

At first glance, the topic outline seems to be a tidy arrangement of points. But would you be able to form a sharp image of what the speaker is saying about working women in the United States? For example, the main point in the topic outline is the word *"preindustrial."* Yet *"preindustrial"* is so broad it could include the first humans to appear in America thousands of years ago. In fact, this point will deal with women between the first European colonization and the advent of the Industrial Revolution. The topic outline point ought to be phrased to leave no doubt.

This is only half the job, though. No matter how refined, a *subject* still needs a *predicate*. Even if point I of the topic outline described women in a specific era (*for example,* "Colonial life for women, 1620–1783"), it is still not clear what idea is being developed: That there were many working women? That their lives were hard? That they participated in all spheres of work? The phrase of the topic outline is expanded into a full sentence by raising and answering such questions. When main point I turns into "In preindustrial colonial settings, the boundaries between men's and women's spheres were indistinct," the direction of the speech will become clearer. For instance, the speaker will probably decide that stories about conflicts between white settlers and Native Americans however interesting, do not belong in this speech.

Full-sentence outlines are not extra work but rather are a necessary tool to demonstrate logical relationships in the speech. Once you think through these relationships with the help of a full-sentence outline, you can proceed to a more spontaneous and fluid oral form of expression, confident that the underlying structure of your speech is sound.

QUICK TIP **You Need a Full-Sentence Outline** The full-sentence speech outline is a tool like your informal research notes (see **16e**), preliminary brainstorming tools (see **17b**), and speaking notes (see **33b**). Although any of these may take an outline form, the full-sentence outline is different. It is a detailed, logical plan of the speech. However, this outline is not an essay. Don't let your outline transform itself into a manuscript speech. (See **28c.**)

20c. Phrasing main points

It is not enough to have main points expressed as full sentences. The sentences must logically encompass the main ideas of the speech. Suppose a speech outline has the following main point:

   I. Many people are unaware of the origins of the paper they use every day.

If this is the main idea, the subpoints should look something like this:

   A. Ursula is utterly unaware of the origin of paper.
   B. Clint is clueless about where paper comes from.
   C. Ned never thought about paper for a minute.
   D. And so on . . .

It is unlikely that the speaker really intends to spend this portion of the speech exposing the ignorance of the general public. More likely, the speaker was planning to talk about where paper comes from. The main point should reflect this goal.

Each main point can be thought of as a *subthesis sentence* that answers two simple questions about that section of the speech: What is it about?, and What about it?

Wrong:

Subthesis sentence:	I first would like to take a few minutes to discuss the origin of paper.
What is it about?	A speaker talking for a few minutes.
What about it?	The topic being talked about is the origin of paper.

Wrong:

Subthesis sentence:	Another interesting point is the origin of paper.
What is it about?	The origin of paper.
What about it?	It is interesting.

Right:

Subthesis sentence:	The origins of paper can be traced to the use of papyrus in ancient Egypt.
What is it about?	The origin of paper.
What about it?	It can be traced to papyrus in ancient Egypt.

At this point, do not include in the outline any transitional phrases that might be part of your oral presentation. Additionally, do not include your supporting evidence in the phrasing of a main point. Keep statistics, testimony, and examples at the subordinate levels. Your main points should express the broader ideas of the speech.

QUICK TIP **Phrasing for Impact** Once you have framed your main ideas so that they are logically and grammatically complete, take time to recast them in language that will highlight them for your audience. In this final phase of refining the outline, you move from organizing points logically to "writing for the ear." Ideas that are phrased in concise, colorful, parallel language are more likely to be remembered by both speaker and listeners. (See also Chapter **29.**)

Critical Thinking Questions:

○ Why is a full-sentence outline preferable to a topic outline at this phase in the speech development process?

○ Why is an outline preferable to a manuscript of your speech at this phase?

○ How might technology help simplify the process of creating and manipulating an outline?

C H A P T E R   2 1

Building Sound Arguments

Through analyzing and synthesizing what we already know, *reasoning* is the process by which we come to understand something previously unknown. Our listeners will not be moved by hearing *what* we think; they want to know *why* we think it. Consequently, the reasoning that should be the foundation of every speech can be seen as the giving of *good* reasons.

To develop a logical line of thought and test its validity, you need to understand how reasoning links key points of a speech together. You also need to become familiar with standard patterns of reasoning and with a few common fallacies. Only then can you decide how best to use reasoning when putting your speech together.

21a. Identify where reasoning is needed

In all persuasive speeches and in some sections of informative, evocative, and invitational speeches, a challenging task confronts the speaker: You must develop lines of argument through reasoning in order to explain why you reached your conclusion. This conclusion is also called a **claim**. Claims are statements that need to be substantiated because they are not taken for granted by your listeners. Your thesis sentence can be thought of as a "super-claim," and your main points are claims that support that super-claim. Even some of the subordinate points have to be reasoned through before they become acceptable.

1 The link from evidence to a claim

Suppose you have a conclusion or claim that you want your listeners to accept, and you have some evidence that you believe supports that claim. Clearly, everyone who confronts the same facts and figures does not automatically come to the same conclusion. What links evidence to a claim—or *warrants* the claim's acceptance—is the process of reasoning. For example, suppose two people are confronted with the fact that more people go to the doctor in countries with national health care programs than in countries with privately funded health care. Person A concludes that this is an argument in support of adopting national health care in the United States. Person B concludes that it is an argument against national health care.

As Figure 21-1 shows, reasoning is what links your evidence—the facts, the examples, the statistics, and the testimony you have collected—to your claim.

2 Familiar patterns

In the health care example, Person A is drawing on a pattern observed in the past—namely, that people who cannot afford a needed service will seek that service when it becomes affordable. This is perfectly reasonable and logical; we all can think of plenty of common examples.

Person B is also being logical and reasonable in linking the evidence of increased medical visits to the claim that a national health care program would be undesirable. This person is drawing on another observed pattern of human behavior—that

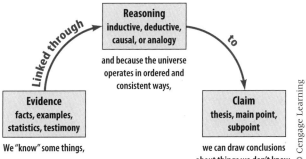

FIGURE 21-1   Reasoning Links Evidence and Claim

people who see a resource as free and unlimited may use it inappropriately and wastefully. There is also plenty of evidence for this view.

The issue here is not what the facts *are,* but what the facts *mean.* There are often many sensible ways to interpret the same piece of evidence. A speaker cannot simply present the evidence and hope it speaks for itself. The speaker must explain the relevance of the evidence and its link to a particular claim.

21b. Inductive reasoning

The most common kind of reasoning is induction. **Inductive reasoning** consists of a series of observations that lead to a probable conclusion. Often, we draw inferences that go beyond what we observe directly. We could not function unless we trusted regularities in events; that is, unless we believed that much of what has happened before will happen again. For example, we step in front of oncoming traffic because we believe, from previous experience, that the cars will obey the red light or the stop sign. Figure 21-2 depicts the process of inductive reasoning.

1   Adequate data

Inductive reasoning depends on collecting enough instances to establish a pattern. Remember the logical tests in the checklist in **16a.1.** A typical line of inductive thought can be portrayed as follows:

Orchid 1 has no fragrance.

Orchid 2 has no fragrance.

Orchid 3 has no fragrance.

....

Orchid *n* has no fragrance.

Therefore, it is probable that all orchids have no fragrance.

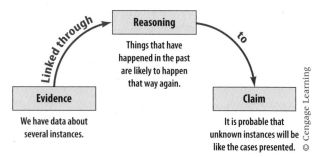

FIGURE 21-2   Inductive Reasoning Draws Inferences from Observations

The extent to which you can generalize from such observations is linked to the extent of your sampling. If you smelled only a few orchids or only the orchids in one corner of a hothouse, you would be less able to make a general conclusion than if you had smelled every orchid in a number of hothouses.

Be cautious about drawing inferences from too few examples. How many cases did you examine? Were they selected fairly? Are the contrary instances accounted for? (See **16b** and **21f**.)

2 Strong probability

The conclusions drawn from induction are always *probable* rather than *absolute*. An inductive conclusion can fall anywhere along this continuum:

		Almost
Possible	**Probable**	**certain**

The degree of certainty depends on the method used in making the observations and on the number of observations made. How strong must this **probability** be before you can consider the conclusion of an inductive argument to be valid—a 51 percent probability, or a 75 percent probability, or a 99 percent probability? It depends.

Would you leap off a 10-foot wall for $1,000? Many people would say yes. It is *possible* that you could be killed, but it is probable that you would escape with minimal injuries. Would you jump from the roof of a three-story building for $1,000? Most people would say no. It is *possible* that you would be unharmed, but not very probable. In both cases, you set the acceptable level of probability by weighing potential risks against potential gains. In inductive reasoning, the acceptability of a probable conclusion always depends on this kind of cost–benefit analysis. (See **24a** and **24d.2**.)

21c. Deductive reasoning

You use a deductive pattern of reasoning when your argument demonstrates how the relationships among established premises lead to a necessary conclusion. In induction, the emphasis is on collecting observable data, whereas **deduction** consists of showing the relationship of accepted premises, according to formal rules. Deduction, then, does not involve bringing new data into play. Rather, it involves rearranging already-known information to discover something new about how pieces fit together, as in scientific breakthroughs, in gossip, and in the English murder mystery. In our everyday lives, we have that "Aha!" experience when we suddenly discover the pattern underlying separate facts and realize their implication. Figure 21-3 depicts the process of deductive reasoning.

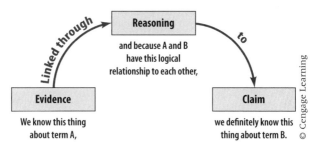

FIGURE 21-3 **Deductive Reasoning Finds the Patterns in What You Already Know**

Because the accuracy of deduction lies in whether it adheres to certain rules, experts in deductive reasoning learn complex symbolic formulas by which they test arguments. For the purpose of this book, we need only touch on the basic concept of deduction: If we know certain things about how two terms—*for example*, concepts and events, or characteristics and events—are related, we can discover other relationships that are logically entailed or implicated:

Term A is related in a known way to Term B.

We know certain things about Term B.

Therefore, we can draw certain conclusions about Term A.

To use deductive reasoning in a speech, you need to turn this formula into a series of steps:

Step 1: Establish that a relationship exists between two terms (the **major premise**).

Step 2: Establish the actual condition/status of one of the terms (the **minor premise**).

Step 3: Show how a conclusion about the other term necessarily follows.

1 Begin with an absolute statement

Step 1 in deduction—establishing the *major premise*—takes many forms. It always involves an absolute relationship between two terms. Below are examples of four common relationships.

- One term may be an intrinsic characteristic of the other: Conflict is inherent in the collective bargaining process.
- One term may be a category that includes the other: All Volkswagens are motor vehicles.
- One term may be inevitably linked to the other: If corporate taxes are cut, then investment will increase.
- The two terms may be the opposite of or exclude each other: Unless we crack down on drunken drivers, fatalities will likely rise.

2 Derive a necessary conclusion

When you have established one of these basic major premises, you have set up a formula that will serve as the link at the top of your arc of reasoning. (See Figure 21-3.) When you move to Step 2, you establish something about one of the two terms—the *minor premise.*

In the context of the major premise "All ducks have webbed feet," a piece of evidence like "Daffy is a duck" is the minor premise, and the resulting implication is that Daffy has webbed feet.

Feed in the data you have, follow the rules of deductive logic, and certain conclusions are inevitably reached:

> We did not crack down on drunken drivers, so traffic fatalities have likely increased.

The beauty of deduction is its certainty. If your listeners accept the premises, they *must* accept the conclusion. The problem with deduction is that, for its conclusion to be absolute, its premises must be absolute. Unfortunately, most absolute statements of relationships are either untrue or trivial. Who needs to argue that ducks have webbed feet? The things we tend to give speeches about are complex issues of public policy, human behavior, and social values. The requirement of having an all-or-nothing beginning premise is so restrictive that true, formal deductive reasoning is rather rare. In speaking (if not in logic class), it is acceptable to use a slightly less rigorous form of deduction and persuade your audience to accept your premises and conclusion as probable. (See **24b** and **24d.2** for more on using the deductive pattern.)

21d. Causal reasoning

You use **causal reasoning** to demonstrate that one event results from another. It is the backbone of all speeches that deal with policy and problem solving. In most cases, if a person says, "I don't favor that policy (or program, or solution)," he or she is really saying, "I don't agree that *X* causes *Y.*" This means that you must carefully scrutinize the relationship between two events and then show your listeners how thoroughly you tested the relationship. Figure 21-4 depicts the causal reasoning process. (See **24c** and **24d.2** for more on using causal claims in your speech.)

1 Test the validity of the relationship

A causal relationship is stronger than mere coexistence or coincidence. Two events may occur together or in sequence without one causing the other. For instance, morning sickness and weight gain often occur together, but neither causes the other; they are

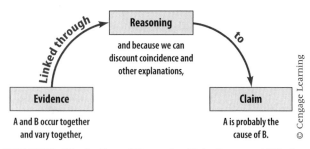

FIGURE 21-4 Causal Reasoning Links Cause and Effect

the result of a third condition, pregnancy. To be sure that the relationship is a causal one, apply these two tests.

Do the alleged cause and alleged effect occur together? To prove that a causal relationship exists, it is not enough to show that the alleged cause is present with the alleged effect. You must show that, in the absence of the alleged cause, the alleged effect does not appear:

> If a rash appears every time you eat tomatoes and never appears when you haven't eaten tomatoes, this is strong evidence that tomatoes cause the rash.

> To prove a causal relationship, you must show both concurrent presence and concurrent absence.

Do the alleged cause and the alleged effect vary together? Another test of causation is whether the magnitude of change in the cause matches that in the effect:

> If one bite of tomato gives you a small rash and consuming many tomatoes gives you a big rash, this is one more bit of evidence to suggest that tomatoes cause your rash.

2 Do not oversimplify

In the worlds of physics and chemistry, there are some straightforward causal relationships:

> Adding silver nitrate solution ($AgNO_3$) to sodium chloride (NaCl) will cause silver chloride (AgCl) to precipitate.

This type of relationship between cause (C) and effect (E) could be represented as

$$C \rightarrow E$$

However, in medicine and in the social sciences—such as politics, psychology, and economics—more complex patterns usually exist.

Some effects have multiple causes

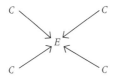

If smoking was the single cause of lung cancer, then every smoker would have lung cancer and every victim of lung cancer would be a smoker. Obviously, this is not the case. Yet research does show that smoking is one causal factor contributing to lung cancer.

Some causes are also effects and some effects are also causes in a long causal chain When we designate a cause of a certain event, we can look at the immediate cause or at a more distant factor. A doctor might say that the cause of a particular death was a cerebral hemorrhage. What, though, was the cause of the hemorrhage? Perhaps a fractured skull, which was caused by going through a windshield, which was caused by the impact of a car with a tree, which was caused by excessive drinking, which was caused by worry over being unemployed, and so on:

$$C \rightarrow (E/C) \rightarrow (E/C) \rightarrow (E/C) \rightarrow E$$

It is sometimes important to point out the cyclical nature of certain causal chains. For example, ignorance about a particular group may lead to prejudice, which in turn results in lack of contact with that group, which perpetuates ignorance. This sort of analysis is far more useful than positing a single cause of racial disharmony.

Some effects result from a one-time cause and some from ongoing causes Effects that are labeled undesirable can be dealt with either by treating the effect directly or by treating the cause that produces the effect. To decide which strategy makes the most sense in a given context, you need to determine whether the cause is one-time or ongoing. For example, what is the cause in a neighborhood that has bare dirt for landscaping, has shattered windows, has broken furniture in the yards, and has residents in need of medical care? If a tornado whipped through the area, emergency relief is an obvious solution. However, if the area is chronically depressed, structural economic reforms would be more appropriate.

21e. Reasoning by analogy

You use **reasoning by analogy** to draw conclusions about unknown events based on what you know about similar events. Figure 21-5 depicts the process of reasoning by analogy.

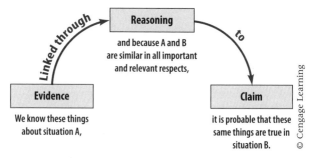

FIGURE 21-5 Analogy Compares Two Things in the Same Category

Reasoning by analogy is a natural and powerful way to make links. People intuitively look to similar examples when they want to understand something. Suppose the president's foreign policy advisors are trying to decide whether to intervene in a foreign country's internal struggles; or a judge is pondering whether to admit expert testimony on battered wife syndrome; or you are wondering whether to take the freeway or back streets to work. From the most far-reaching policy issues to the most mundane everyday decisions, people ask themselves, "What situation like this do I already know about?"

Although reasoning by analogy is so instinctive—or *because* it is so instinctive—you need to choose your analogies carefully.

When you reason by analogy, the two cases should be similar in all relevant and important respects. Do not, as the saying goes, compare apples and oranges. In addition, figurative analogies (such as "Going to war in Vietnam was like tap dancing on quicksand") can have stylistic impact, but they cannot support a conclusion. (See **24d.2** for more on using reasoning by analogy in your speech.)

21f. Common reasoning fallacies

Some people commit reasoning **fallacies** knowingly with dishonest intent. Others commit them due to a lack of practice or skill in doing their own thinking. The good public speaker wants to avoid the appearance of either. Once you have built your speech around sound, logical arguments, go through it to detect any constructions that hint of sloppy thinking. One glaring fallacy in your speech will make all your other conclusions suspect. It is not necessary to learn all the fallacies—over one hundred have been categorized—but you should be familiar with the most common ones.

1   Attacking the person (ad hominem)

The **ad hominem fallacy** substitutes character assassination for solid refutation or persuasion:

> Of course she would say that—what else would we expect from an ignorant piece of trailer trash?

2   The slippery slope

The **slippery slope fallacy** argues that taking the first step in any direction will inevitably lead to going dangerously far in that direction. The image is of someone sliding down a slope without being able to stop.

> If we let the government ban the sale and possession of assault rifles, banning all firearms will be next.

> If we let the government abandon support of the arts, artistic freedom will die.

3   The semantic fallacy

The rich, connotative nature of words, which enhances communication, can also support fuzzy thinking. When midstream shifts of definition are obvious, they can be funny, as in "blackberries are red when they're green." More subtle and dangerous **semantic fallacies,** or shifts in definition, can occur in various critical parts of an argument:

> The free enterprise system, which we all cherish, could not exist without competition. This bill to protect small businesses threatens our whole economic structure. There can be no true competition when one group is given special protection.

In the underlying value premise, the word *competition* is used in the general sense of a market mechanism. In claiming that the bill endangers competition, the speaker uses the term in a much narrower sense, as in "a specific contest between individuals." The semantic fallacy is especially difficult to identify and frustrating to respond to because the syllogistic form of the argument appears to be valid. The problem of identification arises from the slight slippage of definition when a term is used with different meanings in different premises.

4   False dichotomy

A **false dichotomy** is reasoning based on an *either/or* statement when the two alternatives are not really mutually exclusive or when other alternatives exist. Many speeches set up artificial choices:

> Would you rather have a football program or a band and orchestra at our school?

This basic premise so oversimplifies a complex issue that no conclusions can be drawn from it. Do not set up a deductive argument with a false dichotomy as its major premise.

5 Hasty generalization

A **hasty generalization** entails making an inductive leap based on too little evidence. (See **21b.**) This statement makes a faulty leap:

> The administration hid information about the recession. This government can't be trusted.

Time may not allow you, as a speaker, to include all the data that led you to some conclusion. It is especially important, then, to have the unused data at your fingertips so that you can respond to any accusations of hasty generalizations.

6 Confusing sequence with cause (post hoc)

The Latin label for this fallacy (*post hoc ergo propter hoc*) translates as "after the event, therefore because of the event." It is natural to try to understand the world around us by looking for cause–effect patterns. So strong is this motivation that we are frequently guilty of imitating Chanticleer the rooster, who firmly believed that it was his predawn crowing that caused the sun to rise each day.

To avoid the **post hoc fallacy,** never assume causation based on time sequence alone. Test every causal hypothesis against the criteria in **21d.**

7 Setting up a straw figure

The **straw figure fallacy** consists of creating a weak argument, attributing it to the opposing side, and then proceeding to demolish it. The false implication is that all the opponents' arguments are as flimsy as the "straw figure" and could be dismissed with equal ease if time permitted.

Opponents of affirmative action policies sometimes raise objections like this:

> We can't hire people from underrepresented groups without regard for their qualifications. It is not right to hire a mathematician to teach English just because she's a woman.

This claim is misleading because proponents of affirmative action do not advocate disregarding qualifications. The speaker has used an extreme example instead of taking on the complexity of the issue.

8 Extending an argument to absurd lengths (*reductio ad absurdum*)

The **fallacy of the absurd extreme** makes a potentially sound argument appear groundless by extending it to a point where it can be ridiculed. Often, this extension goes beyond reasonable interpretation of the original point. In challenging current methods of criminal sentencing, a speaker might say:

> The average criminal is condemned to a bleak cell, while wealthy wrongdoers lounge around in "country club" facilities. The rationale is that the latter have already been punished by loss of reputation and professional standing. By this reasoning, the celebrity who commits murder might get off with a citation and public embarrassment, while an unemployed ghetto dweller who shoplifts should be put on bread on water, with regular sessions of torture.

Pointing out inequities does not constitute a legitimate argument against the concept that the effect of punishment on the offender can be a valid criterion for a decision about sentencing. This kind of fallacy relies on the ludicrous example making listeners lose sight of the real issue.

9   Circular reasoning

Circular reasoning assumes, as one of its premises, the very conclusion it sets out to establish. Often, circular reasoning comes out of definitional word games:

No sane person would consider suicide, because it is insane to want to take your own life.

Critical Thinking Questions:

○ What is needed for inductive reasoning to be considered valid?

○ What makes "absolute" deductive reasoning difficult to use and how can this limitation be overcome?

○ Which of the reasoning fallacies listed have you heard or read recently?

CHAPTER 22
Informative Strategies

A large part of speaking is explanation—that is, stating an idea and then restating it in a way that develops the basic notion. Unfortunately, explanations can confuse rather than clarify if the speaker has lost sight of which details are essential. It is a real challenge to select the most significant details and present them in the clearest order. How can you most effectively create the mental picture that will aid your listeners' understanding?

22a. Help your listeners grasp information

Base your speech's structure and content on an understanding of how people acquire, process, and retain information.

1   Avoid information overload

When we speak on a topic we know a great deal about, we tend to want to bring our audience up to our level immediately. When we give too much information in too short a time, however, the result is information overload. The informative speaker has to manage a large mass of information and deliver it at the right pace and in the right-sized chunks so it can be useful and meaningful for listeners.

Information-processing research suggests that we cannot comprehend more than seven points (give or take two) at one time. That means selecting five to nine important points for your speeches, depending on the subject and the length of the speech.

2   Use an organizing framework

Have you ever tried to put together a jigsaw puzzle without looking at the picture on the box? Once you see the big picture, you have some idea of how the jumble of pieces is supposed to fit together. Similarly, providing your audience with a sense of the whole picture you will be painting with your speech will help them comprehend the significance of the parts. Avoid overwhelming an audience with details prior to clarifying the big picture.

3   Move from the simple to the complex

Even at the risk of temporary oversimplification, it is advisable first to lay out the most basic concepts and later to introduce qualifiers, exceptions, and interesting details. Think of your listeners as newcomers to town who want to learn the basic route from home to work before learning about shortcuts and scenic detours.

4 Move from the familiar to the unfamiliar

Any group can learn about any subject if you start where the audience is and move along at the proper rate. Teachers will attest that learning proceeds best when they are able to adjust the focus of their instruction to a point just above the current knowledge level of the group. If the instruction duplicates what the group already knows, the material will not be challenging. If the focus is too far above their current level, group members will get discouraged.

22b. Common techniques for clear explanation

The following techniques will help you substantially ease your listeners' path to comprehension.

1 Organizers

Provide your listeners with cues about the structure of the information.

Signposts One organizer is the **signpost.** Verbal signposts, like their physical counterparts, point the way you are going and also serve as a reminder of where you've been. For example,

> First, I'll show you how to make a simple white sauce. Then I'll move on to three more elaborate sauces that start with the basic recipe.

> Finally, from this short description of one novel and three of her poems, you can see once again the two themes that permeate Sylvia Plath's work.

Enumeration Numbering is an obvious organizational cue. For example,

> The many steps in building an apartment complex can be grouped into these three phases:
>
> > One: Finding attractive sites with the proper zoning.
> >
> > Two: Negotiating for the purchase of a piece of property.
> >
> > Three: Contracting with architects and builders.

Acronyms An **acronym** is a word that is formed from the first letters of a series of words and that can be pronounced like one word. For instance, *radar* is an acronym formed from *Ra*dio *De*tecting *A*nd *Ra*nging. Other examples are *RFID,* for *R*adio *F*requency *I*dentification, and HOMES, for *H*uron, *O*ntario, *M*ichigan, *E*rie and *S*uperior (the five Great Lakes).

Slogans, catchwords, and memorable phrases Like acronyms, these types of cues give your listeners a framework for remembering your points. For example,

> So, look at those files in your drawer that you haven't used in a year and assess their real value. Keep in mind Peg Bracken's advice about leftover food: "When in doubt, throw it out."

> Try to do something decisive with each piece of mail as you open it. Apply the "Four D's": Drop the item, Delay the item, Delegate the item, or Do the item.

2   Emphasis cues

Underline and highlight key points with phrases like "this is very important," "if you don't remember anything else," and "here's what it all comes down to."

You can also emphasize points using vocal or physical cues. When you want an idea to stand out, speak more loudly or, occasionally, more softly. Pause before and after the big idea. Step forward. Let your facial expression forecast the seriousness of a point.

3   Examples

When an audience is confused, nothing reassures them like a concrete example. You might begin with a simple, even whimsical, example:

> A "win–win" negotiation has occurred when both parties achieve their important goals without perceiving that they needed to make a major sacrifice. Phil and Dave are roommates, and they both think the other needs to do more around the apartment. After talking about it, they agree that Dave will do all the cooking and Phil will do all the cleaning. Each thinks he got off easy.

Next, you could move to a more complex and realistic example:

> Suppose that you have a used car for sale and that your neighbor wants to buy it but does not have all the cash now. You offer to carry an interest-free note due in six months if your neighbor will take care of your pets and plants for three weeks while you are on vacation.

Finally, you might give an example that is sophisticated, subtle, and complex enough for your audience to apply to situations they may actually encounter:

> Let's see how these principles apply to a typical real estate negotiation. On this chart you will see the seller's and buyer's prioritized needs and bargaining chips.

4 Analogies

Compare the known to the unknown. For instance, you might use this simple analogy to explain a complex process:

> A nuclear power plant is like a steam locomotive. The fireman shovels coal into the furnace, where the heat it gives off turns the water in the boiler into steam. The steam travels through pipes to pistons, where the energy is converted and carried by driving rods to the wheels, pulling long trains of cars down the rails. Substitute a nuclear pile for the coal, a turbine for the pistons, and an electrical generator for the drive wheels, and you have a nuclear power plant.

To reinforce points and reach more listeners, draw analogies from areas of common knowledge such as sports, movies, nature, history, different cultures, and so on.

5 Multiple channels

Your message will be clearer if you send it through several channels. As you describe a process with words, you can also use your hands, a visual aid, a chart, or a recording. Appeal to as many senses as possible in order to reinforce the message. A good rule to follow is this: If a point is very important or very difficult, always use at least one other channel besides the spoken word to get it across.

6 Repetition

People learn and remember what they hear repeatedly. If a principle is important, say it over again, in the same words or in different words. Repeat it. Paraphrase it. Reinforce it. Refer back to it. Then mention it again.

CHECKLIST

Helpful Strategies for Informative Speaking

- ❏ Organize your material so that it is clear and memorable and limit the number of main points.
- ❏ Use signposts and emphasis cues.
- ❏ Plan powerful and plentiful examples and metaphors.
- ❏ Send your message in multiple ways to engage the senses.
- ❏ Repeat important points for emphasis.

Critical Thinking Questions:

○ Why is information overload a speaker's concern?

○ What can a speaker do to avoid overloading an audience with information?

○ Which common technique of clear explanation do you find most difficult and why?

CHAPTER 23

Persuasive Strategies

When you try to change others' attitudes or behaviors, your persuasive effort is more likely to succeed if you understand how and why people change their minds.

23a. Your goals

A strong grasp of purpose is especially important in **persuasive speaking.** When you try to change people, and not simply to educate or inspire them, you are more likely to encounter resistance. It helps to know exactly what your goals are—and what they are not. (See **11c.**) You want to aim for a realistic target.

Some authorities distinguish between persuasive speeches that seek to change behavior and those that try to influence beliefs and attitudes. Although an attitude is a predisposition to respond in a particular way, holding a certain attitude does not guarantee certain behaviors associated with the attitude. People may say they believe in recycling but never drum up the energy to separate their trash. Generally, if you want action, you should define your goals in terms of audience behavior and tell the audience what to *do*—or *not do*—not what to *think*. (See **11d.3** for propositions of fact, value, and policy as speaking goals.)

23b. Audience types

Consider your audience's attitude toward your topic and toward you. (See **12c.**) The following continuum classifies audiences according to their predisposition toward your topic.

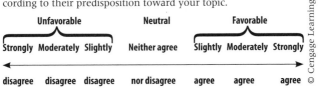

Unfavorable			Neutral	Favorable		
Strongly	Moderately	Slightly	Neither agree	Slightly	Moderately	Strongly
disagree	disagree	disagree	nor disagree	agree	agree	agree

© Cengage Learning

Here are some suggestions on how to deal with favorable, neutral, and unfavorable audiences.

1   Favorable audience

A speaker facing a favorable audience rarely needs to establish credibility. Your listeners, perceiving your position as identical to theirs, approve of you already. Furthermore, a favorable audience will not be thinking of counterarguments that you will need to deflect or to defuse. However, you can solidify or strengthen the attitudes of a favorable audience, or you can cause them to move from theoretical agreement to positive action.

Use emotional appeals to intensify support There is a difference between intellectually agreeing with a position and making a commitment to it. Even once committed, the difference between commitment and action is usually a function of emotional arousal. Out of the vast number of positions we might agree with, there is a much shorter list of issues that we really care about. These issues appeal to our most basic needs, touch on our core values, or have a personal effect on our lives, perhaps through family members, for example.

To get your speech topic on your listeners' short list, appeal to basic values (such as patriotism, humanitarianism, and progress), to basic needs (such as survival, security, and status), or to basic emotions (such as fear, pity, and love).

A major task in speaking to a favorable audience is the creation of personal involvement. First, be very specific about how their lives are affected, and then show them that their actions can make a difference. For example:

> Your $10 check can provide a bed net for a family.

> If you replace those old incandescent bulbs with new fluorescent ones, you can save yourself more than $50 a year.

Get your audience to make a public commitment Invite your listeners to offer suggestions, sign a petition, raise their hands to volunteer, or talk to others. People who have made a public commitment—oral, or written, or physical—are less likely to change their minds.

Provide opportunities for action Make it easy for listeners to take action by offering several specific choices. For example, with people who have shown up at a rally for a candidate, do not say, "Stop by campaign headquarters sometime." Instead, say, "I'd like everyone here to walk a precinct or spend an evening making phone calls. Sign-up sheets are being passed around now." With a favorable audience, do not settle for urging members to do "something." Tell them what you want them to do, and make the execution easy and attractive. If you want them to write letters, give them addresses; if you want them to reduce their sodium intake, give them low-sodium recipes.

Prepare your audience to carry your message to others Audience members can become persuaders in their own right. Each of them may later discuss your topic with coworkers, neighbors, or friends who are neutral or hostile toward it. Give your listeners ammunition for these interactions and make that material memorable and quotable. Provide your audience with ready answers to refute standard counterarguments. (See **23c.3.**) Here is an example:

> You may meet people who tell you that the administration's economic policy is designed to help the average worker. Just ask those people why the greatest tax relief goes to the rich. Have them explain to you why a person who earns $300,000 a year will have a 50 percent reduction in taxes, but a person making $30,000 a year will see only a 6 percent reduction. They may say, "Ah, but we are creating new jobs." Ask them this . . .

This also serves to inoculate your listeners against the persuasiveness of possible counterarguments.

CHECKLIST

Appeals for a Favorable Audience
- ❑ Use emotional appeals to solidify agreement.
- ❑ Seek a public commitment from listeners.
- ❑ Provide your audience with opportunities for action.
- ❑ Give your listeners ammunition to answer opposing points.

---

2 Neutral audience

Audience members can be neutral toward your position because they are *uninterested,* because they are *uninformed,* or because they are genuinely *undecided.*

For an uninterested audience, concentrate on getting and keeping its attention With this sort of audience, draw on all the attention techniques described in Chapter **30,** with special emphasis on concrete illustrations of your subject's impact on audience members' lives. Be sure the facts and statistics you use are relevant to your listeners' experience. Sprinkle your speech with humor and human interest. Make a special effort to deliver your speech in a lively and animated style.

For an uninformed audience, stress clarification Before you can expect people to agree with you, they must have some comprehension of the issue. The main concern is clarity; therefore, use explanations, definitions, examples, and restatements. (See **16a**.) Visual aids can be helpful. Keep your language simple and your organization straightforward.

A direct persuasive appeal should be saved until the very end of the speech.

For an undecided audience, establish credibility The undecided, neutral audience is interested in and informed about your topic but finds the arguments for each side equally compelling. Present new arguments that blend logical and emotional appeals to establish your credibility.

Let your listeners know that you understand their ambivalence. Grant the complexity of the issue and admit that there is truth on both sides. As you present the arguments for your side, stress any recent evidence or new interpretations that might justify a decision. Be sure that you acknowledge and respond respectfully and thoroughly to the main arguments against your position. In short, a well-documented, logical presentation works best for the undecided neutral audience. Appeals to emotions, needs, and values are effective only if used sparingly and clearly interwoven with the logical argument of the speech.

CHECKLIST

Appeals for an Unfavorable Audience

- ❏ Be realistic about what changes you ask listeners to make.
- ❏ Emphasize common ground.
- ❏ Be very thorough in your reasoning and careful with your evidence.
- ❏ Build your credibility by being fair and open-minded and by using humor carefully.

---

3 Unfavorable audience

An unfavorable audience is by no means a belligerent one—*unfavorable* encompasses anything on the disagreeing side of neutral, starting with "slightly disagree." However, the more intensely the audience disagrees, the more members will be predisposed to reject both you and your message. Any idiosyncrasies of appearance and/or style of delivery will allow them to dismiss you as being on the fringe.

Set realistic goals Do not try to do too much with an unfavorable audience. Attitudes change slowly. If most of your audience strongly disagrees, do not expect your 10-minute speech to change its opinion to strong agreement. Even if it means modifying your thesis statement, set a goal that you have a reasonable chance of achieving—such as easing those who strongly disagree over to moderate disagreement, or those who moderately disagree over to a neutral attitude. Do not make a call for action when action is highly unlikely.

Stress common ground However great the differences between you and your audience on any particular issue, there are bound to be places where your opinions and experiences overlap. When you think about the unfavorable audience you face, ask yourself what goals and values you share. Even the intensity of a disagreement between you and your audience over, say, school busing, reveals a common concern for children's education.

Use sound logic and extensive evidence The unfavorable audience is skeptical of your position and will reject most emotional appeals as manipulative. Your only chance to persuade these listeners is to build an iron-clad case supported by impeccable, unbiased evidence. With this audience, you must clearly indicate every step of your reasoning. Discuss and defend even those assumptions that seem obvious to you. Spell out the logical links that hold your argument together. Do not overstate your points; be careful not to claim more than the data allow. Say, "These examples suggest" rather than "These examples prove." Say, "Smoking is one contributing cause of cancer" rather than "Smoking causes cancer."

Use factual and statistical evidence and always cite your sources completely. (See Chapter **16**.) If you mention the results of a survey, for example, tell when, where, and how it was conducted and where it was presented or published. Confront directly the arguments that are foremost in your listeners' minds. Be willing to concede minor points that do not damage your basic case. State the remaining counterarguments fairly and answer them forcefully. Never stoop to ridicule.

Establish a credible image The careful establishment of good character, good sense, and goodwill is essential in a speech to an unfavorable audience. (See **26c**.) Plan every detail of your speech content and of the delivery in order to project an image of a calm, reasonable, fair, well-informed, and friendly person. The careful use of humor can bolster this image while releasing tension and putting the issue in perspective. Direct the humor at yourself, your position, a common enemy, or the ironic aspects of the confrontation. Never direct it at your listeners and their beliefs.

Although you do not want to seem combative, you should remain firm in your position. It is fine to stress common ground and to grant minor points, but do not waffle or be overly conciliatory.

CHECKLIST

Appeals for a Neutral Audience

❑ Use techniques to get and keep their attention.

❑ Make sure your point is clear and understandable; use visual aids.

❑ Acknowledge the complexity of the issue and the merit in both sides.

❑ Establish credibility by presenting the most recent evidence and examples you can find.

❑ Blend logical and emotional appeals.

23c. Organizational patterns

The speech organization patterns discussed in Chapter **19**—chronological, spatial, cause–effect, problem–solution, and topical—grow out of analysis of the speech content. Other patterns can form from retracing the reasoning that led you to your conclusion—inductively, deductively, causally, or analogically. (See Chapter **21**.) Yet another way of ordering points is to consider how your speech unfolds for your listeners. So, if none of the formats based on content or reasoning seems strategically adequate, here are some alternative arrangements.

1   The motivated sequence

Developed by Alan Monroe several decades ago, the **motivated sequence** is one of the most widely used organizers for persuasive speeches.[1] This psychologically based format echoes and anticipates the mental stages through which your listeners progress as they hear your speech.

Attention:	The speaker must capture the audience's attention and motivate audience members to listen to the speech.
Need:	The speaker must bring to light a problem that needs to be resolved.
Satisfaction:	The solution or course of action through which the problem is resolved.

[1]Raymie E. McKerrow, Bruce E. Gronbeck, Douglas Ehninger, and Alan H. Monroe, *Principles and Types of Speech Communication*, 14th ed. (Needham Heights, MA: Allyn & Bacon, 2000).

| *Visualization:* | Psychologically, it is important that the audience see vividly a picture of the benefits of agreeing with the speaker or the dangers of failing to agree. |
| *Action:* | The speech should end with an explicit call for listeners to act. |

Below is an example of a speech that follows the motivated sequence.

Thesis Statement: *We need a light rail system in our county to reduce excessive commuter traffic congestion.*

Attention

Introduction: I was on my way to work, having left home earlier than usual so I could be there in plenty of time for my first important presentation. I heard screeching brakes. It turned out to be only a fender-bender a quarter-mile ahead of me. Nevertheless, I sat in my car, and sat, and sat, while my mood progressed from irritation to outrage to despair. I arrived at work an hour and a half late, just as the meeting was breaking up.

Need

   I. Excessive reliance on automobile transportation to the county's major employment areas is causing severe problems.
     A. Major traffic jams
     B. Pollution
     C. Stress to commuters

Satisfaction

   II. A light rail system should be constructed to alleviate these problems.
     A. Definition of light rail
     B. Proposed route
     C. Proposed funding

Visualization

   III. The new system would be a vast improvement.
     A. Scenario with the light rail system: free parking, time to relax, drink coffee, read
     B. Scenario without the light rail system: increased traffic, gridlock, daily stress

Action

Conclusion: Support the county initiative for a light rail system. Urge your friends to vote for it. Write to members of the county board of supervisors on this issue. Ask your employer to commit to providing free shuttle service from the proposed light rail station to your place of business.

This organization resembles a standard problem–solution speech, but the visualization step makes all the difference. Instead of merely providing a logical need satisfaction in Main Point 2, this speaker has added another psychologically powerful step in Main Point 3. The two scenarios should be developed in detail to drive home the case for the listeners.

It is essential that the attention step be engaging and that the action step be concrete. A complete speech outline utilizing Monroe's Motivated Sequence is available in **Appendix A**.

2   Strongest points first or last

Ideally, all of the arguments and support for your thesis statement should be strong. In reality, however, you will find that you must use materials of varying strengths. People will remember best what is said first (the **primacy** principle) and what is said last (the **recency** principle). In light of this, arranging your arguments either from weakest to strongest (climax) or from strongest to weakest (anticlimax) will be more effective than placing your best points in the middle (pyramidal).

The research on which is stronger, primacy or recency, is far from conclusive. Our best advice regarding what to say first and last is that you consider the importance of your topic to your listeners, your listeners' attitudes toward the topic, and your own credibility level.

3   Dealing with opposing arguments

Generally, it is a good idea to address counterarguments in addition to presenting your own viewpoints. On widely debated topics, these ideas will already be on listeners' minds, and they expect a response. Even on less familiar subjects where you may have the first word, you probably won't have the last. At the end of a straightforward "pro" speech, your audience may agree with you. But if listeners later become aware of powerful opposing arguments, they may discredit your entire position.

Speakers often inoculate their audiences by presenting a few counterarguments and answering them. Then, when these points are brought up later, the listeners will say, "Oh yes, I was warned about this." Inoculation has created "antibodies" to resist the opposing position.

In most cases, answer counterarguments after developing your own position. The only exception is when you know that audience members are highly preoccupied with an opposing position. Under these circumstances, they may not listen to you. If this is the case, respond to the point in question immediately.

Critical Thinking Questions:

○ How should a speaker's audience analysis influence the persuasive strategies employed?

○ How would you persuade a group of high school students to take AP math or science courses?

○ How would an audience in opposition to the speaker's position affect the organization of a speech?

CHAPTER 24
Reasoning

In developing your speech, you must make sure that your evidence is sound. (See Chapter **16.**) Next, you need to cast the arguments into a form that will best help your audience understand them. For example, instead of stating your conclusion or claim after the evidence, stating that claim may be the first thing you want to do when speaking to an audience. Then you develop that thesis or main point by retracing your reasoning in an audience-friendly manner.

24a. The cost–reward analysis of an inductive argument

If you are using induction (see **21b**), you must convince the audience that your conclusion is probable enough to warrant their acceptance. The issue is one of "enoughness." Are your examples sufficient in both quantity and quality? The so-called inductive leap is an apt image. You lead the listeners to a certain point with your data and then ask them to jump across an imaginary divide to the conclusion you see.

Suppose you are advocating a new drug rehabilitation program that has been found to be effective in pilot studies in three different communities. Because you can draw from data in only three cases, you cannot guarantee the program's success with absolute certainty. A member of your audience might ask, "Why should we spend $650,000 for just a two-out-of-three chance that we might help a bunch of junkies?" You cannot change the odds, but you can influence your audience's assessment of the costs and rewards. Tell them how the program, if it works, will benefit the whole community: It will decrease crime, put former addicts back into the workforce, and lower the temptations for adolescent drug use. In addition, minimize the costs: "I know $650,000 sounds like a lot, but it's only 85¢ per citizen." When your listeners reassess the costs and rewards and see them from your perspective, the odds may look more attractive.

Consider another example.

Suppose the conclusion that nuclear power plants are safe could be granted a 95 percent level of probability. However, you do not feel the evidence is sufficient to make the inductive leap and risk a nuclear accident. In this case, you would minimize the rewards—most of the energy we would get from a nuclear plant could be obtained from other sources—and you would maximize the risks by describing just how awful a nuclear accident would be. Your argument would be: "I'm not willing to subject my family even to a 5 percent chance of this sort of destruction just to have a few extra electronic luxuries."

In the case of the drug program, a low probability met the test of enoughness for the speaker. In the case of the nuclear power plant, even 95 percent was not enough. The difference lies in perceptions of risk and reward. No level of enoughness is too high or too low—no inductive argument is innately logical or illogical. The validity is negotiated between you and your audience.

24b. The premises of a deductive argument

One of the advantages of structuring ideas deductively (see **21c**) is that you must state the relationships among the concepts. When you clearly state the major premise on which your argument rests, you call to your listeners' minds certain values and assumptions. They can then apply these concepts when you move on to specific cases in developing your minor premise.

In the following logical arguments, notice how the major premise serves to direct listeners' awareness to a statement that the speaker might otherwise have left implicit.

Major premise: Anyone who has been elected to high office needed to make a number of political compromises along the way.

Candidate J has served as governor and U.S. senator.

Therefore, Candidate J has made a number of political compromises.

Major premise: It has always been the goal of our social welfare system to help recipients become self-sufficient.

Certain current programs encourage dependency and discourage initiative.

Therefore, these programs should be changed.

Sometimes, speakers have so internalized a point of view that they leave out parts of their argument. On controversial topics with diverse audiences, neglecting to lay out every part of the argument is dangerous. In well-developed speeches, speakers take the time to articulate and justify their premises.

24c. Causal claims

Pure, simple causal arguments are rare. (See **21d.**) More common are lines of reasoning that lead to probable causal claims, like the following:

> X was present in these cases and Y occurred.
>
> X was absent in these cases and Y did not occur.
>
> Changes in the amount of X have often led to corresponding changes in the amount of Y.
>
> *Claim:* Therefore, it is probable that X causes Y.

Probable to what degree? To the degree that your examples are sufficient and representative and that conflicting examples are minimized or explained.

With this sort of causal argument, follow the advice in **16b.** Do not overstate your claim. Say, "This is a major cause," and not "This is *the* cause." Say, "There is strong evidence of a causal link between . . ." and so on.

24d. Showing links between evidence and claims

It is not enough to present only a cluster of evidence or a cluster of reasons for a claim. The reasoning process must be made transparent through organization and word choice so that listeners can decide for themselves if it is well conceived and executed.

1 Organization of points

Controversial claims can be found at all levels of a speech; controversial thesis statements, main points, and subpoints all require substantiation. There is not one correct way to display your lines of reasoning in a speech outline, but it is very important that you phrase points to show the connections. Do not simply group "reasons," as in the first example below. Instead reveal your reasoning, as in the second example.

Wrong:

> I. Having a longer school day does not improve learning.
>> A. They tried it at Riverdale High School, and test scores were unchanged.
>> B. They tried it at Glenbrook High School, and test scores actually went down.

    C. At Creekside High School, test scores have gone up even though their school day has not been lengthened.

    D. Braeburn High School shortened their school day, and test scores did not change.

Better:

  I. Having a longer school day does not improve learning.

    A. In cases in which the school day was lengthened, test scores did not improve.

      1. Unchanged at Riverdale High

      2. Went down at Glenbrook High

    B. In cases in which the school day was not lengthened, test scores were not lower.

      1. Improved at Creekside

      2. No change with shorter day at Braeburn

Summary transitional statement: If there was a causal relationship between the length of the school day and learning as measured by test scores, we would logically expect that scores would be higher where the school day is longer and lower where the school day is shorter. I have just demonstrated that this is not the case. Indeed, sometimes the opposite is true. So you can see why I conclude that having a longer school day does not improve learning.

In order for your audience to accept your reasoning, you must differentiate between points and support for the points. Do not use sources in place of reasoning. In the first example that follows, a speaker attempts to support a causal claim by saying that experts have agreed with the claim. But the listeners do not know *why* these people came to the conclusion they did. In the second example, the reasoning behind the causal claim is explained, with experts used to back up specific points.

Wrong:

  I. The use of sexist language perpetuates discrimination against women.

    A. Dr. Deborah Stone says sexist language causes problems.

    B. Professor Lydia Sorenson says sexist language is the root of many social problems.

    C. Linguist Chris Nupriya states that language affects behavior.

Better:

  I. The use of sexist language perpetuates discrimination against women.

    A. Language shapes social perception.

B. Speech that leaves women out can lead to people overlooking women.
   (Cite experts and studies.)
C. If people subconsciously exclude women from certain roles, they discriminate against women.
   (Cite experts and studies.)

2   Word choice

In addition to structuring your speech to highlight your reasoning, you should use words, phrases, and transitional sentences that spell out what your evidence means and how the parts of your argument are linked. Never merely jump from one point to the next. Use phrases that are specific cues to the kind of reasoning you are using. (See **21b, c, d,** and **e.**)

For inductive reasoning
Show the strength of your examples using phrases such as:

One case that supports my claim is . . .

Across many levels of income and many parts of the country, the same pattern holds true. For example . . .

Acknowledge the probable nature of your data by using qualifiers. For example:

Many/Most . . .

Virtually every study in the literature . . .

From these cases, I feel quite confident in concluding . . .

Demonstrate costs and rewards. For example:

I'm willing to bet my tax dollars that this program will work . . .

This is a gamble we can't afford to take . . .

The risks, though they do exist, seem minimal compared to the rewards . . .

For deductive reasoning
State your premises. For example:

Underlying my position is one of the fundamental tenets of our constitutional form of government.

The argument for my claim rests on one basic assumption that I hope you will agree with. It is . . .

Either . . . or . . .

If . . . then . . .

Spell out your reasoning. For example:

Because I've shown you X and Y, . . .

Therefore . . .

From this, it follows that . . .

It seems logical to conclude that . . .

For causal reasoning

Show how the cause and effect are related in a predictable way.
For example:

> In state after state where spending on education went up,
> crime went down.

> This is no coincidence. When X occurs, then Y occurs.

Qualify your causal claims if necessary. For example:

> There may be many causes, but the one I have identified is a
> major causal factor.

> It is highly probable that smoking causes these health problems.

Explain the mechanism of the cause. For example:

> The reason all these experts have concluded that X causes Y
> is that . . .

> I've shown you all these cases in which being abused as a child
> seems to lead to being an abusive parent. Let me explain how
> that happens.

For reasoning by analogy

Stress the points of similarity. For example:

> In Ecuador, as in neighboring Colombia and Peru, . . .

> For 8 of the 10 other universities in our conference, adding wom-
> en's sports to the athletic program has led to more alumni support.

> In a parallel case, . . .

Spell out the link. For example:

> If it worked in New Jersey and Idaho and Georgia, it will work
> in the rest of the country.

> Let's not wait too long on planning for earthquake safety. We put
> off dealing with flood control, and the results have been tragic.

Critical Thinking Questions:

○ What is needed for inductive reasoning to be considered
valid?

○ Why is it necessary to present more than a cluster of
evidence or a cluster of reasons for a claim?

○ Why is it important to make your reasoning explicit
to your audience rather than simply using sources to
support your claim?

CHAPTER 25
Motivational Appeals

This book stresses the role of clear analysis in support of ideas. It also recognizes the importance of making those ideas meaningful to the audience. Love sometimes overrules logic, reverence often transcends reason, and emotion frequently contradicts evidence. To reach your audience as whole persons means presenting your logical case so that it touches listeners' hearts as well as their minds.

25a. The emotional impact you want

Everything you say has the potential to trigger some sort of emotional response in audience members. You can strengthen your speech by selecting main points, supporting material, and language that will engage your listeners' feelings. Positive emotions—hope, joy, pride, love—are surefire motivators. Negative emotions—fear, envy, disgust, and contempt—can also motivate. Why else would roller coasters and horror films be so popular? The motivational effects of negative emotions are less predictable, however. Moderate levels of fear appeal can enhance persuasion but higher levels risk turning off your audience.

25b. The needs of your listeners

The best-known way of classifying human needs is the hierarchy devised by Abraham Maslow.[1] In **Maslow's hierarchy of needs,** shown in Figure 25-1, the lower-level needs have to be met before an individual can become concerned with the needs on the next-highest level. For instance, on the topic of physical fitness, you could appeal to your audience at any of the following levels:

- The effect of exercise in reducing risk of cardiovascular disease relates to *survival needs.*

- *Security needs* might be included by mentioning that physically fit people are more likely to be able to resist or evade an attacker.

- The *need for belonging* can be linked to becoming trim and attractive, as well as to making friends through physical activity.

- *Esteem needs* can be tied into the current popularity of fitness and the social desirability of an active image.

- Fitness can be related to the *need for self-actualization*—the mental and physical satisfaction of reaching one's exercise goals.

[1] Abraham Maslow, *Motivation and Personality,* 2nd ed. (New York: Harper & Row, 1970), 35–58.

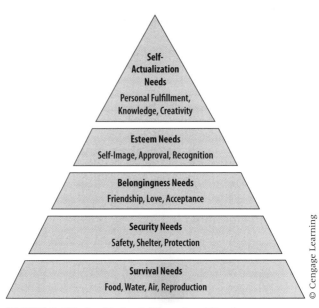

FIGURE 25-1 Maslow's Hierarchy of Needs

© Cengage Learning

You must analyze your audience to determine which needs are most likely to be relevant to them. Listeners whose jobs are in danger and who are struggling to feed their families want to know which local economic program will create jobs. If they are absorbed with their security needs, they are not likely to respond at the self-actualization level. It is counterproductive to aim your emotional appeals too high, and unethical to aim them too low.

25c. The values of your listeners

A **value** is the belief that a particular thing is either good or bad, in the broadest sense of those terms. We *evaluate* concepts, people, objects, events, and ideas every day when we label them just or unjust, wise or foolish, beautiful or ugly, and so on.

1 General values

Although we each choose our values, the choice is rarely totally conscious and rational. Culture has a strong influence, shaping values through families, schools, media, and peers. By knowing the culture of your listeners, the influences on them, and perhaps some of their values, you can make an educated guess about values that might shape their attitude toward your speech topic.

> ● KEY POINT   **Universality of Values***
>
> *Striver:* Values power, status, ambition, health and fitness, material security, courage, perseverance, public image, and wealth.
>
> *Fun-Seeker:* Values excitement, leisure, individuality, pleasure, enjoying life, having fun, adventure, and variety.
>
> *Creative:* Values open-mindedness, beauty, fulfilling work, self-esteem, creativity, self-reliance, freedom, curiosity, knowledge, wisdom, learning, internationalism, and music.
>
> *Devout:* Values spirituality, tradition, duty, obedience, respecting ancestors, traditional gender roles, faith, and modesty.
>
> *Intimate:* Values honesty, authenticity, protecting family, personal support, stable personal relationships, enduring love, romance, friendship, and sex.
>
> *Altruist:* Values being in tune with nature, preserving the environment, justice, social responsibility, helpfulness, equality, social tolerance, and social stability.
>
> *Simeon Chow and Sarit Amir, "The Universality of Values: Implications for Global Advertising Strategy." Journal of Advertising Research 46, no. 3 (September 2006): 301–314. Communication & Mass Media Complete, EBSCOhost (accessed December 14, 2010).

2   Core values

Obviously, all members of a culture do not give the same importance to their shared values. Moreover, any particular issue can touch on many values, on both the pro side and the con. Examples of this value conflict become apparent around election time. Suppose there is a proposed bond issue to build a fine arts complex. A person may be drawn toward approving the bond as a result of valuing beauty and accomplishment. However, this person may also have reservations about taking on a greater tax burden because of a belief in the values of a comfortable, prosperous life and family security. The resolution of this conflict depends on how this person has prioritized these values.

Values that are central to identity are called **core values.** Other values, though important, are not as central. Understanding this, you should try to make reasonable inferences about your listeners' core values and stress them in your speech.

3   Sense of community

Understandably, when people first encounter an issue, they wonder, "How does this affect me and my immediate circle, now and in the near future?" One of the most powerful ways that public speakers can use motivational appeals is to refocus people's awareness on larger frames of reference.

This broader awareness is there and available to be tapped if properly communicated. For instance, when the U.S. public really saw and felt the suffering of the Haitian people following the earthquake in 2010, there was an outpouring of financial support. As a speaker, you can create powerful word pictures to remind listeners of their interdependence with other people and creatures and to transport them into the past and the future. You can use your words to show people the historical and cultural significance of endangered animals and places. You can take listeners into the future and reveal the effects of our environmental policies or our national debt on unborn generations. Link your speech topic to your audience's values in ways that tie into the broadest sense of community and situate the present in relation to the past and the future.

25d. Inappropriate use of motivational appeals

A speech with too much emphasis on feelings can embarrass and offend the audience. If listeners perceive that the speaker is playing on their emotions to the exclusion of sense and logic, they may become angry. It is always a mistake to underestimate the intelligence of an audience. Aside from the issue of effectiveness— advertisers and politicians show that motivational appeals can be effective—there is the question of ethics. (See Chapter **3.**)

Critical Thinking Questions:

○ Which values appeal found in contemporary American media do you find most and least compelling? Why?

○ How does Maslow's hierarchy of needs affect how you might develop a persuasive speech?

○ How could you find out the core and peripheral values of your audience?

CHAPTER 26
Credibility

Your content and delivery determine, to a great extent, whether your listeners believe what you say. However, your audience is also influenced by who you are—or, more accurately, who they think you are. Your **credibility** is that combination of perceived qualities that makes listeners predisposed to believe you.

For centuries, scholars have been fascinated by credibility, from classical discussions of ethos to contemporary investigations of concepts like image, personality, and charisma. Aristotle observed that audiences are most inclined to believe a person they see as having good sense, goodwill, and good character. Modern social scientists have tried to isolate the characteristics that distinguish the most credible speakers from others. Their lists include competence, dynamism, intention, personality, intelligence, authoritativeness, extroversion, trustworthiness, composure, and sociability. You can enhance your credibility, and thus the chances of meeting your speech objective, by projecting these qualities. You can build your speaking image before the speech, and you can take steps to improve your credibility as you are speaking. The first step, though, is to assess your image.

26a. Assess your speaking image

Is your overall credibility high or low? Do people agree with you because of, or in spite of, your personality? Which components of credibility in the *Checklist: Your Speaking Image* are strongest for you? Which need to be developed? If possible, have a friend or two help you with this appraisal. It is very hard to see ourselves as others see us.

CHECKLIST

Your Speaking Image
1. Are you perceived as competent?
   - ❏ Do you have the education, experience, and/or credentials to make you an expert on this topic?
   - ❏ Is your speech based on well-documented, factual information?
   - ❏ Does your delivery show that you are on top of your information, well organized, and composed?
2. Are you perceived as concerned about your audience's welfare?
   - ❏ Have you spoken or acted on behalf of your audience's interests as they relate to your topic?
   - ❏ Do you stress the audience's needs and goals throughout the speech?
   - ❏ Is your delivery warm, friendly, and responsive to the audience?

3. Are you perceived as trustworthy?
   ❑ Is your record one of honesty and integrity?
   ❑ In your speech, do you make an effort to be fair, acknowledging the limitations of your data and opinions and conceding the parts of opposing viewpoints that have validity?
   ❑ Is your style of presentation sincere and not perceived as slick or manipulative?
4. Are you perceived as dynamic?
   ❑ Is your image that of an active, assertive person—a doer rather than an observer?
   ❑ Does your speech have a sense of movement? Do the ideas build to a climax? Is your language lively and vivid?
   ❑ Is your delivery animated, energetic, and enthusiastic?

26b. Build your credibility before the speech

Provide the contact person with information about your qualifications Do not be overly modest when asked for information for advance publicity. Send a résumé that lists your background and achievements. Include clippings, testimonials about your speaking, a list of your books and articles, and a photograph, if appropriate. If there are aspects of your background that you would like to have stressed for a particular speech, be sure to say so.

Manage your image during all contact with the group In your class, service organization, or work group, you know that you have a certain image based on previous interactions. With an unfamiliar audience, virtually all of your interactions with them will affect your credibility. Initially, their entire perception of you will be based on your nonverbal communication and your friendliness, professionalism, and confidence in negotiating arrangements. Even making small talk before the speech will be very influential.

26c. Bolster your credibility during your speech

As you prepare your speech, think about ways to communicate your competence, concern, trustworthiness, and dynamism. The opening minutes of the speech are especially important because first impressions are being formed. (See **31a**.) Many credibility boosters can be woven throughout the speech as well.

1 Present your credentials

Most inexperienced speakers find it difficult to "blow their own horn." Do not be reluctant to provide information about your qualifications to speak about your topic even if you think people already know them. For instance, you might say:

In my five years as a Manager for Target . . .

I've had a special awareness of the barriers the physically handicapped face since 2007, when my brother Dave returned from the Iraq War.

Judgment and tact are important in deciding which qualifications to mention and how to work them into the speech. Our culture frowns upon bragging and name-dropping. Yet false humility is out of place. You can include statements of your qualifications without seeming boastful if you present them matter-of-factly and include only relevant ones.

2 Demonstrate your understanding of your topic

To communicate your expertise, you must show listeners that you have done your homework. Mention the nature of your research when appropriate. For example:

The seven judges I interviewed all agreed on one major weakness in our court system.

I read the minutes of all the committee hearings on this bill and not one expert mentioned . . .

Use concrete examples, statistics, and testimony. Be sure you have your details straight. One obvious error early in the speech can ruin your credibility. The people listening will wonder what other information is wrong.

3 Be sure your material is clearly organized

Appearing competent depends on being in command of the material and seeming to know where you are heading. Listeners may regard you as uninformed rather than unorganized if you wander from topic to topic and apologetically insert, "Oh, one thing I forgot to mention when I was discussing . . ."

4 Present an objective analysis

To demonstrate that you are fair, trustworthy, and of good character, acknowledge the limitations of your evidence and argument, where appropriate. For example:

I'm not saying television is the only cause of these problems. I realize that's an oversimplification. However, I do think that TV has had a pronounced effect on the imaginative thinking of the last two generations.

Also, be sure to acknowledge opposing evidence and opinions. For example:

> Some studies indicate that an alcoholic can return to social drinking, but . . .

Acknowledge self-interest when it exists to prevent the audience from thinking you are trying to hide something. For example:

> It's true I'm a real estate agent and I stand to profit by having folks invest in real estate. However, that's not my main reason for urging you to invest.

If they discover later that you are more partisan than you made it sound, your credibility will suffer.

5   Express your goodwill toward the audience

Let the audience know that your speech is offered to serve their interests. For example:

> I'd do anything to save your families the headaches and heart-aches that go along with having a relative die without a will.

> Taking up cycling has added so much to my life that I'd love to see some of you share in that fun.

26d. Effective delivery

Too many expert and well-prepared speakers lose credibility be-cause they cannot transmit these qualities to their audience. Dropping cards, reading in a shaky voice, fumbling with what-ever is at hand—all suggest lack of competence. Over-reliance on your notes and a lack of facial and/or vocal expression might be interpreted as disdainfulness and detract from perceived goodwill. Hesitancy and uncertainty are sometimes falsely seen as shiftiness or dishonesty. To be seen as a believable source of information and opinion, continue to work on all aspects of delivery covered in Chapters **34** and **35**.

Critical Thinking Questions:

○ How can a speaker create credibility prior to speaking?

○ What can a speaker do to enhance credibility while speaking?

○ What mistakes have you seen destroy a speaker's credibility?

CHAPTER 27
Presentation Aids

Depending on circumstances and context, presentation aids may help you be more effective in communicating your message. A **presentation aid** is an object or technological tool that adds another communicative dimension to your vocal content and delivery. Generally, presentation aids are visual, but they can be aural or audiovisual.

27a. Determine what aids are appropriate

What in your speech could be represented by presentation aids? The first step is to decide whether an aid will help you meet your speaking goal. Then you can move to deciding what form aids will take and what tools you will use to create and present them.

A visual or audio aid can sometimes help you make a point more clearly and quickly than spoken words alone. Conversely, poorly used aids can obscure your ideas and detract from your speech. Presentation aids should *support* your message—not *be* your message. Sometimes you can be tempted to spend more time preparing the aids than preparing your speech.

Another consideration is the context. Especially in the business world, a speaker is expected to have a slide presentation. To do without would jeopardize the speaker's credibility. In contrast, a graduation speech is not expected to have presentation aids. Finding out the expectations of the situation is an important part of the speech planning process.

1   Is a presentation aid needed?

Complex data to compare? Well, there's a possible subject for an aid. Need to intensify an emotional point? Another aid possibility. A recurring theme? Yet another aid possibility.

The two most obvious reasons for using presentation aids are to explain an unfamiliar, complex, or technical idea, and to reinforce a particular message. The approach you use will depend on whether you use continuous or discrete aids. (See **27a.2** and **27a.3**.) A geneticist might use a wire-frame model of the DNA double helix when talking about how that remarkable molecule duplicates itself. A speaker wishing to impress upon an audience the importance of stiffer drunk-driving penalties may choose to reinforce a recitation of traffic fatality percentages with a pie chart. To help the audience understand the differences between blues, grunge, and power metal rock styles, the speaker may choose to play three short audio clips from Cream, Pearl Jam, and Dragon Force.

Don't decide what kind of presentation aid you will use before you have determined what you wish to show. First, figure out what concepts you want to show. Then decide what you'll need to make those concepts concrete and immediate. *Then* determine the best way to present them.

2 What technology will best suit your purpose?

If you've concluded that presentation aids would be useful in your speech, ask yourself, "What am I going to use to make them?" and "How am I going to present them?" To answer these questions, start by investigating the physical environment of your speaking venue. Then think about what aids would work in the space, primarily in terms of visibility and audibility. (See **27b.1**.) You also need to consider how much time you have to prepare your aids; how much time displaying or playing the aids will take; how portable the aids are; what technology is available to you for creating the aids; and what technology is available at your speaking venue for showing your aids.

A multitude of approaches There are many possible approaches to producing these aids, such as posters, flipcharts, PowerPoint slides, or a Prezi. You may decide you want text highlighting your main points, along with a few graphs and photographs to clarify certain points. Additionally, you may wish to add impact to one particular point with text, image, or sound. A quotation may get to the heart of the matter; a photograph may capture the essence of your thesis; or an audio clip might bring a main point to life.

Presentation slides Microsoft's PowerPoint is the best known of many choices. Other **presentation software** includes Keynote, an application in Apple's iWork software suite; Corel Presentations, an application in WordPerfect Office; and specialized packages used by private institutions such as religious organizations, law firms, and medical providers. In addition, free—but less fancy—presentation software is also available, such as Google Docs Presentations and OpenOffice.org Impress and Prezi. Whatever your application, pay particular attention to the design suggestions in **27b and 27c**.

3 Visual representations

The object or a model of it To demonstrate the simplicity of a new lens-to-camera attachment system, you could use the actual camera and lens. If your audience is very large, however, this sort of demonstration might not work because not everyone could see the camera clearly. In this case, you could use a larger-than-life-size model. In contrast, some objects are obviously too large to use, like the USS *Nimitz*, so a scaled-down reproduction is necessary.

Pictorial reproductions You can also use **pictorial reproductions** in the form of photographs, sketches, plans, pictures, slides, overhead transparencies, computer animations, film clips, and video recordings. For example, if the mechanical device that attaches the lens to the camera is complex, you might use a schematic drawing to show the interaction of all the pieces. Again, object size and audience size are important factors in determining which to use and which technology would best serve to prepare and present them.

Pictorial symbols Representation of abstract concepts generally calls for **pictorial symbols** such as graphs, charts, diagrams, and maps.

QUICK TIP **Video Clips: To Use or Not** Video clips have become a popular way to jazz up a speech. Unfortunately they are rarely used well. Effective use is more difficult than most people realize. If you use video, keep it very brief (less than 1/10th of your speech), test and cue it in advance, and have a back up plan.

When speaking on the declining state of the economy, you might use a line graph showing changes in the buying power of the dollar over the past two decades. A speech on local politics might use a map showing city council districts. Figures 27-1 and 27-2 show some common pictorial symbols.

CHECKLIST

Best Uses of Graphs, Charts, and Tables

❏ To make comparisons, especially of differences in quantity or frequency, use a *bar graph* (see Figure 27-2) or *pictogram* (for example, sales by region or number of users of several different computer operating systems).

❏ To show trends or changes over time or to show how one thing is affected by another, use a *line graph* (see Figure 27-2—for example, number of injury accidents each month during a year).

❏ To show relative proportions or percentages of the parts of a whole, use a *pie chart* (see Figure 27-1—for example, world production of heroin by continent).

❏ To show steps in a process or series of related decisions or actions, use a *flowchart* (for example, steps to troubleshoot a problem or to build something).

❏ To show large amounts of data, use a *table* (for example, H1N1 flu infections by age and state).

❏ To juxtapose and compare qualities or characteristics of different elements, use a *grid* (for example, comparison of features of several different models).

Pie Graph

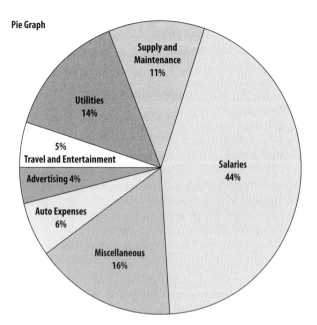

Annotated Map

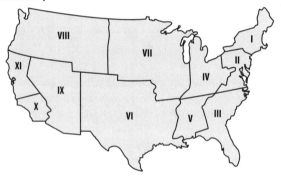

Slogan or Memorable Phrase

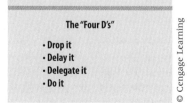

FIGURE 27-1   Pictorial Symbols

(a)

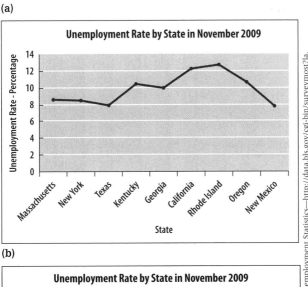

(b)

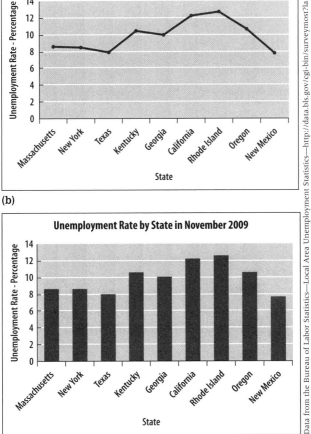

Data from the Bureau of Labor Statistics—Local Area Unemployment Statistics—http://data.bls.gov/cgi-bin/surveymost?la.

FIGURE 27-2   (a) Improper and (b) Proper Choice of
Graph to Match Data Type

Each kind of chart or graph is best suited for a particular kind of information. In general, **line graphs** are better for showing trends than **bar graphs,** and **pie charts** are better for showing relationships of parts to a whole than line graphs. The *Checklist: Best Uses of Graphs, Charts, and Tables* describes the preferred use of each type, along with some examples. Using the wrong type of graph may convey implications that are not present in your data. Figure 27-2 shows U.S. unemployment rates by state using two kinds of graphs. The line graph is the wrong one to use for this information because connecting the state totals with a line implies some kind of trend among them, which obviously makes no sense. The bar graph allows the viewer to see the totals and easily compare them.

27b. Make your aids clear and manageable

The time you spend preparing aids will be wasted if they are hard to see or understand, or difficult to use.

1   Size

The place in which you will be speaking and the size of the audience will determine, to a great extent, the type and size of your aids. If possible, it helps to look over the facility in advance. Stand at the back of the room and envision the scene. Screens for projected presentations and slides should be large enough for everyone in the room to see. Projectors should have focal lengths great enough to fill the screen. With a videotape, make sure that the monitor can be mounted high enough to be seen by people in the back row, or that there are several monitors around the room. Check that your sound equipment is adequate for the size of the room, and check for any background noise in the environment.

If you already have a rough mock-up or draft of one of your aids, such as a poster or a model, place it where you expect it to be when you speak and then walk around the room. If the aid is too small to be seen from every seat, you will need to enlarge it. Lines on charts should be thick and bold. Captions should be concise and large. Model parts should be large enough to be distinguishable. If the room is too large for a poster, a flipchart, or a **whiteboard** to be read by everyone, consider using a slide projector, an overhead projector, or a digital projector. Reduce any aid that is too large for the size of the room. Consider alternatives for an aid that is so unwieldy you will have to wrestle with it.

2   Simplicity

Visual aids should contain only relevant details. Do not crowd maps, charts, graphs, models, and slides with so much data that your audience cannot tell what you are referring to. If there are too many lines on a line graph, audience members are at risk of taking a "wrong turn" while following one line across. Photographs should show the relevant object by itself, or show it more prominently than other objects.

Keep the wording on visual aids simple and familiar. Label parts and ideas with as few words as possible and use color to delineate different parts. The following suggestions will ensure that your PowerPoint slides, overheads, and posters are effective.

1. *Use simple typefaces.* Do not mix more than two typefaces on a slide. Avoid ornate or fancy type and stay away from drop shadows, outline fonts, and other decorative type modifications that add visual "noise."

2. *Use uppercase and lowercase letters in the titles and text.* Sentences in all capital letters are hard to read.

3. *Use a lot of "white space."* That is, do not crowd too much information on one slide or overhead transparency. Keep the information simple; use your speech to fill in the details.

4. *Follow the 3 x5 rule.* Limit the words on a slide to three lines with five words per line.

5. *Look for opportunities to use images rather than text.* Pictures, charts, and graphs can illustrate some ideas better than text-heavy slides can.

6. *Maintain continuity throughout the slides.* Use the same design theme for each slide. For instance, if you use a border or background, put it on all slides; if you use bullets for a list on one sheet, do not use numbers or dashes for a list on another sheet.

27c. PowerPoint and other presentation software

PowerPoint and other presentation software can be considered a mixed blessing to speakers. On the one hand, it is possible to create slides and handouts that are consistent and attractive. On the other, it is too easy to end up reading your slides rather than giving a speech or allowing the technology to overshadow your message.

1 Templates and special effects

Presentation software templates are designed to keep your slides simple. That is, if you use the typefaces in the default sizes, it is difficult to clutter the slides with too many words and ideas. This is good—avoid the temptation to finesse your way around the default type sizes. (Remember the 3 x 5 rule mentioned in **27b.2.**) Instead, look for better ways to organize your material and to pare your language to a minimum. (See Chapters **18** and **19.**)

You can use PowerPoint's animation effects or "builds" to the elements of a slide in a particular order for dramatic effect or to keep the focus on the most immediate point. Use these special effects with restraint; their impact diminishes with overuse. Similarly, exercise restraint with the sound effects that come with the package—"zooping" sounds may be fun with one slide, but they quickly become an annoying distraction.

2 Visual consistency

Used properly, PowerPoint and other presentation software can help you maintain a consistent look throughout your slides. While templates work for keeping the type uniform, the program's settings for color schemes, for slide backgrounds, for patterns, and so on will keep other elements consistent. Even with this help, though, you need to review your slides to make sure no discrepancies have crept in. Look at the captions. Are they all in burgundy 14-point bold Helvetica? Or has one somehow ended up in green 14-point Arial Narrow? How about the placement of elements? Click through the slide show quickly to see if elements seem to jump from place to place. Also, check other features, like transition effects and builds, for their consistency. These can get mixed up. It can be distracting if most slides use a "fade through black" transition but a few use a "wipe right."

3   Clip art

Avoid the temptation to use clip art to "pretty up" your slides or fill white space. Use visual images only when they add clarity to your message or reinforce a point. Because PowerPoint has such wide exposure, some of its clip art images—for example, of business people standing around a table or the ubiquitous business handshake—can make your message seem dull. Additionally, too many images peppered around your text can be distracting. Images in different styles—a line drawing of a person followed by a cartoon image of a person, for instance, or a low-resolution bitmap image followed by a sharp PostScript image—can be distracting as well.

Figures 27-3 and 27-4 show two text-based slides, the first of which violates many of the design guidelines in **27b** and **27c.** In Figure 27-3 the creator has tried to fit too much into the text, making it a "read-along" slide. Clip art in different styles fills the white space and does nothing to advance the message.

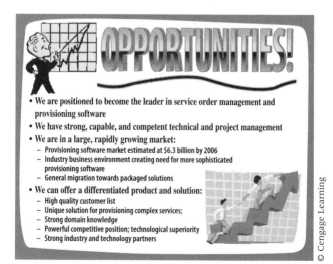

FIGURE 27-3 **Overworked Text Slide**

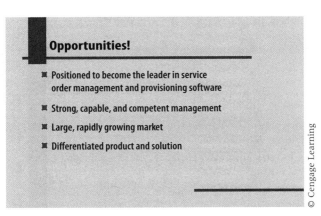

FIGURE 27-4 Effective Text Slide

The modification to the type in the slide title makes it hard to read. The slide in Figure 27-4 provides a better approach. Instead of full sentences, it uses key phrases, making the message clear while supporting, rather than supplanting, the speaker. The type is large and readable and is not competing with extraneous clip art for the viewers' attention.

Critical Thinking Questions:

○ What determines whether you should use a particular presentation aid?

○ What presentation aids would improve the speech you are currently developing?

○ What advantages and disadvantages do presentation aids offer the speaker? The audience?

CHAPTER 28. **Modes of Delivery**

Select a mode of delivery that is appropriate to your topic, audience, and occasion.

CHAPTER 29. **Language and Style**

Choose words and constructions that make your ideas clear and memorable. Respect the power of language.

CHAPTER 30. **Capturing Attention and Interest**

Adapt your speech material so that it captures your listeners' attention and retains their interest.

CHAPTER 31. **Introductions and Conclusions**

Lead your listeners into and out of your topic with a carefully planned introduction and conclusion.

CHAPTER 32. **Polishing Your Speech**

Unify your speech by weaving in supporting materials and by using transitions between ideas.

CHAPTER 33. **Practicing Your Speech**

Use practice sessions to get feedback and polish your delivery.

CHAPTER 28
Modes of Delivery

Decide early if your speech will be **impromptu** (off-the-cuff), **extemporaneous** (planned and practiced in advance), **manuscript** (written out and read with expression), or **memorized** (presented word for word). Settle on the predominant mode you will use, but be aware that no speech is purely *one* mode. For example, even in an extemporaneous speech, it is often advisable to write out the introduction and conclusion and to commit them mostly to memory. Any speaker who accepts questions must be prepared to offer some impromptu answers.

28a. The extemporaneous mode

Extemporaneous speaking is the most common mode of delivery. You should use it in all but a few special cases because it makes for a more conversational and flexible presentation. In this mode, you prepare extensively, constructing the progression of ideas with the aid of an outline, planning your content thoroughly, and practicing until you are comfortable and conversational. You never commit yourself to a rigid, exact sequence of words.

Prepare an extemporaneous speech in four steps:

1. *Begin with a fully developed outline.* Follow the recommendations in Chapters **17** through **20** in order to arrange your material in a logical and effective manner.

2. *If you have used a full-sentence outline, convert it to a keyword or key-phrase outline.* A full-sentence outline is written English, not spoken English, and if you use it for the wording of your speech, the result may be dull and lifeless. For this reason, we suggest that you convert the full-sentence outline to a **keyword or key-phrase outline** that enables you to develop the speech aurally as you proceed through Step 3.

3. *Word the speech.* Working from the keyword outline, practice putting your ideas into words. The second time through, some clumsy phrases will have disappeared as you play with sentence structure, rhythms, and so forth. Third time, fourth time, fifth time through—your topic is becoming more and more familiar, giving you the freedom to relax and to allow yourself to experiment with construction. You will also discover that several ways of expressing a set of thoughts may be equally effective.

4. *Convert your brief outline to speech notes.* See **33b** for directions on how to transform your content to easy visual cues that you can refer to while speaking.

28b. Speaking impromptu

No one should give an important speech in the impromptu mode, but sometimes we may be called on to give a speech unexpectedly. On these occasions, follow these four simple steps.

1 Keep your composure

Remind yourself that you speak all the time in conversations without extensive preparation. You should have realistic expectations for yourself and not fall apart if you fail to deliver your most polished performance. Do not apologize. Speak slowly and confidently.

2 Select a theme

Quickly list several possible approaches to the topic. Do it mentally or, if time permits, with pencil and paper. By thinking beyond the most obvious approach, you may discover a way to link your topic to a subject you are conversant with.

3 Select an organizational framework

You will not have time to make an extensive outline, but you can hook your topic to a simple framework like one of the following:

Past–present–future

Pros and cons

Concentric rings, progressing from immediate concerns to universal concerns (for example, home, school, community; or locally, regionally, nationally, internationally)

Domains or different spheres touched by the topic (for example, political, social, and economic spheres, or practical, theoretical, and moral implications)

After you have organized your main points, find one way to support or develop each idea, such as an explanation, an example, a story, a fact, or a statistic.

If time permits, jot some notes. Even a few keywords on a napkin can reassure you and keep you on track once you have started to speak.

4 Plan your first and last sentences

By having introductory and concluding sentences, you avoid the aimless rambling that is so characteristic of impromptu speaking. When you know your task is to start with Sentence A and finish with Sentence B, you have a reference against which to judge ideas that occur to you as you are speaking.

28c. Manuscript speeches

Limit your use of **manuscript speaking** to the following situations:

- The time allotted is specific and inflexible (for example, the broadcast media)
- The wording is extremely critical (for example, sensitive and emotionally charged topics)
- The style is extremely important (for example, a major speech of tribute)

There is a widespread misconception that speaking from a manuscript is the easiest and safest mode of delivery ("I'm not an experienced speaker, so I'd better write it out"). However, a bad manuscript speech is much worse than a bad extemporaneous speech. Stilted phrasing, monotonous vocal delivery, and lack of eye contact are all perils facing a novice speaking from a manuscript.

A poorly delivered manuscript speech is marked by a singsongy cadence, gasping for breath between overlong sentences, and a quick glance up from the page between paragraphs. To deliver a manuscript speech smoothly, practice reading and rereading your manuscript out loud until you are comfortable with it and will be able to make eye contact with your audience occasionally. You should neither sight-read nor memorize the text; instead, you should become familiar with its flow and rhythm.

Start with a full-sentence outline for good organization. However, for the actual wording of the speech, "talk" the speech out and onto the paper. You need to check your composition against your ear more than your eye. As you write and rewrite, keep saying it aloud, listening for the rhythms of oral style. (See Chapter **29.**)

CHECKLIST

Manuscript Readability

- ❑ Print out the manuscript on a printer, on heavy paper, with triple spacing and with wide margins.
- ❑ Use capital and lowercase letters in standard sentence format. Make sure the print is dark and legible.

KEY POINT **Manuscript Delivery**

- Retain a conversational style of speaking.
- Be familiar enough with your content to sustain eye contact.
- Memorize the wording in a few places (for example, first and last sentences) where audience contact is crucial.

28d. Memorized speeches

By definition, giving a **memorized speech** means giving a manuscript speech—without the manuscript. The only times you should give a memorized speech are when the speech is to be short and the situation is inappropriate for holding a manuscript. These occasions are most often ceremonial—giving a toast, presenting a plaque, or accepting an honor.

1. *Memorize the structure of the speech before memorizing the speech word for word.* Memorize a few keywords that help you internalize the main sequence of ideas.

2. *Read the speech aloud several times and then work on learning it paragraph by paragraph.* Always keep your mind on the meaning. Do not try to learn sentences in isolation. Rather, work on whole paragraphs at a time, reinforcing their logical and conceptual unity.

3. *As you practice, visualize giving the speech.* Avoid thinking of your speech as lines of text in a social vacuum. You do not want to be startled and lose your concentration when you realize that you are actually facing a roomful of people.

4. *Do not go into a trance when delivering the speech.* Once again, be comfortably familiar with your material so that you can maintain eye contact and establish a rapport with your audience.

5. *If you go blank, switch to the extemporaneous mode and recall the structure of the speech rather than groping for the next word.* Speaking along the general lines of the point you know you were trying to make, you can collect your thoughts and click back into what you have memorized.

Critical Thinking Questions:

○ Which delivery style creates the feeling of a conversation with the audience?
○ How are the impromptu, the manuscript, and the memorized styles useful to an extemporaneous delivery?
○ What are the disadvantages of extemporaneous speaking?

CHAPTER 29
Language and Style

In the context of speaking, **style** is your choice of words and the way you put them together. "Good" style involves choosing and combining those words so that your audience can easily understand and remember your ideas. Good style is the use of clear, appropriate, vivid, and varied language.

29a. Oral and written styles

Although oral style and written style use the same components, they differ in some important ways. Readers can reread passages to make sure they understand an idea. Listeners have only one contact with each word, and their memory is the only instant replay. Consequently, a speaker is more likely than a writer to use repetition to ensure comprehension. Oral style employs more signposting, internal summaries, and internal previews to make the organization clear. (See Chapter **32**.) Shorter sentences and words of fewer syllables are characteristics of oral style as well. Sentence fragments are common in speaking, as are contractions. Even in a formal setting, a speech will be more conversational than an essay on the same topic. Table 29-1 illustrates some key differences between oral and written style.

TABLE 29-1	Comparisons of Written and Oral Styles
Written Style	**Oral Style**
As mentioned above . . .	As I said a few minutes ago . . .
One cannot avoid individuals with this characteristic.	We can't avoid people like that.
Hypothetically, the government might . . .	Imagine this. Suppose Uncle Sam . . .
That is unlikely to result.	Well. Maybe.
Subjects were randomly assigned to either a control group or one of three experimental treatment groups. The four groups were pretested for initial attitudes toward the topic and then posttested after each experimental group had received a persuasive message containing one of three levels of fear appeals.	Here's how we did our research. First, we randomly assigned the subjects to four groups. Next, we gave all four groups a pretest to see what attitudes they held toward the topic. Then, three of the groups heard persuasive messages. One had a high level of fear appeals, one a medium level, and one a low level. Last, we posttested the attitudes of all four groups, including the control group that received no message.

29b. Clear language

To construct clear messages, you must do two things. First, clarify your own thoughts. Know exactly, not approximately, what you want to communicate. Second, consider who the receivers of your message are and what the words are likely to mean to them.

1 Be precise

To avoid fuzzy communication, seek out the word that means precisely what you wish to convey and use it in a structure that illuminates its meaning. Do not say a person was *indicted* for robbery if, in fact, you mean *arrested* (much less serious) or *convicted* (much more serious). Be sure you know what an unfamiliar word means before using it. Be careful with words that sound similar but have no similarity of meaning. For example, *allusion* means "a passing mention" and *illusion* means "a false perception." Some other troublesome near-homophones can be found in **Appendix C,** which is located online at the Speaker's Compact Handbook companion website.

2 Be specific and concrete

The more specific and concrete your words, the less is left to your listeners' imaginations. When a speaker says, "NCAA academic standards for college athletes are ineffective," one listener may think, "Yes, they are racist," and another may think, "Yes, they are too low." But the speaker may feel that the standards are too high. Table 29-2 gives examples of specific, concrete language.

3 Be concise

Express yourself with no more words than you need to effectively convey your meaning. Sometimes speakers use long words, extra words, and convoluted constructions for the reasons listed in Table 29-3. Most often, though, wordiness results from lack of discipline. It takes time and effort to find the best wording. The clear speaker makes every word count.

TABLE 29-2	Specific, Concrete Language	
Do Not Say	**If You Mean**	**Or If You Really Mean**
We need to attract individuals.	We need to attract customers.	We need to attract grocery shoppers.
This will cause problems.	This will be expensive.	This will cost $2,500 we don't have.
Our committee has studied it.	Our committee researched and discussed it.	Our committee read documents, heard testimony, and deliberated for several hours.

TABLE 29-3	Reasons and Repairs for Bloated Language	
Reason	**Uneconomical**	**Economical**
To hide meaning by using doublespeak.	*We sustained losses through friendly fire.*	*We shelled our own troops.*
To avoid responsibility by using the passive voice.	*It has been determined that your services are no longer needed.*	*I have decided to fire you.*
To soften unpleasant messages by using euphemism.	*Jesse has gone on to his reward.*	*Jesse died.*

29c. Appropriate language

Different audiences and topics require different approaches. Based on your audience analysis, you must decide how formal to be; which part of your personality to project; and how specialized your language should be. Your age, status, and personality also determine what language is appropriate for you. The vocabulary and stylistic level suitable for a senior executive differs from those for a teenager or a poet-in-residence.

Language is not fixed. New words and phrases are always coming into our language and others are fading out. Meanings change, as do standards of appropriateness.

1   Level of formality

Just as you dress differently for formal and casual events, so should you tailor vocabulary and usage to fit the situation. In general, the more formal the occasion, the more serious the tone, the more subtle the humor, the more elaborate the sentences, the greater the number of figures of speech, and the greater the departure from everyday word choice.

More formal occasions include debates, presentations of policy statements, and ceremonial speeches. Less formal occasions include business conferences, roasts, rallies, and after-dinner speeches.

2   Jargon and slang

Both jargon and slang can be used to create a bond with a specialized audience. At times, **jargon,** the special vocabulary of a particular group, can also allow you to get a point across more quickly. **Slang**—popular, nonstandard catchwords and phrases—when used at the appropriate moment, can enrich the texture of your language. However, the perils of jargon and slang are substantial.

You may confuse your audience with technical terms or sacrifice your credibility by using slang expressions that are offensive or out-of-date.

3 Substandard usage

The audience's perception of a speaker's competence has a large bearing on the speaker's credibility. Although acceptable usage varies, many words and constructions are rated substandard by consensus. Speakers who use *ain't* for *isn't* or who get sloppy with noun–verb agreement will find that many in the audience do not give serious consideration to their ideas. Of course, you can sometimes break the rules for dramatic effect, like capping your opposition to a proposal with "Ain't no *way*!" **Appendix C,** located on the companion website**,** gives some examples of standard versus substandard language.

> QUICK TIP   **Not All Nonstandard Language Is Substandard**   Sometimes, when people try to "standardize" the language others use, they are actually trying to change the content or to mold the identity of the speaker. Women should not have to talk like men. People from New Orleans should not have to talk like they are from Connecticut. You will not feel comfortable or seem authentic if you totally abandon your own language style. Strive to find a way to maintain your own cultural, ethnic, and individual identity while still speaking in a credible way.

4 Respectful and inclusive language

Referring to a group or individuals by the name they prefer is a sign of respect. Make a reasonable effort to learn which term of identification people prefer. You can make a commitment to flexibility. It is worth the temporary inconvenience of changing a language habit if that change is highly symbolic and important to your audience.

Some guidelines for the use of inclusive language can be found on the websites of various universities and publishers, for example:

http://ucommunications.colorado.edu/services/ style-guide/inclusive-writing.

29d. Vivid, varied language

Your message may never get past your listeners' short-term memory if you do not infuse it with vigor and a sense of newness. Energize your language with the following verbal devices.

1   Imagery

When you describe something, put the senses and the imaginations of your listeners to work:

> *Not:*   The life of the long-haul trucker is rough.
>
> *But:*   The long-haul trucker pulls to the side of the road, and even though the truck is stopped, his arms still throb to the rhythm of hitting four hundred miles of highway expansion joints. The harsh roar of the engine leaves him with an infuriating ringing in his ears.

2   Stylistic devices

Enliven your language through figures of speech and structuring words and phrases.

Simile and metaphor   You can add vigor to your speaking by connecting objects or ideas to vivid images. A **simile** makes a comparison between two things ordinarily dissimilar, as in, "When she came in from shoveling off the walk, her hands were like ice." No one would mistake a hand for a piece of ice but, in this case, they share the characteristic of extremely low temperature. A **metaphor** equates two unlike things, as in, "Her hands were ice cubes."

Personification   You can bring objects or ideas to life by providing them with human qualities. We know that no room is really *cheerful,* that winds do not actually *whisper,* and that the economy cannot actually *limp.* Nevertheless, such images are effective descriptions because they reflect human behavior.

Hyperbole   For emphasis, you may deliberately overstate a point in a way that is clearly fanciful. For example:

> "This paperwork will be the death of me."
>
> "I thought of nothing else for the next three days."

Repeated words or phrases   By repeating keywords or phrases, you make your listeners feel that your points are snowballing to a certain conclusion. You can use parallel structure to add emphasis. You can also use repetition to introduce consecutive ideas. For instance, a speaker can build a sense of urgency by repeating the phrase "We must act now to . . ." as each problem is presented. Or you might end several sentences with the same words as in this example:

> "What remains? Treaties have gone. The honor of nations has gone. Liberty has gone."
>
> —*David Lloyd George*

Alliteration and assonance These devices repeat the same sound. Whether it is with consonants (**alliteration**) or vowels (**assonance**), this repetition can make an idea more memorable, or at least charge it with a sense of poetry.

For example, Bill Clinton shared these alliterative words in his Convention Acceptance Address: "Somewhere at this very moment a child is being born in America. Let it be our cause to give that child a happy home, a healthy family, and a hopeful future." Assonance is visible in this example from Jesse Jackson's address at the 1984 Democratic National Convention: "Our flag is red, white and blue—but our nation is rainbow, Red, yellow, brown, black, and white, we're all precious in God's sight."

Antithesis When you want to contrast two ideas, certain sentence structures can dramatize the differences. **Antithesis** uses forms like these:

> Not . . . , but . . .
>
> Not only . . . , but also . . .

In his speech after receiving the 2001 Nobel Peace Prize, Kofi Annan combined antithesis, alliteration and assonance, and repetitive structure:

> "Today's real borders are not between nations, but between powerful and powerless, free and fettered, privileged and humiliated."

3   Original language versus clichés

The power of figurative language lies in the images stimulated in the listener's mind. After too many repetitions, the original impact is lost. "Fresh as a daisy" once summoned a picture of a bright, dew-studded blossom. At the first turn of the phrase "it went in one ear and out the other," its aptness produced pleasant surprise. Now both expressions are likely to be processed as just empty words. They have become clichés.

Certain fad words attract a following and are used to the exclusion of many good (and fresher) synonyms. Examples include *cutting edge, iconic, and 24/7.* Invest the time needed to select original combinations of words and phrases that capture the image, mood, or thought you want to get across.

4   Sentence rhythm

Although oral style is characterized by simpler, shorter phrases with some repetition of words, you are not trying to bore your audience. The "singsonginess" associated with bad poetry can creep into a speech if you fail to vary the rhythm of your sentences. Use parallelisms and repetition sparingly.

Consider this plodding passage whose sentences have the same length and structure:

> The association's annual convention should be user supported. The convention is attended by a core of regulars. The average association member doesn't benefit from the convention. These average members shouldn't have to bear more than their fair share.

Recasting the sentences will create a more memorable paragraph:

> The association's annual convention should be user supported. Who attends the convention? A core of regulars. The average association members, who don't benefit from the convention, shouldn't have to bear more than their fair share.

Critical Thinking Questions:

- ○ Why is a choice of words considered a choice of "worlds"?
- ○ When might a speaker intentionally use abstract words over more concrete language? What effect would such a usage achieve?
- ○ What are the implications for a speaker who makes poor choices relating to language and style?

CHAPTER 30

Capturing Attention and Interest

When you give a speech or presentation, your words are competing for attention with every other sight and sound in the room and with every daydream in the mind of each listener. The better you understand the psychology of attention, the more likely you will receive the compliment most appreciated by speakers: a sincere and simple "That was an interesting speech!"

30a. How to enliven your speech

The following techniques will help you catch and keep your listeners' attention.

1 Concrete, real-life examples

Examples are always more interesting when they are specific and real. Never say "a person" or "one" if you can give a name. Use famous people, members of the audience, or even hypothetical characters; give place names, brand names, dates, and specific details.

2 Your listeners' self-interest

Often, when people say, "So what?" they are really saying, "What's it to me?" Do not assume that the benefits of your particular approach are obvious. Motivate your audience to listen by spelling out the rewards. Do careful audience analysis and tap into as many of your listeners' needs and values as possible. (See Chapter **25.**)

> You don't have to be a vegetarian or a gourmet cook to benefit from these menu ideas. By serving just a few meatless meals a week, you can save 30 to 100 dollars on your monthly grocery bill, while providing a healthier diet for your family.

3 Storytelling

A well-constructed story commands the interest of nearly everyone. Notice how the excellent feature articles and the documentary films share many of the qualities of good fiction or drama. A speech, even if it is an annual report, can captivate an audience if it unfolds in a narrative fashion with suspense, conflict, intriguing characterizations, lively bits of dialogue, and a moment of climax leading to the denouement. Your speech need not promise to make your listeners rich or famous if it takes them outside their experience in an engaging way.

4 Humor

Humor is both powerful and tricky. An infusion of humor into any speech can ease tension, deflate opponents, enhance the speaker's image, and make points memorable. It needs to be appropriate to your personality and to the situation. A string of unrelated jokes and stories or aimless clowning pulls the focus away from your topic. Constructing a transition that huffs and puffs to tie in an unrelated joke is a waste of time.

What is important is the ability to spot a potentially humorous idea and to craft it into a genuinely funny moment in your speech. Look for the humor in your everyday experience. The boring, frustrating, and mundane aspects of life all have their humorous elements. Take note of the everyday things that make you laugh on your job, in your relationships, on television, and in the newspaper.

Topically organized books of humor and websites like **www. humorlinks.com** or **www.joke-archives.com** can sometimes yield just the gem you need to catch people's attention. Be selective, though, choosing only material that is relevant, appropriate, and fresh.

If you do choose to use jokes, you should plan and practice them carefully. To succeed, you need to draw on the writer's attention to word choice and the performer's sense of presence and voice.

5   Variety and energy

Change attracts attention! Sameness is dull! If your content or delivery becomes totally predictable, audience members' interest will start to wane. Vary your forms of support—do not rely on only examples, only statistics, or only testimony. Draw support from many domains.

Whenever possible, give the speech a sense of movement. Use images of activity. Use vivid verbs and stay in the active voice as much as possible. For instance, instead of saying, "Five new businesses can be seen downtown," say, "Drive down First Street and you will see five new businesses."

In your delivery, it is important to remember the use of vocal variety and physical movement. Who wants to listen to a deadpan speaker monotonously delivering a presentation while standing woodenly behind a podium? (See **34b** and **35.**)

30b. How to involve your audience

If you have done a thorough audience analysis, you should be able to build many references about the audience into the speech. There are always more opportunities to adapt to your audience once you start your speech. Here are examples of some techniques you might try.

Use the names of people in the audience "Suppose Ms. Silver's [you nod toward a listener] hardware business is expanding so rapidly that she decides to take out a loan to enlarge her store."

Refer to the person who introduced you and to the other speakers "As Dave was saying . . ."

Refer to details in the immediate setting or from shared experience "And all of that expensive atom-smashing machinery was housed in a room not half the size of this one."

Use audience participation techniques "Can I have a show of hands?" "How many people here . . . ?"

Make liberal use of the word *you* "You've probably seen . . ." "Now, I'll bet you're saying to yourself . . ." "You could undoubtedly give me a dozen more examples . . ." "In your city here . . ."

Critical Thinking Questions:

○ What is wrong with opening your speech by saying, "Hello, my name is . . ."?

○ How can you ensure your speech will capture and maintain your audience's attention?

○ What can you do to regain your audience's attention?

CHAPTER 31
Introductions and Conclusions

A carefully composed introduction and conclusion can crystallize your relationship with your listeners.

31a. The introduction

A speech **introduction** prepares your listeners to hear your ideas. Both speaker and audience need a period of adjustment before getting to the meat of the speech. The audience needs to get used to a speaker's appearance, mannerisms, and style of talking; you, the speaker, need to settle into your role.

1   Project confidence before starting

It is important to realize that your speech really starts before you start speaking. The moment the attention shifts to you, you need to begin to develop a rapport and prepare your audience to listen to you. Stand up and, if necessary, move confidently to the position from which you will speak. Then pause in order to engage audience members' attention before you begin speaking.

2 Engage the audience's attention immediately

You don't want to risk leaving your opening sentences to the inspiration of the moment. You need strong opening material that will carry the speech forward.

Start with a sentence that leaves no doubt that you are beginning. Avoid false starts and apologetic or tentative phrases such as "Can you hear me now?" or "I'm sorry, but before I begin . . ." Tone is almost as important as content here. Your immediate purpose is to command the attention of your audience. (See Chapter **30**.)

Your **attention-getter** (a few sentences to capture the audience's attention and invite them to listen) can be a joke, a brief story, an apt quotation, a startling statement, or a provocative question. Be imaginative, and even a little dramatic, but do not go too far. Avoid contrived and gimmicky openings such as flicking off the room lights and asking, "Are you in the dark about . . . ?" Your attention-getter should also be consistent with your personality and the situation. Avoid adopting an unnatural style; not only will you be uncomfortable, but your audience will sense that you are not being yourself.

With this in mind, consider the following possible attention-getters from the "Bite Back: speech about malaria in **Appendix A.** Kayla Strickland starts by saying: "It's just a mosquito, right? To us it is, but to half the world it is also fever, vomiting, aches, jaundice, anemia. It is seizures, comas, lung inflammation, cardiovascular collapse, kidney failure, paralysis. It is speech impediments. It is stillbirths and maternal deaths and low birth-weight babies. It is blindness. It is deafness. It is malaria."

Attention-getters need not always be catchy or clever; however, it is essential that you begin your speech with a few well-planned sentences that say, in effect, "I know where I'm going and I want you to come with me—it will be worth your while."

3 Turn attention into interest

Before you can ask your audience to concentrate on the substance of your message, you need to transform their attention into interest by orienting them psychologically. This psychological orientation has two parts: establishing a good relationship with your listeners and motivating them toward your topic.

Establish a relationship Speakers can seem distant from the audience because of their role and status. Use your introduction to create a personal bond with your listeners. You can do this with, among other things, references to everyday, common occurrences. You want to set a tone of collaboration with your audience. (See **30b** and the *Checklist: Connecting with Your Audience*.)

CHECKLIST

Connecting with Your Audience

❑ Establish credibility. (See Chapter **26**.)

❑ Establish common ground by pointing out shared backgrounds, experiences, interests, or goals.

❑ Refer to the setting or occasion to establish your personal connection to the speaking situation.

❑ Flatter your audience with a personalized compliment based on your audience analysis.

❑ Refer to the person who introduced you or to some other person who is present. Build a relationship with the audience by showing that you know one of its members.

❑ Use humor. (See **30a.4**.)

Motivate your audience toward your topic This motivational step is often overlooked, but it is the pivotal step of the introduction. You need to reassure your listeners that there are good reasons for them to be warming the seats; that your topic has a link with their own experiences and is, thereby, worthy of their attention. Chapters **25** (Motivational Appeals) and **30** (Capturing Attention and Interest) are especially relevant for this step.

4 Provide a logical orientation

Now that your audience is *motivated* to listen, you must be sure they are *prepared* to listen. In the **logical orientation,** you show your listeners how you will approach and develop your topic—in effect, giving them an intellectual road map. In this phase of your introduction, you show the larger whole into which your speech fits and the way you have divided your topic. Show your audience the context of your topic by using one or more of the following approaches.

Fit your topic into a familiar framework Consider this statement:

> Turkey is located south of the Black Sea, east of the Aegean Sea, and north of the Mediterranean Sea. Turkey shares its southern border with Syria and Iraq, and its eastern edge borders Iran, Armenia, and Georgia.

Here, the unknown is linked to the known in a geographical sense. You can also relate your topic to some schema, chart, organizational structure, or process with which your audience is already familiar.

The speaker can also connect an unfamiliar topic to the familiar by using an analogy:

> When the traffic lights break down on a busy corner, you see a traffic cop standing in the middle of the intersection, blowing a whistle and telling impatient motorists where to go. In effect, that is what I do as crisis manager at the Metacom Corporation.

Place your topic historically The historical context helps listeners learn about the events that led up to your topic. One of the most famous speeches by an American, Abraham Lincoln's "Gettysburg Address," used this simple form of introduction:

> Fourscore and seven years ago our fathers brought forth on this continent a new nation, conceived in liberty and dedicated to the proposition that all men are created equal. Now we are engaged in a great civil war, testing whether that nation or any nation so conceived and so dedicated can long endure. We are met on a great battlefield of that war. We have come to dedicate a portion of that field, as a final resting place for those who here gave their lives that that nation might live. It is altogether fitting and proper that we should do this.

Place your topic conceptually Just as you can place your topic in time or space, so can you locate it in the world of ideas. By showing your listeners how your speech fits in with familiar theories, concepts, and definitions, you prepare them to listen. For example:

> You are familiar with the law of supply and demand as it relates to goods and services. Let me review this basic market mechanism with you, because I want to ask you to apply these same essential principles to our system of information exchange.

Provide new definitions and concepts If you use unfamiliar terms and concepts in your speech, or use familiar terms in unfamiliar ways, prepare your audience.

Here is how you might introduce an unfamiliar term:

> By logistics, I'm referring to the art and science of moving something exactly where it needs to be, exactly when it needs to be there. Logistics done well means that sellers more efficiently connect with buyers. And that means more profitability and growth opportunities.

Orient the audience to your approach to the topic The second step in a logical orientation—once you have shown how your speech fits into some larger context—is to preview the structure of your speech. By previewing your speech, you give your listeners a framework on which to attach your main points, improving their understanding and recalling your ideas.

In most introductions, you will explicitly state one or more of the following: your topic, thesis, title, or purpose. For example, "I would like to persuade you to change your vote on this bond issue." At times, you also want to tell what you are *not* talking about—essentially explaining to your audience how you have narrowed your topic.

Here is an example, derived from the comic book outline in **Appendix A,** of a speaker spelling out what the speech will not cover:

> I am not going to tell you which comic books are currently the best investment. Nor am I going to explain how to treat and store comic books so that the acid in the paper won't turn them into yellow confetti. I *am*, however, going to tell you some things about comic books that will help you better understand their place in American popular culture.

You must also decide whether to give an exact **preview** of the points you are going to cover or a general overview of your topic. Explicit previews are useful in the majority of speeches and essential for speeches with fairly technical or complex topics. In a preview, the speaker gives the listeners a reassuring road map to carry through the speech, one that they can refer to if they start to get lost.

5   Make your introduction compact

Generally, the introduction should take 10–15 percent of your speaking time. Organize your opening in a natural narrative style to avoid an introduction that is disjointed and overlong. Often it is more important to fulfill the *functions* of getting attention and providing psychological and logical orientation than to progress mechanically through these three steps. Whenever possible, select material that fulfills more than one function. In addition to combining parts of the introduction, it is often appropriate to omit steps altogether. A presidential speech can begin, "My fellow Americans, tonight I want to talk about the serious problem of international terrorism." Attention, credibility, and motivation to listen are assumed.

31b. The conclusion

Just as you led your audience into your topic step by step in the introduction, you must lead them out again in a conclusion, tying all the threads together and leaving the audience with a sense of fulfillment or closure. Like the introduction, the conclusion should be precisely planned and practiced, almost to the point of memorization. Social scientists tell us that people are most likely to remember what they hear last, so you should choose your words carefully.

1   Provide logical closure

Although you have already demonstrated the interconnectedness of your points and ideas in the body of the speech by the use of transitions and internal previews and summaries, you still need to tie it all together at the end for your audience.

Summarize the main ideas In all but the shortest of speeches, include an explicit restatement of your thesis and main ideas. A conclusion can reinforce the pattern that has been implicit all along. This can be used for either inductive or deductive lines of reasoning, when the relationship among points needs to be spelled out. (See Chapter **21**.)

Reconnect your topic to a larger context A conclusion can be more than a summary. In the introduction, you drew your speech topic out of some broader context. After developing your ideas, you may want to show how they tie back to the original larger picture. In other cases, you might want to build on the points you established to highlight broader implications or ramifications of your topic. If you have introduced new definitions and concepts or familiar definitions and concepts in unfamiliar ways, use the conclusion to reinforce your use of them.

2   Provide psychological closure

Making your main points fit together logically for your audience is not enough. Members should walk away psychologically satisfied with your speech—you need to have touched them. When you plan your conclusion, think about what your listeners need; what you want them to understand and agree with; and how you want them to feel at the end of the speech.

Remind the audience how the topic affects them In the introduction, you make the topic personal to your audience. During the speech itself, you make your examples and manner of speaking appropriately personal. At the end, you bring the topic home again and show your listeners why they have a stake in what you described. Here is an example:

> I've told you how malaria affects us, showed a way of fighting it, and revealed the benefits that we would see by being rid of it. So what can you do to take your bite out of malaria? Buy a net. Ten dollars will provide the funds for a treated net, its distribution, and education for the happy owner. I bought one through biteback.net. Roll Back Malaria recommends Malaria No More and Nothing But Nets. You may be saying, "One net? What will that accomplish?" Consider the African proverb: "If you think you're too small to make a difference, try sleeping in a closed room with a mosquito."

Make an appeal Part of the psychological wrap-up of a speech can be a direct **appeal** to your audience, especially in a speech to persuade. Ask them directly to behave in a certain way or ask them to change their attitudes. An appeal can be strengthened by a statement of your own intent: "I plan to give blood tomorrow morning, and I hope to see you down there."

3   End with a clincher

It is as important to plan your last sentence as it is your first. Every speech needs a powerful, memorable closing—in a word, a **clincher.** While trying to devise a good exit line, speakers who have not prepared one tend to keep summarizing or they simply stop short.

One type of effective clincher ties back to the attention-getter. This can be an answer to the provocative question you asked initially or a reference to your opening joke or story. Then you can take it one step further in light of your thesis, as Kayla did in her *Bite Back* speech:

> Just take a look at the benefits we've been over, and you can see that a simple bed net is probably one of the best investments you could ever make. The mosquito will always be a nuisance, but it doesn't have to be a killer.

Another type of clincher is a proverb, aphorism, quotation, or bit of poetry. Martin Luther King, Jr., ended his historic "I Have a Dream" speech by evoking the words of an old spiritual: "Free at last, free at last, thank God Almighty, we are free at last."

The delivery of your clincher is as important as its content. Do not mumble your final sentence in a throwaway voice or spend the last few speaking moments gathering up your notes. Be familiar enough with your clincher that you can deliver it while maintaining eye contact with your listeners.

31c. Common introduction and conclusion pitfalls

1. *Don't* begin with "Before I start, I'd like to say . . . ." You have already started. (See **31a.1.**)

2. *Don't* begin with an apology like "I'm not really prepared" or "I don't know much about this, but . . . ." (See **31a.2.**)

3. *Don't* use an attention-getter that has no real link to your topic. Avoid the temptation to stretch a point so you can start with an unrelated joke that you think is hilarious. (See **31a.2.**)

4. *Don't* make your introduction disproportionately long. (See **31a.5.**)

5. *Don't* use stock phrases like "Unaccustomed as I am to public speaking" or overworked apocryphal stories. Ask a friend to give an honest critique of your trove of expressions and anecdotes. (See **29d**.)

6. *Don't* startle your audience by bursting out of a yogalike trance into an explosion of oral energy. This is a favorite of high school orators. Engage your audience before you start. (See **31a.1**.)

7. *Don't* read your introduction or your conclusion. If you have memorized them, be sure they do not sound mechanical. These are times when you should maximize eye contact and keep your inflection natural and conversational. (See **34b**.)

8. *Don't* end with an apology: "I guess I've rambled on long enough," or "I don't know if I've made this clear," or "I'm not usually this hyper; it must be the coffee."

9. *Don't* trail off. Do your audience the courtesy of wrapping things up and using a clincher. (See **31b.3**.)

10. *Don't* introduce a new point in your conclusion. The body of your speech is the place for new points. (See **18a**.)

11. *Don't* make the conclusion disproportionately long. It is a summary and ending.

12. *Don't* end in a style or mood that is at odds with the rest of the speech. You do your listeners a disservice if you have kept them laughing up to the very end and then hit them with a stark recitation of doom.

13. *Don't* use the phrases "in conclusion" or "in summary" in any part of the speech other than the actual conclusion. You will lose part of your audience while they reorient themselves to the fact that the speech is continuing when they thought it was winding down. (See Chapter **32**.)

Critical Thinking Questions:

○ What attention strategy would you recommend for the comic book speech at the end of **Appendix A**?

○ Why should the introduction be limited to about 10 percent of the speech length?

○ What are the dangers associated with a weak conclusion?

○ How might the conclusion of a persuasive appeal differ from that of an informative speech?

CHAPTER 32
Polishing Your Speech

When you have completed your research, selected and organized your points, and added an introduction and conclusion, one final step remains: smoothly and gracefully tying all the components of your speech together. This helps avoid choppiness and provides listeners with a unified presentation that is easier to follow. Figure 32-1, at the end of the chapter, illustrates how the speech components flow together.

32a. Weave in supporting materials smoothly

When you have chosen appropriate definitions, facts, examples, statistics, and testimony, you still have to present these materials effectively. You want to emphasize their quality, make them clear and understandable, and incorporate them appropriately in relation to the points they support.

1   Vary the lead-ins

Do not introduce all your examples, statistics, and other supporting material with the same phrase: "Some figures about this are . . . Some figures about that are. . . ." There are many possibilities for lead-ins:

> To support this idea . . .
>
> _____ put it well, I think, when she said . . .
>
> What causes this situation? One answer to that question was offered by _____ when he wrote last year . . .
>
> There are several examples of this. Let me share just two.

To introduce a direct quotation (in contrast to a paraphrase), be sure to indicate to your listeners the boundaries of the quoted material. You can do this by saying, "and I quote . . ." followed by "End of quotation." In some cases a subtle change in your voice or posture is enough.

2   Cite specific sources

By giving credit for your supporting materials, you build your own credibility as you show the range of your research. You are also providing information your listeners are almost certain to want. Very few audiences will settle for "studies show . . .," "one researcher found . . .," or "a friend once told me . . . ." To evaluate your statements, listeners need to know where the information came from.

This does not mean that you are required to present regulation footnotes in oral form, citing volume and page numbers. Nor do you need to recite an authority's complete biography or necessarily explain a study's design intricacies. Although you should know the *who*, the *why*, the *when*, and the *how* of every bit of data you use, you will probably mention only a couple of these in introducing them.

3 Give adequate citations

The form an oral citation takes is, like many choices in speaking, dependent on the context. In some speaking situations, there is a rigid and stylized form, as in the college debate or speech contest. Otherwise, you can choose how much information you need to include about the source, according to how much you think your audience needs to hear to accept the source as legitimate. If your audience has a favorable attitude toward your thesis, you will not need as much source information as you will if they have an unfavorable attitude. (See **7d**.)

Here are three examples of citation density. The first introduces the information with no citation at all. The second presents the name of the source, which indicates that you are not picking numbers out of the air. The third example is fairly dense, giving your listeners enough information to jot down and use to check your source if they so wish.

No citation

> Only 17 percent of all bicycle accidents are car–bike collisions. In only 10 percent of those collisions was the car overtaking the bike from the rear.

Light citation

> According to transportation engineer John Forester, only 17 percent of all bicycle accidents are car–bike collisions. In only 10 percent of those collisions was the car overtaking the bike from the rear.

Dense citation

> In his 1993 book, *Effective Cycling*, published by MIT Press, transportation engineer John Forester notes that only 17 percent of all bicycle accidents are car–bike collisions. In only 10 percent of those collisions was the car overtaking the bike from the rear.

If you must be dense in your citing, be as conversational as possible. Avoid the "big parenthetical speed bump" that interrupts the flow of a sentence, as in "Transportation engineer John Forester notes (*Effective Cycling*, MIT Press, 1993) that only . . . ." It may take a few more words to come up with a smooth version, but the result will be more natural to the ear.

32b. Use signposts to link points

Transitional sentences, phrases, and words serve as bridges between points. They also signal how two ideas are related. Clear and evocative connectives are more important in speaking than in writing because the spoken message is fleeting. In this book, for example, we can show the relationships among ideas by indenting, capitalizing, punctuating, and using different typefaces. As a speaker, however, you do not have access to these devices. You need to use verbal signposting techniques to show how your points relate. (See **22b.1.**) You can help your listeners follow the overall structure of your speech by the generous use of signposts like these:

> The second cause of inflation is . . .
>
> To show you what I mean, let me tell you a couple of stories.
>
> What, then, is the solution to this three-part problem I have outlined?
>
> In summarizing this entire argument, . . .
>
> The final point we should consider is . . .

Do not worry about using too many signposts. Your audience will appreciate them.

1   Connectives that reflect logical relationships

The connectives you choose should highlight the organizational structure of the speech. Here are two examples. The first shows an effect-to-cause structure and the second shows a chronological structure.

Thesis Statement: . . .

> I say that for three reasons. First, [main point I]
>
> This situation is also due to [main point II]
>
> Last of all, we can attribute the problem to [main point III]

or

Thesis Statement: . . .

> Initially, [main point I]
>
> Next, [main point II]
>
> Finally, [main point III]

Points can be related in a number of ways. Table 32-1 lists common connective words and phrases that can be used to tie main points to one another, main points to subpoints, subpoints to one another, supporting evidence to arguments, and introductions and conclusions to the body of the speech.

TABLE 32-1	Connective Words and Phrases That Signal Relationships

Relationship	Connective Words
Chronological	First, second, third Next, then Following
Cause–effect	So, since, thus Therefore, hence Consequently, as a result Due to, because
Part-to-whole	One such, another The first (second, third) of these For instance, for example Illustrative of this, a case in point
Equality	Similarly, additionally Another Of equal importance
Opposition	But, though, however On the other hand, conversely In spite of Nonetheless, nevertheless

2   Internal previews and summaries

Sometimes, connectives between main points should take the form of **internal summaries** or **internal previews** that pull together two or three main points.

Internal Preview

> Once your résumé has been prepared, the next step in job seeking is to list specific job openings. The three best sources here are newspaper and Web listings, campus placement service, and word-of-mouth recommendations. We will examine the pros and cons of each of these.

Internal Summary

> Because the problems in our department were affecting morale and because we had found they were caused by poor communication, we instituted an unusual training program. Let me tell you about it.

Internal Summary and Preview

> I have told you why we need to reduce our dependence on the automobile, and I hope I have convinced you that a light rail system is the best alternative for our city. Now, you are probably asking two questions: "What will it cost?" and "How will it work?" I want to answer both of these questions. First, the question of cost.

QUICK TIP **Premature Summaries** Do not say "In summary" anywhere but in the conclusion. Carefully qualify your internal summaries by using phrases like "So, to summarize this first idea" or "Let me review the points so far."

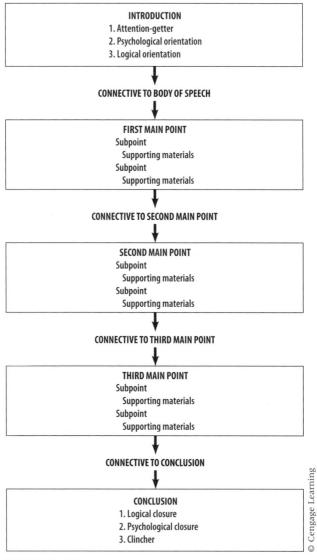

INTRODUCTION
1. Attention-getter
2. Psychological orientation
3. Logical orientation

CONNECTIVE TO BODY OF SPEECH

FIRST MAIN POINT
Subpoint
  Supporting materials
Subpoint
  Supporting materials

CONNECTIVE TO SECOND MAIN POINT

SECOND MAIN POINT
Subpoint
  Supporting materials
Subpoint
  Supporting materials

CONNECTIVE TO THIRD MAIN POINT

THIRD MAIN POINT
Subpoint
  Supporting materials
Subpoint
  Supporting materials

CONNECTIVE TO CONCLUSION

CONCLUSION
1. Logical closure
2. Psychological closure
3. Clincher

© Cengage Learning

FIGURE 32-1 Speech Structure Chart

Critical Thinking Questions:

- ○ How is your credibility as a speaker affected by the clarity of your citations?
- ○ What is wrong with vague connectives such as "next" or "also"?
- ○ How are connectives similar to bridges between ideas?
- ○ What is the benefit of an internal preview or a summary to the listener?

CHAPTER 33
Practicing Your Speech

Start practicing your speech aloud well before the presentation. Using the three stages of practice sessions enables you to finalize your points, get specific feedback from others, and polish your delivery. Whenever possible, form a support group of other learners, colleagues, or friends. See **2d** for a discussion of constructive feedback.

33a. The three stages of practice

Your practice sessions need a timetable. You should plan your practice sessions, write down a schedule of steps and phases, and adhere to it. Table 33-1 shows possible timetables for different kinds of speeches with different amounts of advance notice. Use this table as a guide to create a schedule for your speeches.

1 Stage 1: Flesh out your outline

During these early developmental sessions, you will transform your outline of ideas into a speech by adding the elements of language and delivery to the logical framework of your outline.

Begin by internalizing your outline. Read it over a number of times, becoming familiar with the flow of the logic. Sit at your desk or a table and talk your way through the outline. Try to explain the ideas to yourself.

At this point, pick a quiet spot and start to put together the speech as it will actually be given. Stand up and give the speech out loud in your speaking voice. Visualize the speech situation and mentally put yourself there.

Sometime during this stage, you will have made the first draft of your speech notes. These will evolve. They can be revised according to how things shape up as you tinker with the wording.

		Preliminary Analysis, Research, and Outline Completed	
Type of Speech	Commitment Made to Speak		Stage 1: Early Practice Sessions (Development)
Major policy address	Several weeks before	1 week before	1–2 weeks before: Discuss ideas with colleagues. 5–6 days before: Talk through speech once a day.
Classroom speech	10 days before	4 days before	4–10 days before: Talk about speech with friends. 4 days before: Read outline several times; practice aloud twice.
Routine oral report in a business meeting	24 hours before	Evening before	Afternoon or evening before: Talk through basic ideas with friends or colleagues. Evening before: Practice aloud 1–3 times.

TABLE 33-1 Example of Practice Schedules

2 Stage 2: Get feedback

After you have become comfortable with your material but before you do the final polishing, seek feedback on your speech. If you solicit feedback on content, style, and delivery before you have finished shaping your basic speech, you will miss getting help on those parts that have not yet been crystallized. If the feedback comes too late in the schedule, you will not have the time to incorporate it comfortably.

Practice in front of others Just as people are good sounding boards for the development of your ideas, as described in **10c,** so are they the best source of feedback. As you rehearse your speech for colleagues, family members, or friends, imagine that you are in front of your actual audience. Do not leave things out. Do not talk *about* your speech. Give your speech.

Ask for honest feedback on content and delivery, but do not necessarily take any single person's comments as the last word. Everyone has quirks and prejudices. Feedback from a group of people is preferable because it gives you a sampling of responses.

Stage 2: Middle Practice Sessions (Feedback)	Stage 3: Final Practice Sessions (Refinement)
4 days before: Videotape speech, review with advisors, repeat.	Beginning 3 days before: Practice aloud once a day; read notes or outline once a day. Day of speech: Practice aloud once; review notes just before speaking.
3 days before: Give speech to friendly critic, receive feedback, practice aloud one more time.	Beginning 2 days before: Practice aloud 1–3 times a day; read outline and notes several times. Day of speech: Practice aloud once; review notes just before speaking.
Morning of meeting: Give report to colleague if possible.	Day of presentation: Practice aloud once; review notes just before leaving for meeting.

You should not ask, "How'd you like my speech?" Answers like "It was nice" or "I thought it was okay" do not help you much. Lead your critics with a few specific questions and seek clarification of their answers. Begin with these two questions:

- "What did you see as the single most important thing I was trying to say?" If they do not come up with your thesis sentence, you must look at your structure again.

- "What were the main ideas I was trying to get across?" They should answer with your main points.

It is important to get answers to these two questions before moving on to finer points of development and delivery. (See the *Checklist: Questions to Elicit Useful Feedback.*) Everything else is insignificant if your reason for speaking is not being understood.

Videorecord your practice session A video is the next best thing to a human critic. When you play back your performance, try to get outside of yourself and see the image as that of a stranger. In this case, you may temporarily shift your focus from your message and your imagined audience to yourself as a speaker. Become the audience and ask yourself the questions you would ask to solicit feedback from other people. A hazard to avoid here is being too self-critical. Seeing yourself on tape can be devastating if you notice only the aspects that need improvement. Look also for things you are doing right. It can be helpful to watch the video with a friend or a coach who can give you a more balanced perspective.

CHECKLIST

Questions to Elicit Useful Feedback
❏ Did my ideas flow in a logical sequence?
❏ Did the speech hold your attention? What parts were boring? Confusing?
❏ Did I prove my points?
❏ Did my introduction show you where I was going?
❏ Did the conclusion tie the speech together?
❏ Did I sound natural?
❏ Did I have any distracting mannerisms?

QUICK TIP **Practicing in Front of a Mirror** With a mirror, it is hard to make a detached assessment of the details of your presentation. When you watch yourself there, you divide your attention between what you are saying and how you are saying it. Practicing in front of a mirror can do more harm than good. However, if you have no other way to check on the visual impact of your posture, gestures, and facial expressions, it may be worthwhile to practice before a mirror just once.

3 Stage 3: Make refinements

By this time, you should be committed to a basic version of your speech while maintaining the flexibility of the extemporaneous mode. You should not be making radical changes.

Make the final practice sessions as realistic as possible. If you are going to use presentation aids, they should be ready early enough to include in your final practice sessions. The same holds true for the final draft of your notecards. Check yourself against your time limit. Practice your speech standing up, at the rate and volume you will be using. Speaking with rudimentary mechanical amplification to a large audience, for example, will use more breath than will the conversational volume used in early practice. You need to unabashedly boom out your speech in the final practice sessions if that is what it will take to be heard when you actually give the speech.

Continue reading through your notes and outline, but do not think of these activities as a substitute for the formal practice sessions. Save the hours just before the speech for one final run-through and for getting into the proper, relaxed frame of mind.

33b. Speech notes

Speech notes are not the same as your outline; they serve different functions. An outline is used to ensure logical organization. **Speech notes,** in contrast, are used as a guide and a safety net while you are actually speaking.

Like your outline and wording, your notes should go through several drafts. Do not feel committed to the first thing you write.

1   Keywords, key phrases, and material to be cited directly

Unlike your outline—in which your points must be parallel, mutually exclusive, and in full sentences—your speech notes do not have a rigid, regulation form. A point can be represented by a word, a sentence fragment, or an actual sentence or two. (See Figure 33-1.) What goes into your notes depends on what you find you need during practice.

While practicing, you may also find that you want more than just a keyword reminder to get through an important, but tongue-twisting, sentence or to ensure that you remember an especially eloquent turn of phrase. Your notes may also contain material that you will be citing exactly, such as long quotations or complicated statistics.

Keep in mind, however, that your notes should remain *notes.* If you make them too extensive and detailed, you risk moving out of the extemporaneous mode and into the realm of the manuscript speech. Your notes should be referred to, not read from.

2   Format

There are many contexts in which your speaking can occur. (See **Part 2.**) These will dictate—to some degree—the format your

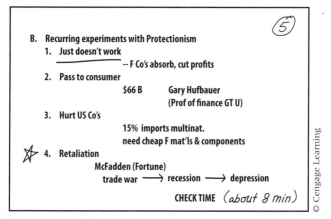

FIGURE 33-1   Speech Notes

notes take. The invited speaker at a world affairs forum may use four six-inch cards. An attorney in court does not look out of place referring to a legal pad while speaking. A project manager can glance at the PowerPoint note page on her laptop screen covering the content of her slides. For all of these instances, however, the advice in **33b.1** still applies.

If you choose to go the notecard route, a few medium-sized cards can easily become an extension of your hand as you gesture and move about. They will not be distracting to your listeners if you seem comfortable with them. Whatever medium you choose for your notes, do not be coy about using them—refer to them honestly. A surreptitious peek will not fool your listeners into believing that you are speaking without aids.

Do not go to the other extreme and get lost in your notes. You should be able to look down, see what is next, and then talk about it. If you find yourself burying your nose in your notes, you have not prepared them correctly.

Speech notes with presentation software PowerPoint and other presentation software will give you the option of entering notes to accompany your slides. This is where you can put the tongue twister, the precise data, or the short quotation. Adjust the font size so that it is easy to read. Also, feel free to mark up the output with the other visual cues as illustrated in Figure 33-1.

CHECKLIST

Formatting Speech Notes

❏ Words and phrases should be large, well spaced, and uncluttered.

❏ Use visual cues (such as large card numbers, underlining, indenting, stars, highlighting, different colors) to make it easy to find what you want at a glance.

❏ Add time notations to keep on track—writing, for example, "If more than eight minutes, skip to [card six/ point four/slide ten]."

❏ Mark optional sections of the speech if appropriate—for example, highlight in yellow to mean "Include this if the audience seems uncertain about my point. Otherwise, omit it."

33c. Timing your speech

In a speech class, there may be penalties for not reaching a minimum time limit. In most other settings, no one is going to be upset if you take only 15 of the 20 minutes you have been given.

However, taking 40 minutes when you have been allotted 20 can disrupt the schedules of other speakers and audience members.

Often, you cannot tell for sure how much time your speech will take until you have gotten well into the practice sessions. In extemporaneous practice, you will experience variations in length as you work with forming your ideas and with the style and rhythm of your speaking. Most inexperienced speakers practice at a speaking rate faster than the one they find necessary for clarity during the speech itself. The more realistic your practice, the less likely you are to incorrectly estimate your time.

To clock your speech, do not glue your eyes to the sweep hand of your watch. Merely note the time when you begin and when you finish. A sweep hand can induce unnatural behavior such as speaking at twice your normal rate for the last minute if you think you are running long or slowing your delivery to a tired shuffle.

There are more sensible ways to solve problems of length. The first step is to time the parts of your speech. You can have a helper jot down the times of your main points on your outline as you practice, or you can time yourself with a tape recorder.

Look at the relative proportions of the parts of your speech: introduction, body, conclusion. Generally, the body should make up 75 percent of your speech. Does an extended story make the introduction too long? Also, look at the relative proportions of your main points. Are you spending half your time on only the first main point? Is it worth it?

When your delivery time becomes consistent, mark the cumulative times of the parts in your notes. For example, you might print "2 min" at the bottom right of your notes on the introduction, "5 min" after the first main point, "8 min" after the second, and so on. (See Figure 33-1.) This will make it easier if you need to adapt your speech to audience feedback or if you have a last-minute change in the program.

Some people have internal clocks that are accurate enough that they do not need external cues. If yours is not that well developed (and most of ours are not), feel free to use the timer on your phone or have a colleague in the audience give you prearranged time signals. Avoid excessive reliance on the clock. Become comfortable with your presentation by practicing and timing your speech.

KEY POINT **Practice Out Loud** Sitting and thinking about your speech or reading over your outline or notes is no substitute for rehearsing the speech aloud. Oral practice is essential to get comfortable with phrasing and to check your timing. Do not let "speaker's block" make you put off working orally until the last moment.

Critical Thinking Questions:

○ Why is practicing mentally rather than orally a pitfall?

○ How many times should you deliver your speech aloud to be fully ready?

○ How can technology aid the practice phase of speech preparation?

PART 8

Presenting Your Speech

CHAPTER 34
Vocal Delivery

As important as preparation, organization, content, and style are, the essence of the speech is still your spoken words. What a waste of time and brainpower it will be if what you have to say cannot be heard or understood. You must be aware of the mechanics of transmitting sound: articulation, breath control, projection, and so on. At the same time, your most important goal is to develop a style of vocal delivery that sounds natural and conversational.

34a. Speak to be heard and understood

1   Volume

For the inexperienced speaker, the appropriate **volume** will sound too loud. This is understandable because speeches must be louder than normal conversation.

The only thing that will make loud speaking more comfortable and natural is, of course, practice. In the early stages, you have to ignore the feedback on volume that you receive from your own ears and rely on a friend or perhaps a recording device set some distance away. What you are aiming for is a louder voice that retains the rhythms and inflections of your normal conversation. You want to be loud but not to yell like a drill instructor. As you practice, you will discover that this requires more air for each phrase and that you need to develop breath control in order to keep your breathing pauses in normal patterns.

Create a mental image of propelling your voice to the far corners of the room. You will then find yourself doing things that naturally aid projection, such as keeping your head up and opening your mouth wide.

2   Rate

Generally, you will need to speak more slowly than you do in daily conversation. To be sure you have timed the speech realistically, practice at the rate and volume you will actually use. An average **rate** of speaking is around 125–150 words per minute.

The need to speak a little louder and a little more distinctly will require extra breath. It will be more natural to pause to breathe between phrases than to rush through the last few words of a sentence and gasp for air.

3   Enunciation

The audience can miss information because of distance from the speaker and because of distracting noise. Therefore, it is important to work on crisp, precise **articulation.** Use your tongue, teeth, and lips to pronounce every sound. Be sure you say "government" rather than "goverment" and "hundred" rather than "hunnerd." Do not mumble, run words together, or swallow whole phrases. (See **34d.2** for a discussion of chronic articulation problems.)

You can enunciate properly and still sound natural. It merely takes some practice incorporating precision into your normal conversation. You are not trying to create a separate "speaking persona."

4   If you have an accent

If you have a regional accent or if you are not a native speaker of American English, you may be concerned about being understood. Do not try to eliminate or hide your accent. Your manner of speaking is part of your unique personality. The differences can add interest and charm to your presentation. To ensure comprehension, follow these suggestions:

1. Do not start out with the most important material. Use your introduction to let the audience adjust to the pronunciations and patterns of emphasis that differ from their own. Usually, this will take less than a minute.

2. Speak more slowly and distinctly than you do in daily conversation.

3. Be alert to feedback. If you see confused faces, repeat ideas slowly. Unclear vocabulary or mispronunciation of a key word may mystify your listeners. Try several synonyms for important words.

4. Consider using visual presentation aids and gestures to reinforce the meaning of key phrases.

If you are a non-native speaker of English, you may find these two simple tips useful in increasing your intelligibility:

1. Prolong your vowel sounds. In contrast to many other languages, spoken American English carries more meaning in vowels than in consonants. It may sound odd to you but make a conscious effort to extend vowel sounds. Maaaaake eeeeeach laaaast a looooong tiiiiime.

2. Also blend the end of one word into the beginning of the next so each phrase sounds like one long word. This reduces the perceived choppiness of much accented English.

34b. Vocal variety

You can use your voice to underscore and reinforce your message. Without variations in **pitch,** rate, and volume, everything you say has equal importance.

Suppose your speech on air pollution contained these two sentences:

When the pollution levels are high, my hair feels gritty, and I have to wash it more often.

Every time pollution reaches the "Alert" level in our city, more people with chronic respiratory problems die.

Delivering these sentences in the same tone could imply equal importance, yet clearly dying is worse than dirty hair. Changes in pace and emphasis reveal to your audience what is significant, funny, or serious, as well as a range of other emotions.

34c. Standard pronunciation

Some regional differences in the ways people pronounce words are inevitable and cause no problem for public speakers. If, however, a person says "warsh" instead of "wash" or "ax" instead of "ask," many listeners will consider this substandard. They will draw conscious or unconscious conclusions about the speaker's educational level, credibility, and intelligence. This sort of linguistic snobbery can be unfair, but it is easier to change some of your pronunciations than to change everyone else's attitudes.

1   Identify words that you habitually mispronounce

Look over the list in **Appendix C,** located online, and see if you make any of the identified pronunciation errors. If you find one or two words that you mispronounce, you can easily work on correcting them. If you find five or more, you may need help in the form of coaching or coursework. Due to factors in your background or perhaps a lazy ear for the finer distinctions of speech, you probably are also mispronouncing several other words. Here, too, feedback from your practice audience can alert you to errors of which you were unaware.

2   Check the pronunciation of unfamiliar words

Your reading vocabulary and your speaking vocabulary are different. There can be words you frequently see and understand yet rarely hear spoken. Without exposure and feedback, you might develop your own way of mentally pronouncing them and mistakenly add a sound or reverse sounds. If you give a whole speech about the "Electorial" College (instead of "Electoral"), your listeners might wonder just how knowledgeable you really are. They may be confused or amused if you constantly refer to the need for a counselor to listen "emphatically" when you think you are saying "empathically," a word that means something entirely different. Check words you encounter in research but do not use regularly to be sure you have them right. The online Dictionary.

com has an audio pronunciation for each word (**http://www. Dictionary.com**).

Refer to these sources for questions of pronunciation:

- Jean Yates, *Pronounce It Perfectly in English*, 2nd ed. (with four audio CDs). Hauppauge, NY: Barrons Educational Series, 2005.
- A Free Online Talking Dictionary of English Pronunciation, http://www.howjsay.com

34d. Distracting vocal characteristics

Your reason for speaking is undermined when your listeners begin to pay less attention to what you are saying and more attention to how you are saying it; for example, "That's the fifteenth time she's said 'quite frankly,'" or "Why doesn't he clear his throat?" Your voice and speech style should not distract from your ideas.

Distracting speech habits are difficult to identify and even more difficult to change. Vocal mannerisms become so familiar to you and your closest associates that they are overlooked. To a new audience they are blatant. Follow the suggestions in Chapter **33** for receiving feedback. For an objective perspective on your performance, use video or audio recordings and get feedback from knowledgeable friends.

1 Problems of voice quality

The resonant, musical voice you view as an ideal may be beyond your reach, but there is, of course, no one perfect voice for effective speaking. Although the quality and timbre of your voice are determined to a great extent by your larynx and by the size and shape of your nasal cavities, you can still have a pleasing voice unless you are hampered by one or more of the following problems.

- Harshness, hoarseness, or stridency, giving an impression of anger or gruffness
- Breathiness, thinness, or weakness, resulting in a soft, childish-sounding voice that lacks authority and power
- Nasality or denasality, producing either whiny or stuffed-up qualities

2 Problems of articulation

Many people have speech problems that are not severe but that are sufficiently distracting to impede good communication. Listen closely to your speech for irregularities in the way you produce consonant sounds or blends of consonants. Many articulation errors take the form of *substitutions,* such as "*d*ese" for "*th*ese." Also common are sound *distortions:* the hissing or whistling *s* and the lazy *l* or *r*. Less frequently encountered articulation errors are *additions* (like "ath*a*lete" for "athlete," "real*a*tor" for "realtor") and *omissions* (like "doin'" for "doing," "reg*l*ar" for "regular").

3 Irrelevant sounds and phrases

Do not be afraid to pause between sentences or thoughts when you speak. Avoid filling those pauses with meaningless sounds and phrases. When a speaker is nervous, a one-second pause can seem like a 10-second stretch of dead air and the temptation to fill it with something can be great. Consider these questions:

- Do you use **vocalized pauses**: "uh," "um," "er"?
- Do you fill pauses with other nonspeech sounds: lip smacking, tongue clicking, throat clearing, snuffling?
- Do you unconsciously insert a giggle after every sentence?
- Do you repeat certain words or phrases excessively, such as one from the following list?

Here is a list of words and phrases that lose their meaning when allowed to spread throughout a speech:

okay?

y'know

see

like

I mean

or whatever

and so on and so forth

et cetera

in other words

you might say

4 Repetitious inflection patterns

There are logical and natural places in sentences to vary the pitch of your voice. For instance, in English, the pitch usually goes higher at the end of a question or deepens to add emphasis. In normal conversation, we use a variety of inflections without having to think about it. In public speaking, however, there can be a tendency to deliver every sentence with the same inflectional pattern regardless of the sentence's meaning or grammatical structure. This happens when the speaker is not thinking about the content of the speech, and is nervous, or reading from a manuscript, or recalling a memorized text. A monotone, hypnotic pattern of inflection can easily lead to drooping eyelids in the audience.

5 Self-improvement versus professional help

Self-improvement When you identify a problem and your motivation to correct it is strong, you may devise a simple plan of action. Books and recordings are available to provide exercises in breathing and projection. These also have exercises, like tongue twisters, that make apparent the muscle groups used to produce certain sounds properly. You can start with resources such as these:

Goldes, J. *The Dialect Coach*. Retrieved from **http://www. thedialectcoach.com**

Mayer, Lyle Vernon. *Fundamentals of Voice and Articulation*. Boston: McGraw Hill, 2008. For a deeply ingrained habit, you may choose to map out a program of behavior modification. This approach, which has been quite successful helping people to lose weight or quit smoking, is based on the premise that habits, which develop gradually, are best eliminated gradually. New behaviors are substituted for old ones and the new behaviors are rewarded.

CHECKLIST

Steps to Behavior Modification

1. Assess your present behavior. Quantify the frequency of the distracting habit.
2. Set a specific, realistic goal. If you say "okay?" after nearly every sentence—perhaps 20 times in a 10-minute speech—resolve to cut down to 10 times.
3. Do not simply estimate your progress. Have a friend tally the occurrences or tape each speech yourself. Keep a written chart of your progress.

Professional help Some problems of vocal delivery are difficult to diagnose or solve without professional help. In seeking help, consider the nature and seriousness of your vocal problem, as well as the time and money you are able to commit. Then consult the appropriate professional person, such as a speech therapist, a voice coach, a public-speaking teacher, or a consultant.

Critical Thinking Questions:

○ What is the danger of speaking too fast or too slow?
○ Should a person with an accent eliminate his or her accent in order to be better understood? Why or why not?
○ Why does vocal variety make a speech more "listenable"?

C H A P T E R 3 5
Physical Delivery

Much of how your listeners respond to you is a result of what they see rather than what they hear. Do shaking knees and fidgeting fingers contradict your confident words? Slouching posture and a grim expression can reveal the lie in "I'm so happy to be here!" When practicing and delivering your speech, be aware of the visual image you are creating. As with vocal delivery, the goal with physical delivery is to be natural and to avoid any actions that will contradict your verbal message.

35a. Appearance

As you get ready for your speech, consider what your hairstyle, grooming, and clothing might communicate to your audience. You should show that you took care in preparing and that you consider the event important enough to expend some energy in trying to look good.

Ideally, your clothes should provide a tasteful and unobtrusive frame for your personality and your remarks. Be aware of regional, cultural, and occupational norms. There is no need to be drab. However, your audience could be distracted by loud colors, busy patterns, showy jewelry, unorthodox combinations of apparel, and clothing they consider too revealing. Avoid apparel that could weaken your credibility.

35b. Distracting mannerisms

Distracting mannerisms fall into two categories: those you have all the time, such as tucking your hair behind your ear or pushing your glasses up on your nose; and those you have only when giving a speech, such as noisily fanning and squaring up your notecards or rocking back and forth on your heels. Few acts are inherently distracting; it is the repetition of an act that becomes distracting. As with vocal mannerisms, you are probably unaware of the frequency of the act until someone points it out. Therefore, the first step toward eliminating the problem is becoming aware of it. Sometimes this awareness is sufficient to stop the mannerism, or you may want to adapt the behavior modification techniques described in **34d.5.**

35c. Posture

As a general rule, you should stand when speaking. This focuses audience attention on you and gives you a better view of your listeners. Of course, there are exceptions. As a member of a panel discussion, you should follow the lead of the moderator. If, however, you can learn to be comfortable speaking without a lectern—with your weight evenly distributed; your notes grasped casually in one hand at waist level; and no props of any kind for support—you can easily adapt to any setting. Appropriate variations might include leaning across the lectern to show deep involvement or sitting on the edge of a desk or table to signal the shift to an informal mood. Draping yourself across the lectern, lounging at the side with one elbow extended, or standing in an off-center posture are incompatible with the energetic and controlled image of a polished public speaker. In addition, be careful never to lock your knees. This can make you light-headed or even faint.

35d. Movements

You can give a perfectly good and proper speech standing behind a lectern. However, most speeches can be aided by movement at appropriate times. Taking a few steps to the left or right or moving closer to your listeners can add variety and emphasis to your speech. You also establish immediacy with the segment of the audience that you move toward. Moreover, physical movement during a speech is a constructive way to release tension.

Make your movements purposeful. Pacing nervously around the room is distracting. If you are going to move, be decisive. Take at least two or three normal paces diagonally or directly forward.

The timing of your movement can reinforce your ideas. Generally, it is best to remain in one place when explaining complex material or when delivering your most emotional examples or powerful arguments. Physical movement works best at transitional points, signaling to the listeners a change in mood, content, or form.

35e. Gestures

What you should do with your hands in a speech is exactly what you do with them in normal conversation. For some people, using their hands in this manner means hardly using them at all. For others, it means gesturing a great deal. Whether you gesture a little or a lot, you do it to describe, to point out, to enumerate, to emphasize, to entreat, and so on.

There is no need to plan what gestures go with your speech. If you are absorbed with your topic and with communicating it to your listeners, your gestures will emerge spontaneously at the appropriate points. This will happen only if your hands are free to move. Too many speakers immobilize their hands completely due to either the panicky need to cling to something or the desire to prevent uncontrolled movement. Do not lock yourself into any of these gesture-inhibiting stances:

The bear hug: Arms across the chest—one of the most common ways of getting a grip on yourself

The flesh wound:	One arm hanging useless at the side and the other hand serving as a tourniquet above or below the elbow
The choirboy/girl:	Hands clasped at waist level with fingers entwined
The fig leaf:	Demurely crossed hands that are strategically placed

Actually, all of these are perfectly acceptable *transitory* postures. The problem with them does not lie in the position of the limbs, but in the temptation to leave them in that position—statue like—while concentrating only on what is coming out of your mouth.

So, what *do* you do with your hands? First, do nothing distracting such as nervously shredding notecards, drumming on the table, scratching, or making other kinds of unproductive hand movements:

| *The Lady Macbeth:* | Hands wrung compulsively and continuously to wash out the "stain" of having to speak |
| *Happy pockets:* | Keys, change, and other pocket articles set to jingling by restless hands become the sound competing with the speaker's voice |

Second, do nothing contrived—no rehearsed gestures. What matters most is that your arms, wrists, and fingers are relaxed so that your hands can move naturally if you need that movement.

35f. Eye contact

In any speech, even a manuscript speech, you should have eye contact 85 percent of the time, looking down only to read technical material or to refer briefly to your notes. Most important, be sure to maintain eye contact throughout your introduction and conclusion and during the most significant points and the most pivotal arguments.

Be familiar enough with your material that you can look at as many members of your audience as possible—as often as possible. Maintaining eye contact allows you to read your listeners' faces to get feedback on how your message is being received. Faking eye contact by looking between heads or over heads of the people in the back row misses the whole point.

Actually look into the eyes of the individual audience members and hold that contact for at least three seconds. Do not skim across rows of faces. Move your eye contact randomly throughout the room. Do not fall into a head-bobbing pattern—left, center, right, center, left. . . .

> QUICK TIP **Smile** The expression that has the same meaning in every culture is the smile. Most public speakers underuse or misuse this powerful tool. A constant, fixed, jaw-aching grin is as bad as a deadpan expression. A smile at a sad or serious moment is inappropriate. However, remind yourself to smile genuinely whenever it can reinforce your message. It is one of the easiest ways to establish rapport, show your goodwill, and put you and your audience at ease.

Critical Thinking Questions:

○ How does physical delivery affect speaker credibility?

○ How can movement be used to enhance a speech and to maintain audience attention?

○ What impact does eye contact have on audience attention and, later, retention? Why?

CHAPTER 36
Using Presentation Aids

Your presentation aids should be a seamless part of your speech—whether discrete or continuous, hand-held or projected, seen or heard—and not an interruption. Choosing appropriate aids that supplement and augment your points will go a long way toward easing this blending. (See Chapter **27.**) Beyond the structural appropriateness of the aid or aids you select, there are a few simple things you can do to smooth your aids' introduction.

36a. Practice with your aids

Your aids should be prepared early enough so that you can practice with them several times. (See **33b.2.**) This will alert you to any changes that might be necessary. Become comfortable with them so that you do not fumble around during the presentation.

> QUICK TIP **Presentation Aid Practice Time** Spend twice as much time practicing with your aids as you spend developing them. This strategy will help you to keep your aids simple, and it will ensure that you spend substantial time practicing them. This practice time will help ensure that audio aids are cued to the proper place and that files and slides are in the proper sequence.

36b. Have your aids ready to go

For audio/video aids, have the segment or CD cued to the spot so that you only need to press a button. If you are projecting off a computer, have the program launched and the file(s) open. Don't subject your audience to a search through multiple folders for the right file.

36c. Face the audience

Be so familiar with your material that you can look at your listeners while explaining a visual aid. Often, speakers make the mistake of speaking to the projection screen or wall instead of to their audience. Doing so communicates a lack of concern for the audience.

36d. Keep talking

Avoid long pauses when demonstrating a process. If there is some complexity or if many steps are needed to produce your desired result, you might take a hint from cooking shows and prepare a series of aids to demonstrate the various phases. For example, a speaker could say, "Then you apply glue to the two blocks, press them together like this, and let the bond dry. Here are some that have already dried. Now, I'll show you the next step. . . ." When you cannot avoid a time lag because you need to demonstrate some process, have a planned digression—perhaps some bit of history related to the process—to fill the gap.

36e. Do not become secondary to your presentation slides

A common scene at business conferences is a large screen dominating a room holding dozens or hundreds of people. Dwarfed by the screen, a speaker is partially hidden behind a bank of computer monitors, hunched over in the dim light, clicking away at the mouse while talking into the body mike, and often commenting on some glitch with the system. Obvious problems here are the lack of connection with the audience because of the darkened room; the focus on the machine; the confinement of the speaker to the space in front of the computer; and the "aid" becoming an impediment.

If you are in a situation in which PowerPoint or other presentation software will be used, take steps to counteract the potential difficulties. Enlist a colleague or friend to operate the computer so that you are free to move around and make eye contact with the audience. If you cannot avoid operating the equipment or if you must compensate for dim lighting, use vocal variety to counterbalance immobility and lack of visibility. (See **34b.**) If possible, use the slides for key illustrations and points but leave the screen blank the rest of the time.

36f. Do not let your aids become distractions

Keep your visual aids out of sight—turned off, covered, or turned away from your audience—until you are ready to use them. Remove or recover them immediately after they have served their purpose. If you are using a projector, turn it off if you aren't using it in order to eliminate the cooling-fan noise. For a continuous visual aid like a PowerPoint presentation of charts and graphs that support particular points, use a blank slide between each content slide. Similarly, be cautious about using video in your speech. Too many speakers think a lively video will make up for their own lack of preparation. This is rarely true.

Refrain from passing objects around the room. It will cause a ripple of inattention. This rule is flexible, especially if you are dealing with an unusual object and a small audience. Still it is probably best to share the item *after* the speech—say, during the discussion period. By the same token, handouts should be distributed after a speech. You want the audience to listen now and read later. (Of course, there are some contexts, primarily business, where this is not necessarily the norm.) (See Chapter **7**.)

> QUICK TIP **Avoiding Presentation Aid Fiascoes** Practice carefully; arrive in plenty of time for setup; and bring interface cables, pins, tape, extension cords, extra projector bulbs, flashdrive backups, and the like in order to ensure that what you envision comes to pass.

If you are using electronic aids, find the outlets in the room and actually test both your aids and the outlets for proper functioning. If you are being provided with equipment, insist that it come with spare bulbs, batteries, and so on. If you are using a computer, make sure it is compatible with the projection system. It is also wise to e-mail yourself a backup copy of any slide presentation you plan to use.

Finally, presentation aids are most distracting when you are clumsy with them. Be sure that your charts are in the right order, your models are set up, and your equipment is in perfect working order.

Critical Thinking Questions:

- ○ Why is it important to spend more time practicing with presentation aids than creating them?
- ○ What advantages and disadvantages do presentation aids offer the speaker? The audience?
- ○ What presentation aids would improve the speech you are currently developing?

CHAPTER 37

Answering Questions

The **question-and-answer period** is a great opportunity to further the goals of your speech. While you spoke, you attempted to address the needs of your audience, and now you can see how close you came. From your listeners' questions, you can learn what points are unclear or what arguments and objections they have. Communicate an eagerness to interact with your listeners and to hear their ideas on your topic.

Do not forget to use your delivery skills even though the speech is over. Maintain eye contact and avoid fidgeting or mumbling.

37a. Come prepared

As you prepare your speech, anticipate the questions that will arise naturally from each of your points. You can also have the friends who listen to your practice sessions ask you questions afterward. Although you can never predict the exact questions that will come up, certain ones are more probable than others. Rehearse aloud possible answers to the most complicated and difficult ones in the same way as you prepare the "planned" portion of your speech. This is how public figures prepare for news conferences.

Ideally, your research has been so extensive that you have much more material than you were able to use. You have reviewed this extra material so you are familiar enough with the content to use it in response to questions.

37b. Invite questions and be direct in your answers

Do not worry if there are not any questions immediately or if at first there are long pauses between questions. It usually takes listeners a moment to collect their thoughts. In some cases, you can start the ball rolling by asking a question of the audience.

Call on questioners in the order they sought recognition and maintain eye contact while a question is being asked. If you are not sure you understand the question, paraphrase it and ask the questioner if it is accurate. When both of you are satisfied, restate or paraphrase it for the entire audience and direct the answer to them.

Be sure you answer the question. To avoid oversimplification, you want to elaborate, expand, or qualify your answer. However, if your discussion becomes too complicated, you will appear to be avoiding the issue. Consequently, always include a direct one-sentence answer in your response to a question. For emphasis, place this sentence first or last, as in these examples:

First: *Yes, I do oppose building nuclear power plants,* at least until several safety questions are answered satisfactorily. My reasons include . . .

Last: . . . So, because of all these serious problems I see, my answer to your question would be *Yes, I do oppose building new nuclear power plants at this time.*

QUICK TIP **What to Do If You Don't Know the Answer** Do not try to bluff your way through. Rather, admit that you do not know. If you have some idea where the answer might be found, tell the questioner about the source. Ask other audience members to help you out by volunteering what they know. Additionally, you might promise to look up the answer if the listener wants to get in touch with you later.

37c. Manage self-indulgent questioners

The purpose of a question-and-answer period is to clarify issues for the entire audience. When individual audience members attempt to use this time for detailed consultation on a specialized problem or to get on their favorite soapbox, you have an obligation as speaker to bring the interaction back on its true course. Be prepared to keep control of the situation by dealing in a firm and tactful manner with several types of distracting questioners.

- *The person who wants to give a speech.* This person may agree or disagree with you or may have a favorite ax to grind that is only tangentially related to your topic. It becomes obvious that, rather than asking a real question, the person is taking advantage of an assembled audience. It is rarely effective to ask, "What is your question?" The person will just say, "Don't you agree that . . ." or "What do you think of the position that . . ." and continue for another five minutes. You have to jump in at the end of a sentence, manufacture a question somewhat related to the person's ramblings, answer it, and recognize another questioner on the opposite side of the room.

- *The person who wants to have an extended dialogue.* This person might begin with a genuine question but, after you respond, may refuse to relinquish the floor by countering with follow-up questions, commenting on your answer, or opening new lines of discussion. The best way to deal with this sort of person is to end the exchange firmly but with a compliment: "Thank you, you've given me quite a number of interesting insights here."

- *The person who wants to pick a fight.* Intellectual confrontation and probing, penetrating questions are to be expected—and even welcomed—from audience members who disagree with you. But sometimes questioners become inappropriately argumentative and mount hostile, personal attacks against a speaker. Rather than seeking an answer to a question, they are trying to destroy your credibility. Do not let them succeed by becoming angry or by defending yourself against generalized name-calling. Pick out the part of such a person's diatribe that contains the kernel of a question, paraphrase it, and answer it calmly and reasonably. For example:

Q: What about all this poisonous junk that you greed-crazed despoilers dump into our rivers to kill our children and whole species of animals?

A: The questioner has brought up the valid and difficult subject of toxic waste disposal. What is our company doing about it? Well . . .

In short, respond to these disruptive people diplomatically. Do not take cheap shots or direct humor at them to shut them off.

Likewise, when you are taken aback by incomprehensible questions or questions that demonstrate gross ignorance or misinformation, you should react positively. Avoid language that embarrasses the questioner or points out errors. For example:

Not: You've totally confused fission and fusion!

But: Many of those problems relate to nuclear *fission.* The *fusion* reaction is quite different. It works like this . . .

Try to find ways to dignify bad questions and turn them into good ones. Your listeners' empathy is with the questioner, who may be nervous or confused. Your efforts to put others at ease will earn you an audience's goodwill.

Critical Thinking Questions:

○ How might the process of responding to a question be similar to or different from the process of giving an impromptu speech?

○ How should you handle a question whose answer you do not know?

○ What should be your goal in responding to self-indulgent questioners?

APPENDIX A

Sample Speeches and Outlines

This appendix contains an informative, an invitational, a persuasive, and a commemorative speech. It also includes a sample outline for an informative speech—the "comic book outline" referred to in various chapters of this handbook. An annotated version of the popular persuasive speech outline for Hans Erian's "No More Sugar" is available via *The Speaker's Compact Handbook* companion website.

The 54th Massachusetts

Informative speech by Nathanael Dunlavy[1]

It was eighth grade history class, and I hated, absolutely hated, history. But as another boring week began, I heard what was music to my ears: "Class, this week we're going to watch a movie." The movie was called *Glory*. It was about the Civil War and the raising of the first black regiment from the Northeast.

Every year in the month of February, our country celebrates Black History Month. We recognize the efforts of such African Americans as Harriet Tubman, Booker T. Washington, and Martin Luther King, Jr. However, today I will not be speaking on such notable names as these, but on quite the contrary. I'll be speaking about what review author Jeff Shannon calls a noble, yet little-known, episode of history: the 54th Massachusetts. After watching *Glory*, I became intrigued with the Civil War and began doing research on it, specifically the events surrounding the 54th Massachusetts. It all began on January 1, 1863, when Abraham Lincoln signed the Emancipation Proclamation, allowing for the first time in this nation's history the opportunity for men of color to sign up and fight for their country. Today, I'll be discussing the formation of the 54th Massachusetts, the racial difficulties they faced, and the Battle of Fort Wagner. Let's begin with the formation of the troops.

In March 1863, the regiment simply known as the 54th was formed in Readville, Massachusetts. The man who would be colonel and in charge of the men was Robert Gould Shaw, the 25-year-old son of a prominent Boston abolitionist family. Although he was young, he was already a veteran of the

[1]Used with permission.

battlefield. Civil War historian William James notes that from the time Shaw accepted the preferred command, he lived but for one object, and that was to establish the honor of the 54th Massachusetts. On May 28, 1863, a parade honoring the men cheered them on as they left Boston to fight for the Union. With the men trained, suited up, and ready for battle, next I'll be discussing the racial difficulties the men faced.

The 54th was comprised mostly of free men who had never been slaves or had to face the types of racial prejudices that were to come. First, according to Civil War author and lecturer Kathy Dahl of BitsofBlueandGray.com, instead of the promised Army wage of thirteen dollars a month, because they were black troops, they would receive ten dollars a month—minus three dollars for clothing. Then, despite intense training and fighting readiness, the regiment was only ordered to do basic manual labor. Then in June 1863, Shaw was given orders to have his men burn and loot a small town in Georgia. Shaw saw this as a Satanic action, and in a letter to his wife he writes, "I fear that such actions will hurt the reputation of black troops and those connected with them." Performing only manual labor with little pay and the possible disgrace brought upon them with the burning of the town, this will take us to the last point: the Battle of Fort Wagner.

On July 16, 1863, the men of the 54th saw action and were successful in their attempts. That night, under the secrecy of darkness and in a torrent of rain, the 54th trudged through mud and hazardous terrain for eight hours, and on the morning of July 18, Colonel Shaw accepted the honor of leading his troops in the assault on Fort Wagner. The fort was to be taken by bayonet in hand-to-hand combat. At dusk, Shaw and his men began their assault. In front of the fort was a moat followed by a 30-foot wall of sand. Confederate fire opened. Nearly blinded by gun smoke and fire, Shaw led his men up to the top of the hill. With a final charge of "Forward, 54th!" Colonel Shaw was shot through the heart, falling face down into the fort.

William Carney, a member of the regiment, saw that the flag bearer had been shot and lay dead in the moat. Carney climbs down the hill, races into the moat, grasps the flag, and begins his ascent back to the top. In the process, Carney is shot through the leg, the shoulder, the arm, and in the head. With orders to retreat, Carney clutches onto the flag, gets on his hands and knees and crawls back down the hill, which is now covered with the bodies of fallen comrades, and flees some five hundred yards to safety. Before collapsing, his only words were, "Boys, I only did my duty; the flag never touched the ground." The next day, the body of Colonel Shaw and three hundred of his men were thrown into a sandy ditch and buried. Thirty years later, William Carney would become the first African American in this nation's history to be awarded the Congressional Medal of Honor and become the public symbol of the many unsung heroes of the 54th Massachusetts. Because of the efforts of the 54th, more black troops were enlisted, and President Lincoln credited the raising up of African American troops as helping to secure the final victory.

In conclusion, we have covered the formation of the 54th Massachusetts, the racial difficulties they faced, and the Battle of Fort Wagner. There have been many years removed since that eighth grade history class, but the images of those brave men serve as constant reminders that although their names may remain ambiguous, their place in our nation's history lasts forever. The courage and legacy of the 54th is encapsulated best in the words of an unknown author that read: "Glory was not to be found in victory, but in their willingness to keep fighting for what they believed in."

Four-Day School Week: An Invitational Dialogue

Invitational speech with discussion by
Courtney Felton[2]

General purpose: To invite

Specific purpose: To explore with my audience the idea of changing the five-day high school week to a four-day week.

Thesis statement: Today I want to explore with you the idea of high schools changing from a regular five-day-week schedule to a four-day schedule with longer days.

Seven hours! That's almost enough sleep for a night. Or perhaps a solid day's worth of skiing. Or the time it takes to travel by plane across the country. Seven hours is also roughly the amount of time high school students spend in school in one school day. Take a second to imagine what it would have been like not having school on Fridays when you were in high school. This would have you with an extra seven hours you hadn't had before! That would have been seven hours to do countless activities.

The National Conference of State Legislatures states, "Supporters of the shortened week also boast of improved morale and increased attendance (by both students and teachers), open Fridays for sporting events and doctor appointments, and more time to spend with loved ones."

This idea of having a shorter high school week has been a topic of interest for me. Since all of us go to school—even though now it's college—I have a feeling it may be a topic that you might want to explore as well. Today I want to explore with you the idea of schools changing from the normal schedule of a five-day week to a four-day week with longer school days.

[2]Used with permission.

Since I don't have a solid opinion on whether or not this would be beneficial to all schools, I'd like to share two of the many perspectives on this issue, one for and one against. I'd also like to hear your feedback on the issue.

I'd like to start by addressing the pros of a four-day school week. Perhaps the most significant issue right now in education is the idea of budget cuts. Cutting back on one day of school per week saves on expenses such as transportation, utilities such as heat for the school, food expenses, and the other costs to keep a school open.

Another advantage to having only four days of school is the option to hold sporting events on Fridays. And if students are free on Fridays, the attendance at games could increase. A March 12, 2009, Associated Press article from FoxNews.com, accessed on March 9, 2010, explains that "about 85 percent of the district's athletic events are scheduled on Fridays, so a Monday-to-Thursday school week means fewer Friday absences as students and teachers prepare for or travel to games."

A third advantage to the shortened schedule is the idea of having more time to spend with family or friends, taking care of doctor appointments, or being able to schedule any other week-day activity that one may not have time for on a five-day school schedule.

Exactly how many schools are actually doing this, though? An article from the *Wall Street Journal,* accessed on March 9, 2010, states, "Of the nearly 15,000-plus districts nationwide, more than 100 in at least 17 states currently use the four-day system, according to data culled from the Education Commission of the States."

While, in my opinion, all of these aspects seem appealing, I want to address another side of the issue and consider the views of those opposing the change. Each of the articles I looked at on FoxNews.com as well as the NCSL site discussed the following issues.

While the shorter week appears to be helpful in saving money, it may cause parents to take on the cost burden. With their children home during a normal workday, parents have to find extra child care.

Another important problem opponents of the four-day schedule discuss is the increased length of the school day. As current students, some of us may feel like the school day is already long enough. Adding to the length may make high school students even more tired, less able to concentrate, and could hinder their learning time while at school. And extending school further into the day cuts into students' time for extracurricular activities on days other than Friday.

In addition, while an extra day off leaves time for family time and other activities, some parents—and even students—are afraid of how students will actually use this time off.

Finally, it is important to consider the current school reform movement. A research brief prepared by the Principles Partnership of the Union Pacific Foundation explains, "Some educators are concerned that the four-day week may appear to be inconsistent with the new emphasis for more time in school."

Now that we have explored both sides of the issue, as well as opinions of students, teachers, and parents, I think it is important to hear your opinions as well as ideas that I may not have addressed yet.

Courtney and her audience discussed the issues related to moving from a five-day to a four-day week in high schools. To encourage audience members to share their views, she prepared the following questions in advance:

- To begin, by a show of hands, who would like to keep the current school schedule?
- And who would want to change the high school week to four longer days rather than five?
- For those of you who want to change, what aspect of changing is most appealing to you?
- For those of you who think the current schedule should stay, what isn't appealing about changing for you?
- For those of you who were athletes in high school, how do you think changing this schedule would have affected your athletic schedule? Practice time, game time, et cetera?
- As a high school student, would you personally have been able to concentrate and work at the level you did on a five-day week for a longer amount of time at school?
- If you had had one extra free day, do you feel like you would have worked better as a student?
- What types of things would you have done with an extra day?
- What aspects of the four days of the week would have been hindered by your longer day at school?
- Are there any other drawbacks or benefits you want to share that I didn't cover?

When the discussion was over, Courtney concluded her speech.

Thanks for sharing your ideas and opinions. I think that really helped shed some more light on the situation and how students really feel about the issue.

We've heard today some of the views in favor and some against changing the current five-day high school week to a four-day week with longer days. For students, perhaps a shorter week would allow for more time outside school, but it could also cut into sports practice time and extracurricular activities. For parents, finding day care could be an issue, but for the schools, it could be a way to save money.

On the whole, though, I think there are multiple perspectives to consider, and I've enjoyed being able to talk about some of them with you.

A. Sample persuasive speech outline (1)
Bite Back
by Kayla Strickland

Notice that the main points listed here are never stated in precisely those words in the speech transcription. The outline is a logical plan—a place to set down main points in propositional form, to fit the subpoints beneath the main points, and to fit support beneath the subpoints. Uncluttered with transitions and extra words and being properly indented, the outline allows the reader to see the basic speech development at a glance.

Along with the outline of the body of the speech, we include the thesis sentence and identify the text that delineates the parts of the introduction (attention-getter, psychological orientation, logical orientation) and conclusion (logical closure, psychological closure, clincher).

> **General purpose:** To persuade
>
> **Specific purpose:** To persuade my audience to get involved in the fight to end malaria.
>
> **Thesis statement:** Malaria, a disease that stunts economic growth, education, health care productivity, and takes thousands of lives every day, can be stopped and reversed within our lifetime.

I.   Introduction

Attention: It's just a mosquito, right? To us it is, but to half the world it is also fever, vomiting, aches, jaundice, anemia. It is seizures, comas, lung inflammation, cardiovascular collapse, kidney failure, paralysis. It is speech impediments. It is stillbirths and maternal deaths and low-birth-weight babies. It is blindness. It is deafness. It is malaria.

Reveal topic: The disease is caused by a little parasite from the genus *Plasmodium* that is carried from human to human via mosquitoes. It invades and ruptures red blood cells, reproducing rapidly, and every day this process takes thousands of lives and stunts economic growth, child development, and health care productivity.

Credibility: You've most likely heard of malaria as a distant problem—something that affects Africa and poor people in jungles. But what if I told you that this disease actually has global implications that affect you and me? And what if I also told you that we have the ability to stop this disease and reverse the negative effects it has on economics, education, health care, and life expectancy?

Preview: Today I would like to talk about why malaria is a problem, what can be done to fight it, and what the benefits of ending malaria would be.

Transition: We have the ability to deaden malaria's sting. This is a reality. But today it is not yet accomplished, so let me share with you some other realities.

II. Need step

A. Malaria has killed a million people just this past year, according to estimates by the Centers for Disease Control and Prevention.

   1. The disease has it out for the most vulnerable members of society—pregnant women, children, and groups living in conflict areas.

   2. The Roll Back Malaria Partnership (RBM)—made up of representatives from the World Bank, the World Health Organization (WHO), and UNICEF, among others—points out that nearly a third of malarial deaths occur in areas racked with the stresses of war, food shortages, displacement, and civil unrest.

B. You are probably beginning to see that lives are not the only cost of malaria.

   1. RBM reports that malaria costs Africa US$12 billion dollars each year.

      a. Some causes are productivity losses due to illness-related absences from work, and diminished foreign investment and tourism.

      b. The same report stated that the cost on poor families for prevention and treatment of malaria is around a fourth of their annual income.

      c. Poverty keeps communities sick, and sickness keeps communities in poverty.

   2. Malaria also overloads the health care infrastructure in affected countries.

      a. The disease renders the infrastructure less efficient to tackle other health concerns like HIV/AIDS and tuberculosis.

      b. The Global Strategy and Booster Program, published by the World Bank, estimates that malaria consumes close to 40 percent of all public spending on health in Africa.

      c. Up to half of the beds in African hospitals are occupied by malaria victims.

   3. You can imagine that when most of these beds are filled by children, education and child development are hampered.

a. Kids who stick through the horrible malarial pains and fevers are likely to experience recurrent episodes.

    i. They can be left with severe brain damage and physical impairments like paralysis, deafness, and blindness.

    ii. These afflictions negatively affect their ability in school and inhibit them from adding to the prosperity of their communities.

b. These many costs of a mosquito bite suggest that malaria is a wide-reaching, global problem.

Transition: So now let's talk about what can be done to fight it.

III. Satisfaction step

    A. There are many methods of malaria prevention.

      1. These methods range from insecticide sprays to antimalarial drugs.

      2. An efficient combination of them is the only way that malaria can be stopped.

    B. But there is no time to cover all of the methods here, so I would just like to introduce one: the simple bed net.

      1. The progression of malaria is dependent on continued contact between humans and mosquitoes.

      2. Bed nets sever this contact for ten dollars apiece.

      3. Improved technology allows nets to be treated by insecticides as they are manufactured, weaving a chemical barrier into the physical one.

        a. This means that they prevent infection and kill mosquitoes at the same time.

        b. These insecticide-treated nets, called ITNs, are a tried and true method of malaria prevention.

        c. A 2007 WHO report on ITNs said that they have been shown to avert around half of malaria cases and to reduce deaths in children under five by nearly 20 percent.

Transition: We see that malaria is a global problem. We see a simple, proven solution to the problem. Now let's see the benefits of ending malaria.

IV. Visualization step

    A. The UN (United Nations), along with many international organizations, set eight international development goals to be met by 2015.

    1. These are known as the Millennium Development Goals.

    2. Addressing the problem of malaria has the potential to impact six out of these eight goals.

       a. Eradicate extreme poverty and hunger.

       b. Achieve universal primary education.

       c. Reduce child mortality rate.

       d. Improve maternal health.

       e. Combat HIV/AIDS, malaria, and other diseases.

       f. Develop a global partnership for development.

    3. Poverty is a worldwide problem, so any actions that take steps against it, like those laid out by the MDGs, offer rewarding returns on our investments.

B. Imagine economic productivity restored in Sub-Saharan Africa.

    1. The weight of poverty will be a little less crushing.

       a. Men and women can remain at work instead of in hospitals or at home looking after sick children.

       b. They can grow their crops, raise their livestock, build their trades.

       c. Poor families will no longer have to make a decision between buying antimalarial pills or food.

    2. Trade and tourism will increase.

    3. Government funds will no longer be sucked dry by mosquitoes.

    4. The health care infrastructure will be freed up to take on other issues like HIV/AIDS and TB.

    5. Children will stay in school.

       a. Their futures will not be clouded by the uncertainty and fear that a mosquito's pinprick used to bring.

       b. The minds of future generations will be free to excel and contribute to their families, their communities, their countries, and the entire world.

Transition: In conclusion, I've told you how malaria affects us, showed a way of fighting it, and revealed the benefits that we would see by being rid of it.

V. Action step

Summary: So what can you do to take your bite out of malaria?
Call for action: Buy a net. Ten dollars will provide the funds for a treated net, its distribution, and education for the happy owner. I bought one through biteback.net. Roll Back Malaria recommends Malaria No More and Nothing But Nets.

    You may be saying, "One net? What will that accomplish?" Consider the African proverb: "If you think you're too small to make a difference, try sleeping in a closed room with a mosquito." Just take a look at the benefits we've been over, and you can see that a simple bed net is probably one of the best investments you could ever make.

Closing: The mosquito will always be a nuisance, but it doesn't have to be a killer.

References

Centers for Disease Control and Prevention (CDC). "Disease," (February 12, 2010) http://www.cdc.gov/malaria/about/disease.html (accessed November 11, 2010).

Centers for Disease Control and Prevention (CDC). "Malaria Facts," (February 12, 2010) http://www.cdc.gov/malaria/about/facts.html (accessed November 11, 2010).

Roll Back Malaria Partnership. "Looking Forward: Roll Back Malaria," (2004) http://www.rollbackmalaria.org/docs/rbm_brochure.pdf (accessed November 11, 2010).

The World Bank. *Rolling Back Malaria: The World Bank Global Strategy and Booster Program,* (2005): 15.

World Health Organization. "Insecticide-Treated Mosquito Nets: A WHO Position Statement," *Global Malaria Programme* (2007) http://www.who.int/malaria/publications/atoz/itnspospaperfinal.pdf (accessed November 11, 2010).

United Nations. *United Nations Millennium Development Goals,* (2010) http://www.un.org/millenniumgoals/index.shtml (accessed November 11, 2010).

D.   Commemorative speech transcript

Remarks on a Historic Day in Egypt

Special occasion speech by President Barack Obama[3]

Good afternoon everybody. There are very few moments in our

Go to your CourseMate for *The Speaker's Handbook* and click on **WebLink 36.2** to watch a video of this speech.

lives where we have the privilege to witness history taking place. This is one of those moments. This is one of those times. The people of Egypt have spoken, their voices have been heard, and Egypt will never be the same.

By stepping down, President Mubarak responded to the Egyptian people's hunger for change. But this is not the end of Egypt's transition. It's a beginning. I'm sure there will be difficult days ahead, and many questions remain unanswered. But I am confident that

---

[3]Barack Obama, "Remarks by the President on Egypt," (February 11, 2011) http://www.whitehouse.gov/the-press-office/2011/02/11/remarks-president-egypt.

the people of Egypt can find the answers, and do so peacefully, constructively, and in the spirit of unity that has defined these last few weeks. For Egyptians have made it clear that nothing less than genuine democracy will carry the day.

The military has served patriotically and responsibly as a care-taker to the state, and will now have to ensure a transition that is credible in the eyes of the Egyptian people. That means pro-tecting the rights of Egypt's citizens, lifting the emergency law, revising the constitution and other laws to make this change ir-reversible, and laying out a clear path to elections that are fair and free. Above all, this transition must bring all of Egypt's voices to the table. For the spirit of peaceful protest and perseverance that the Egyptian people have shown can serve as a powerful wind at the back of this change.

The United States will continue to be a friend and part-ner to Egypt. We stand ready to provide whatever assistance is necessary—and asked for—to pursue a credible transition to a democracy. I'm also confident that the same ingenuity and en-trepreneurial spirit that the young people of Egypt have shown in recent days can be harnessed to create new opportunity—jobs and businesses that allow the extraordinary potential of this gen-eration to take flight. And I know that a democratic Egypt can advance its role of responsible leadership not only in the region but around the world.

Egypt has played a pivotal role in human history for over 6,000 years. But over the last few weeks, the wheel of history turned at a blinding pace as the Egyptian people demanded their universal rights.

We saw mothers and fathers carrying their children on their shoulders to show them what true freedom might look like.

We saw a young Egyptian say, "For the first time in my life, I really count. My voice is heard. Even though I'm only one per-son, this is the way real democracy works."

We saw protesters chant *"Selmiyya, selmiyya"* ("We are peace-ful") again and again.

We saw a military that would not fire bullets at the people they were sworn to protect.

And we saw doctors and nurses rushing into the streets to care for those who were wounded, volunteers checking protesters to ensure that they were unarmed.

We saw people of faith praying together and chanting, "Mus-lims, Christians, we are one." And though we know that the strains between faiths still divide too many in this world and no single event will close that chasm immediately, these scenes re-mind us that we need not be defined by our differences. We can be defined by the common humanity that we share.

And above all, we saw a new generation emerge—a genera-tion that uses their own creativity and talent and technology to call for a government that represented their hopes and not their fears, a government that is responsive to their boundless aspirations. One Egyptian put it simply: Most people have discovered in the last few days . . . that they are worth something, and this cannot be taken away from them anymore, ever.

This is the power of human dignity, and it can never be denied. Egyptians have inspired us, and they've done so by putting the lie to the idea that justice is best gained through violence. For in Egypt, it was the moral force of nonviolence—not terrorism, not mindless killing—but nonviolence, moral force that bent the arc of history toward justice once more.

And while the sights and sounds that we heard were entirely Egyptian, we can't help but hear the echoes of history—echoes from Germans tearing down a wall, Indonesian students taking to the streets, Gandhi leading his people down the path of justice.

As Martin Luther King said in celebrating the birth of a new nation in Ghana while trying to perfect his own, "There is something in the soul that cries out for freedom." Those were the cries that came from Tahrir Square, and the entire world has taken note.

Today belongs to the people of Egypt, and the American people are moved by these scenes in Cairo and across Egypt because of who we are as a people and the kind of world that we want our children to grow up in.

The word *tahrir* means "liberation." It is a word that speaks to that something in our souls that cries out for freedom. And forevermore it will remind us of the Egyptian people—of what they did, of the things that they stood for, and how they changed their country, and in doing so changed the world.

Thank you.

E. Sample informative speech outline

Thesis Statement With their scope, history, and influence, comic books are an interesting component of American popular culture.

I. Comic books are not merely "comic" but rather explore a range of subject matter.
   A. Funny animal comics and kid comics are parables and parodies of the human condition.
      1. Elmer Fudd and Bugs Bunny: Tradition versus the pioneering spirit.
      2. Barks's ducks: Epic adventure and human foibles.
      3. Harvey's rich kids: Capitalism with a human face.
   B. True-love and teen comics present a hackneyed, boring, and sometimes disturbing picture of male/female relationships.
      1. True-love girl meets, loses, gets, marries boy (and vows never to be so stupid as to put her needs above his again).

    2. Teen comic girl fights other girls for the favors of a jerk male like Archie, who her father thinks is a twerp.

    3. True-love and teen comics foster the "us versus them" view of the male/female world.

C. Western and adventure comics concentrate on the triumph of good over evil.

    1. Western cattle barons learn that six-gun-slinging saviors arise naturally from oppressed common folk.

    2. Adventure stories pit virtuous types against the blind malice of uncaring nature.

D. Horror and mystery comics investigate ethics and morality while titillating and scaring readers.

    1. Eternal punishment for an unethical choice is a recurring theme of horror comics.

    2. The tempting hedonism of wrongdoers is graphically displayed in mystery comics—until the ironic twist of fate appears on the last page.

E. Superhero comics manifest the unspoken and sometimes frightening fantasies and aspirations of the American people.

    1. Superman is the supremely powerful spokesman and policeman for the American definition of the "right way."

    2. The jackbooted hero, Blackhawk, was created in World War II to fight totalitarian fire with fire.

    3. Mar-Vell personifies the desire for total knowledge and the wisdom needed to use it.

    4. Spider-Man is the embodiment of the perennial underdog triumphant.

II. Comic books started as anthologies of another medium but soon grew into a separate art form, developing along a path of its own.

A. Early comic books were mostly reprints of Sunday newspaper comic strip sections.

    1. "Foxy Granpa" was reprinted in a number of comic books just after the turn of the century.

    2. The following decades saw strips like "Mutt & Jeff," "Little Orphan Annie," and "Moon Mullins" reprinted.

    3. Reprint books in the thirties included such titles as "Tarzan" in Tip Top Comics and "Terry and the Pirates" in Popular Comics.

B. By 1938, the majority of comic books contained original work and, with the appearance of Superman, the golden age of comics began.

    1. Detective Comics was the first single-theme, all-original comic.

     2. Superman, the first costumed superhero, was featured in Action No. 1.

     3. More than 150 titles were in print by the end of 1941.

  C. During the decade after the war, comic books for the most part went into a slump.

     1. With the Axis powers defeated and the Cold War not yet focused, the perceived need for superheroes lessened and sales of their books slacked off.

     2. Many horror, mystery, superhero, adventure, true-love, and teen comics fell before the wave of censorship, following the publication of *Seduction of the Innocent.*

     3. Funny animal comics and kid comics retrenched behind the strongest series.

  D. By the late fifties, comic books had started to recover, overcoming their tarnished image.

     1. In creating the Comics Code Authority, publishers hoped to reassure worried parents and legislators.

     2. The silver age of comics began with the reintroduction of long-idle golden age characters.

  E. In the early sixties, the trend toward emphasizing characterization, motivation, and involvement with issues initiated a new and still-developing era in superhero comics. The effects were eventually felt in the other comic genres.

     1. The Fantastic Four, Spider-Man, and the Hulk were the first fallible and self-questioning superheroes.

     2. Comic books became accepted by a wider, more literate audience.

     3. Concern with ethical and even political questions became more evident, even in kid comics and funny animal comics.

III. Comic books have an effect beyond their entertainment value.

  A. Comic books are a unique and vigorous art form.

     1. Comic books have developed exciting and innovative methods for transcending the static nature of the panel format (series of distinct pictures across and down the page) to produce a sense of motion and drama.

     2. The art of comics is not confined to the work within a single panel but also touches the arrangement of panels on a page.

     [as a result]

B. Comic books can influence other media.
   1. Many filmmakers' use of split screens and quick cuts demonstrates a stylistic adaptation of the comic panel format.
   2. Camp and pop art drew heavily on comic book themes and styles.
      [and as a result]
C. Comic books are in demand with collectors.
   1. Some issues of rare comics can bring prices in the thousands of dollars.
   2. Every year there are many large conventions around the United States where comics can be bought, sold, and traded.

APPENDIX B

Citation Guidelines

Two standard formats for citing references in reference lists are APA style, as set out in the *Publication Manual of the American Psychological Association,* and MLA style, as set out in the *MLA Handbook for Writers of Research Papers.* (See **16d.**) The following is a sampling of reference citations for print and nonprint sources in both styles. Some of the sources, especially those from the Internet, may lack one or two pieces of information shown in these templates (for example, page numbers, a Digital Object Identifier [doi], or even a date). Try to find as much information as you can—at least enough so that your readers can locate and evaluate your sources. In MLA style, include the URL (Web address) for online sources only if they cannot be easily found by a Web search for the document's title.

In your speech, the reference to each source should include the first element in its entry—the author's name or the title of the work if no author is named.

Selected Entries in APA and MLA Styles

Publication Manual of the APA, 6th ed. (2010): References	*MLA Handbook, 7th ed. (2009): Works Cited*
Print Sources	
Book, single author	
Lastname, A. A. (Date). *Title of book.* City: publisher.	Lastname, Firstname. *Title of Book.* City: publisher, date.
Morrison, T. (2008). *A mercy.* New York: Knopf.	Morrison, Toni. *A Mercy.* New York: Knopf, 2008.
Book, two authors	
Lastname, A. A., & Lastname, B. B. (Date). *Title of book.* City, state: publisher.	Lastname, Firstname, and Firstname Lastname. *Title of Book.* City: publisher, date. Print.
Crossan, J. D., & Reed, J. L. (2001). *Excavating Jesus: Beneath the stones, behind the texts.* San Francisco: Harper SanFrancisco.	Crossan, John Dominic, and Jonathan L. Reed. *Excavating Jesus: Beneath the Stones, behind the Texts.* San Francisco: Harper, 2001.
Book, edited	
Lastname, A. A. (Ed.). (Date). *Title of book.* City: publisher.	Lastname, Firstname, ed. *Title of Book.* City: publisher, date.

Publication Manual of the APA, 6th ed. (2010): References	*MLA Handbook, 7th ed. (2009): Works Cited*
Sebold, A., & Pitlor, H. (Eds.). (2009). *The best American short stories 2009*. Boston: Houghton.	Sebold, Alice, ed., and Heidi Pitlor, series ed. *The Best American Short Stories 2009*. Boston: Houghton, 2009.

Chapter or reading in edited book

Lastname, A. A. (Date). Title of chapter. In A. A. Lastname (Ed.), *Title of book* (pp. pages). City: publisher.	Lastname, Firstname. "Title of Chapter." *Title of Book*. Ed. Firstname Lastname. City: publisher, date. Pages.
Baldwin, J. (2002). Sonny's blues. In J. G. Parks (Ed.), *American short stories since 1945* (pp. 225–245). New York, NY: Oxford University Press. (Reprinted from *Going to meet the man*, by J. Baldwin, 1965, New York: Vintage).	Baldwin, James. "Sonny's Blues." *American Short Stories since 1945*. Ed. John G. Parks. New York: Oxford UP, 2002. 225–45. Print. Rpt. of "Sonny's Blues." *Going to Meet the Man*. New York: Vintage, 1965.

Book, no author or editor, second or subsequent edition

Title of book (Edition). (Date). City: publisher.	*Title of Book*. Edition. City: publisher, date.
The New York Public Library Desk Reference. (3rd ed.). (1998). New York: Macmillan.	*New York Public Library Desk Reference*. 3rd ed. New York: Macmillan, 1998.

Periodical, scholarly journal article

Lastname, A. A. (Date). Title of article. *Periodical, volume*, pages.	Lastname, Firstname. "Title of Article." *Title of Journal* volume. (date): pages.
Spigel, L. (2009, January). My TV studies . . . Now playing on a YouTube site near you. *Television & New Media, 10*(1) 149–153.	Spigel, Lynn. "My TV Studies . . . Now Playing on a YouTube Site Near You." *Television & New Media* 10.1 (Jan. 2009): 149–53.

Periodical, magazine article

Lastname, A. A. (Date). Title of article. *Periodical, volume*, pages.	Lastname, Firstname. "Title of Article." *Periodical*, date: pages.
Anderson, J. L. (2009, October 5). Gangland: Who controls the streets of Rio de Janeiro? *The New Yorker, 85*, 46–57.	Anderson, Jon Lee. "Gangland: Who Controls the Streets of Rio de Janeiro?" *New Yorker* 5 Oct. 2009: 46–57.

Newspaper article

Lastname, A. A. (Date). Title of article. *Newspaper Title* [city name in brackets if necessary], pages.	Lastname, Firstname. "Title of Article." *Newspaper Title* date [edition if named]: pages.
Temple, J. (2009, October 18). Tribe teams with Google Earth to make a stand in the Amazon. *San Francisco Chronicle*, pp. A1, A11.	Temple, James. "Tribe Teams with Google Earth to Make a Stand in the Amazon." *San Francisco Chronicle* 18 Oct. 2009: A1.

Publication Manual of the APA, 6th ed. (2010): References	*MLA Handbook, 7th ed. (2009): Works Cited*

Nonprint and Internet Sources

Episode in television series

Lastname, A. A. (Writer), & Lastname, A. A. (Director). (Date). Title of episode [Television series episode]. In Lastname, A. A. (Producer), *Series title*. City, state: network.	Lastname, Firstname, dir. [*or* perf., narr., prod. If the show rather than a person is your focus, start with episode title.] "Episode Title." *Series Title*. [Any relevant names, for example, director, performers, narrator, producer]. Network. Station, city, date of broadcast. Television.
Ward, G. C. (Writer) & Burns, K. (Director). (2001). Gumbo [Television series episode]. In K. Burns & L. Novick (Producers), *Jazz*. Washington, DC: WETA.	Burns, Ken, dir. "Gumbo." *Jazz*. Narr. Keith David. PBS. WETA, Washington, DC, 8 Jan. 2001. Television.

Sound recording

Writer, A. A. (Date). Title of song (Recorded by B. B. Artist if different from writer). On *Title of album* [CD *or* Record, Cassette, etc.]. City, state: Label. (Date of recording if different from song date)	Lastname, Firstname, comp. [*or* cond., perf., etc]. "Title of Song." Perf. [*or* Cond.] Firstname Lastname. *Title of Recording*. Label, date. CD [*or* LP, Audiocassette, etc.].
Bach, J. S. (1727). Cantata BWV 82: Ich habe genug (Recorded by Lorraine Hunt Lieberson, mezzo soprano, Craig Hunt, conductor, and the Orchestra of Emmanuel Music). On *Bach cantatas BMV 82 and 199* [CD]. New York, NY: Nonesuch. (2002)	Bach, Johann Sebastian, comp. "Cantata BWV 82: Ich habe genug." Perf. Lorraine Hunt Lieberson. Orch. of Emmanuel Music. Cond. Craig Hunt. *Bach Cantatas BMV 82 and 199*. Nonesuch, 2002. CD.

Internet document (nonperiodical, no author)

Document title. (Date). Retrieved from address	"Document Title." *Title of Website*. Sponsor/publisher of site, date of publication [*or* n.d.]. Web. Date of retrieval. <Address if necessary>.
King Institute encyclopedia: Martin Luther King, Jr. and the global freedom struggle. (n.d.). Retrieved from http://mlk-kpp01.stanford.edu/index.php/encyclopedia/encyclopedia_contents	"King Institute Encyclopedia: Martin Luther King, Jr., and the Global Freedom Struggle." *King Institute Home*. The Martin Luther King, Jr., Research and Education Institute, Stanford University. n.d. Web. 20 Oct. 2009. <http://mlk-kpp01.stanford.edu/index.php/encyclopedia/encyclopedia_contents>.

Publication Manual of the APA, 6th ed. (2010): References	MLA Handbook, 7th ed. (2009): Works Cited
Internet periodical article	
Lastname, A. A. (Date). Title of article. *Periodical Title, volume*(issue). Retrieved date from address	Lastname, Firstname. "Title of Article." *Periodical Title* volume.issue: pages [*or* n.p.]. Date of publication. Web. Date of retrieval. <Address if necessary>.
Rose, M. (2009, March 11). Screaming mummies. *Archaeology* (online feature). Retrieved March 1, 2011 from http://www.archaeology.org/online/features/screaming_mummy/	Rose, Mark. "Screaming Mummies." *Archaeology*: n.p. 11 Mar. 2009. Web. 20 Oct. 2011. <http://www.archaeology.org/online/features/screaming_mummy/>.
Blog post	
Lastname, A. A. (Date). Title of post [Web log post]. Retrieved from address	Lastname, Firstname. "Title of post." *Title of Blog.* Sponsor/publisher of website, date [*or* n.d.]. Web. Date of retrieval. <Address if necessary>.
Picard, R. G. (2009, March 28). Everyone's not atwitter [Web log post]. Retrieved from http://themediabusiness.blogspot.com/search/label/Blackberry	Picard, Robert G. "Everyone's Not Atwitter." *The Media Business.* Robert G. Picard, www.robertpicard.net, 28 Mar. 2009. Web. 20 Oct. 2009. <http://themediabusiness.blogspot.com/search/label/Blackberry>.
E-mail	
(Personal communication not included in reference list.)	Lastname, Firstname. "Subject Line." Email to Firstname Lastname. Date.
	Thor, Leifur. "Info on the Design Science Initiative Project." Email to Doug Stuart. 2 May 2009.
Interview conducted by the speaker	
(Personal communication not included in reference list.)	Lastname, Firstname. Personal [*or* Telephone] interview. Date.
	Thor, Leifur. Telephone interview. 5 May 2011.

GLOSSARY

A

acronym A word or abbreviation created from the first letters of each word in a phrase. **(22b.1)**

ad hominem fallacy An error in reasoning that consists of attacking a person identified with a position instead of refuting the position itself. **(21f.1)**

agenda A planned order of events for a meeting or group function. It provides structure and helps minimize conflict over what will be discussed, in what sequence, and, perhaps, for how long. **(7f.1)**

alliteration A stylistic device that consists of the repetition of a consonant sound. For example, "big, brutal bullies" is stronger and more memorable than "large, mean bullies." **(29d.2)**

antithesis A stylistic device that consists of two contrasting ideas set up in opposition. **(29d.2)**

appeal Any part of a speech designed to evoke a response from the audience. A direct appeal is often found in the conclusion of a speech when the speaker asks the audience to take a particular action. **(31b.2)**

articulation The ability to produce the sounds of speech correctly so that words are understandable. **(34a.3)**

assonance A stylistic device that consists of the repetition of a vowel sound. "People are dreaming of pie in the sky, by and by" repeats the long *i* sound, which makes it memorable. **(29d.2)**

attention-getter The opening one or two sentences of a speech introduction designed to immediately engage the listeners' interest. **(31a.2)**

B

bar graph A format for displaying data that compares related items by representing their amounts with columns or bars of different lengths or heights. **(27a.3)**

C

causal reasoning The justification for an argument claiming that one thing is the direct result of another. A causal claim should not be confused with mere coincidence or correlation. **(21d)**

cause–effect pattern A way of organizing speech points that begins with the origin of the situation and moves to the consequences. **(19a.3)**

central idea The core idea of a speech and the touchstone for its development; less formal than a thesis sentence (a subject–predicate assertion). **(11d.1)**

chronological pattern A way of organizing speech points that follows a time order; it might be historical or it might follow the steps in a process. **(19a.1)**

circular reasoning An error in reasoning that occurs when a speaker assumes the truth of the conclusion and uses it as the starting point for developing an argument, instead of building a case for the conclusion. **(21f.9)**

claim A proposition that a speaker advances as a conclusion. The claim might be the thesis of the speech, a main point, or a sub-point. Typically, a claim is a controversial statement that does not earn automatic acceptance but needs to be proven by the development of an argument. **(21a)**

clincher The carefully thought-out closing sentence of a speech conclusion that is memorable and gives a sense of finality. A good speech can be spoiled if it just "trails off" without a clincher. **(31b.3)**

cognitive restructuring A treatment for communication apprehension that involves discovering the underlying statements driving one's fear, analyzing their logic, and replacing them with more realistic statements. Regularly repeating the statements can eventually restructure the way a person thinks about speaking. **(4d.2)**

concept mapping A nonlinear technique for organizing ideas in order to develop the main points of a speech. A circle diagram or notecards are used to group similar ideas. **(17b.2)**

context Features such as time, space, and degree of formality that shape the core message of a speech. Specific contexts, such as the workplace or the political arena, have norms that shape public speaking in them. **(5)**

coordinate points Points of equal importance in an outline, for example, points I, II, and III, or points A, B, and C. **(18d)**

core values Beliefs about right and wrong that are central to the identity of the person who holds them. These values are very difficult to change. **(25c.2)**

credibility A speaker's believability over and above the logical message and the emotional impact of the speech. Credibility comes from the ability to project qualities such as competence, trustworthiness, concern, and dynamism. Other things being equal, speakers perceived as having these qualities will be more persuasive. **(26)**

D

deduction A form of reasoning that demonstrates how the relationship among established premises lead to a necessary conclusion. The deductive relationship is often expressed in an if/then or either/or syllogism. **(21c)**

E

evocative Designed to call forth an emotion or shared feeling. An evocative speech is sometimes called a speech to entertain, but evocative speaking is broader and can arouse feelings of sympathy or grief as well as feelings of happiness or amusement. **(9)**

extemporaneous The most common mode of delivery. An extemporaneous speech is a structured speech delivered in a conversational manner from general notes. The speaker is thoroughly familiar with the order of points and subpoints and with key phrases, but the speech is not written out or memorized. **(28, 28a)**

F

factual example Specific, directly verifiable or commonly accepted instance used to illustrate or to prove a general point. **(16a.1)**

fallacies Errors in reasoning that make a particular argument or position invalid. **(21f)**

fallacy of the absurd extreme (*reductio ad absurdum*) An error in reasoning that makes a potentially sound argument appear groundless by extending it to a point where it can be easily ridiculed. **(21f.8)**

false dichotomy An error of reasoning that results from the assumption that there are only two alternatives in a situation when in fact there are many. **(21f.4)**

full-sentence outline A plan for a speech that states each main point and at least the first level of subpoints in complete subject–predicate sentences. This attention to detail helps ensure that every part of the speech is logically related. **(20b)**

H

hasty generalization An error in inductive reasoning that results from making a premature inductive leap and basing a generalization on insufficient data. **(21f.5)**

hypothetical example A plausible story created by the speaker to illustrate a point. In contrast to factual examples, hypothetical examples can be used only to clarify a point but not to prove it. **(16a.2)**

I

impromptu A mode of delivery that requires the speaker to speak without formal preparation. An impromptu speech can, however, have elements of other types of speeches, such as a theme, planned first and last sentences, appeals to the audience, and lots of examples. **(28)**

inductive reasoning A pattern of reasoning in which a series of specific observations lead to a probable general conclusion. **(21b)**

internal preview A forecast in the course of a speech of one or more points that will be covered. This is a device to unify a speech and to emphasize key points. **(32b.2)**

internal summary A restatement in the course of a speech of one or more points that have been covered. Like the internal preview, this is a device to unify a speech and to emphasize key points. **(32b.2)**

introduction The opening section of a speech that serves to get attention and orient audience members before the first main point is developed. **(31a)**

J

jargon Terms that relate to a particular activity and are familiar to the people who practice this activity. **(29c.2)**

K

keyword or key-phrase outline A tool used in speech preparation. It consists of words and phrases to be used and is more developed than brainstorming tools, such as concept mapping, but less detailed than a topic outline or a full-sentence outline. **(28a)**

L

line graph A format for displaying data represented as points connected by lines; it indicates changes over time or distance. **(27a.3)**

logical orientation A section of the introduction to a speech that provides the speech's intellectual framework, often including the thesis sentence and previewing the main points. **(31a.4)**

M

main points The ideas that are central to the development of the thesis of a speech. **(18a)**

major premise The basic statement about a relationship between two terms that underlies a deductive argument. **(21c)**

manuscript speaking A mode of delivery in which the speech is written out word for word (preferably in the oral style). The speech is practiced until it is familiar enough to sound conversational when it is delivered. **(28c)**

Maslow's hierarchy of needs A ranking of human needs from basic survival needs through needs for security, belonging, and esteem, and culminating in the need for self-actualization. **(25b)**

memorized speech A mode of delivery in which the speech is written out (preferably in the oral style) and then practiced until it can be delivered word for word. **(28d)**

metaphor A stylistic device that equates two different things; for example, "My job is a nightmare." **(29d.2)**

minor premise The part of a deductive argument that introduces some data. **(21c)**

motivated sequence An organizer for persuasion that is based on the mental stages through which listeners progress during a speech. **(23c.1)**

P

persuasive speaking A speech that has the purpose of changing the behavior or attitudes of the audience members. **(23a)**

pictorial reproductions Presentation aids that visually depict an object; examples are photographs, sketches, and videos. **(27a.3)**

pictorial symbols Presentation aids that represent abstract concepts; examples are graphs, charts, diagrams, and maps. **(27a.3)**

pie chart A format for displaying data as segments of a circle; it shows the relative size of parts of a whole. **(27a.3)**

pitch How high or low a speaker's voice is. Speakers should try to use a pitch that is natural, and they should occasionally vary their pitch to reinforce meaning. **(34b)**

post hoc fallacy An error in reasoning that results from assuming that an event that follows another event is caused by the first event. This error confuses sequence with cause. **(21f.6)**

presentation aid An object that adds another communication dimension to a speaker's content and delivery. **(27)**

presentation software Computer software such as PowerPoint that is used to create presentation slides. **(27a.2)**

preview An organization tool that gives listeners a road map of the topics to come. **(31a.4)**

primacy The persuasive effect of placing a point first or early in a speech in order to give it greater impact or make it memorable. **(23c.2)**

primary audience outcome The most important result that a speaker wants to achieve, phrased in terms of what the audience will do after the speech. **(11c.3)**

probability The condition that exists when a conclusion is likely to be true but cannot be established with absolute certainty. When speakers try to persuade listeners, they often compare costs and benefits so that the "odds" favor their position. **(21b.2)**

problem–solution pattern A way of arranging the main points of a speech that begins with a description of something that needs changing and moves to a proposal for the remedy. **(19a.4)**

project proposal A workplace presentation in which a plan and its rationale are described; examples are research proposals and sales presentations. **(7c)**

project status report A workplace presentation that describes the progress on a project. This interim report is used to reassure colleagues or customers about what is being done, to alert them to any problems, and to seek feedback. **(7d)**

proposition of fact A claim that something is or is not true. **(11d.3)**

proposition of policy A claim that a certain course of action should or should not be adopted. **(11d.3)**

proposition of value A claim that something is good or bad. **(11d.3)**

PSR statement A problem–solution–result (PSR) statement is a brief but memorable personal success story that states a problem, describes a solution, and lists the results; it should be delivered in 90 seconds or less. **(7a.4)**

public speaking A communication setting in which one person has primary control and direction of the resources of communication. It may occur in a formal or informal setting, but it involves preparation, and the focus is on the speaker for all or most of the time. **(1a)**

Q

question-and-answer period A time allotted after the conclusion of the main speech when audience members can ask for clarification or elaboration on the topic. **(37)**

quotation The words of another person. Quotations are used because their language is more powerful than the speaker could create or because the person being quoted has some special credibility. Direct quotations use the exact words of another, and indirect quotations paraphrase another person's words; both should be attributed to the source. **(16c.1)**

R

rate The speed at which one speaks. Ideally, the rate must be fast enough to hold attention, slow enough to be understood, and varied as necessary to enhance meaning. **(34a.2)**

reasoning by analogy A form of reasoning in which conclusions can be drawn about unfamiliar events or things based on what is known about familiar events or things. **(21e)**

recency The persuasive effect that comes from placing a point last or late in a speech to give it greater impact or make it memorable. **(23c.2)**

S

semantic fallacy An error in reasoning that occurs when a word is used in different senses in different parts of the argument. **(21f.3)**

signpost An organizational technique that keeps listeners informed about how a speech is unfolding. Signposts can tell what has been covered, what is still to come, and when changes in direction are about to occur. **(22b.1)**

simile A stylistic device that compares two different things, such as "Managing a group of scientists is like herding cats." **(29d.2)**

slang Popular, nonstandard words and expressions. **(29c.2)**

slippery slope fallacy An error in reasoning that claims the first step in some direction will inevitably lead to a disastrous outcome. **(21f.2)**

spatial pattern An organizational pattern according to some relationship of components in space; examples are geographical regions or galleries in a museum. **(19a.2)**

speech notes Working notes designed for quick reference and easy readability during a speech. They contain key words and phrases, organizational cues, and information that must be cited exactly. **(33b)**

statistical evidence Data that have been systematically collected and coded in numerical form. **(16b)**

straw figure fallacy An error in reasoning that proceeds from stating an argument in weaker form than its advocates use and then proceeding to demolish that weak argument. **(21f.7)**

style The effective use of language. Style consists of being clear and concise and using various linguistic devices to enhance the impact of language. **(29)**

subordinate points The lesser points that support or elaborate on the main points of a speech. **(18d)**

supporting materials The parts of a speech that expand on or prove the claims made in main points or subpoints. These examples, definitions, statistics, and testimonies are the building blocks of a speech. **(16)**

T

team presentation A speech prepared and delivered collaboratively by a small group of presenters, each of whom typically has special expertise or perspective. **(6d, 7b)**

testimony A form of supporting material that reports the experience or opinions of another person, who is typically an expert or has direct experience with the topic. **(16c)**

text A message captured in words. All the nonverbal, psychological, and cultural factors that surround this core message and help shape its meaning are called the *context.* **(5)**

topic outline An outline that identifies the points to be covered and the relationships among them but does not spell out all the logical connections that are present in a full-sentence outline. **(17b.1)**

topical pattern A way of organizing the main points of a speech that grows naturally out of a topic that does not lend itself to sequential or spatial organization. **(19a.5)**

training presentation Usually a series of workshops or seminars related to the workplace; the goal is to teach a specific set of work-related skills or body of knowledge. **(7e)**

V

values Beliefs about what is good and bad (or wise or foolish, just or unjust, pretty or ugly, etc.).**(25c)**

vocal variety Changes in the tone and pitch of the voice to provide interest and emphasis; the opposite of monotone. **(34b)**

vocalized pauses Filler phrases such as "um," "er," "y'know," and "like" that break the fluency of speaking and can be distracting to listeners. **(34d.3)**

volume The loudness or softness with which one speaks. **(34a.1)**

W

whiteboard A board with an erasable shiny surface that can be used during a speech for quick drawings or words. **(27b.1)**

INDEX

CHECKLISTS

QUICK TIPS

KEYPOINTS